ENHANCING
PARENTING SKILLS

ENHANCING PARENTING SKILLS

A Guide Book for
Professionals Working with Parents

Edited by

Kedar Nath Dwivedi

JOHN WILEY & SONS

Chichester · New York · Weinheim · Brisbane · Singapore · Toronto

Other Wiley Editorial Offices

John Wiley & Sons, Inc., 605 Third Avenue,
New York, NY 10158-0012, USA

Wiley-VCH Verlag GmbH,
Pappelallee 3, D-69469
Weinheim, Germany

Jacaranda Wiley Ltd, 33 Park Road, Milton,
Queensland 4064, Australia

John Wiley & Sons (Asia) Pte Ltd, 2 Clementi Loop #02-01,
Jin Xing Distripark, Singapore 129809

John Wiley & Sons (Canada) Ltd, 22 Worcester Road,
Rexdale, Ontario M9W 1L1, Canada

Library of Congress Cataloguing-in-Publication Data

Enhancing parenting skills: a guide book for professionals working
with parents / edited by Kedar Nath Dwivedi.
p.   cm.
Includes bibliographical references and index.
ISBN 0-471-97661-X
1. Child rearing—Study and teaching.   2. Parenting—Study and
teaching.   3. Parents—Services for.   I. Dwivedi, Kedar Nath.
HQ755.7.E54   1997
649'.1'071—DC21   97-17408
                                                                    CIP

British Library Cataloguing in Publication Data

A catalogue record for this book is available from the British Library

ISBN 0-471-97661-X

Typeset in 10/12pt Palatino by Mackreth Media Services, Hemel Hempstead
Printed and bound in Great Britain by Redwood Books, Trowbridge, Wilts
This book is printed on acid-free paper responsibly manufactured from sustainable forestation,
for which at least two trees are planted for each one used for paper production.

With warm affection and esteem,
this book is dedicated by the editor
to Rory Nicol, Professor of Child Psychiatry
at the Greenwood Institute of Child Health, Leicester.

CONTENTS

ABOUT THE AUTHORS

Dr Harold Behr, MB, Bch, FRCPsych, DPM, MInstGA, formerly Consultant Child Psychiatrist at the Central Middlesex Hospital, London, teaches and supervises at the Institute of Group Analysis and practices psychotherapy at The North London Centre for Group Therapy. He has published in the field of adolescent and family group work, training of group therapists and group analytic theory.

Dr Dorit Braun, MA, PhD, the Chief Executive of the National Stepfamilies Association and formerly a Locality Purchasing Coordinator, Northamptonshire Health Authority, has a background in adult, community and health education. She has worked within the statutory and voluntary sectors, and has devised, run and managed a wide range of work with primary care practitioners, much of which has focused on aspects of parent and family education. She has written many practical guides for professionals, has devised and run national training programmes, and undertaken a variety of research projects to gain insights into parents' needs from parent education. She has a Masters in Social Research in Health Care from Warwick University and a PhD in Political Economy from Manchester University, for which she conducted a study of the pharmaceutical industry in Columbia. She is a single parent of three sons.

Kathleen Cox is a Chartered Educational and Clinical Psychologist who is a founder member of the Stepfamily Telephone Counselling Service. She has two grown-up daughters and two stepsons. She was formerly Senior Educational Psychologist for a large Metropolitan Borough and is now in private practice. She is in partnership with her husband in running a business of Chartered Psychologists writing reports for legal purposes. These often include stepfamily issues such as contact between non-resident parent and children.

Jo Douglas is a Consultant Clinical Psychologist and Head of the Clinical Psychology department at the Great Ormond Street Children's Hospital. She has had a special interest in the emotional and behaviour problems of young children for many years and has published extensively in this area. At present she is the Director of the Feeding Programme for young children with severe and chronic eating difficulties in the hospital.

Dr Kedar Nath Dwivedi, MBBS, MD, DPM, FRCPsych, is Consultant in Child, Adolescent and Family Psychiatry at the Child and Family Consultation Service and the Ken Stewart Family Centre, Northampton, and is also Clinical Teacher in the Faculty of Medicine, University of Leicester. He graduated in medicine from the Institute of Medical Sciences, Varanasi, India, and served as Assistant Professor in Preventive and Social Medicine in Simla before coming to the UK in 1974. Since then, he has worked in psychiatry, is a member of more than a dozen professional associations, and has contributed extensively to the literature (nearly 40 publications) including editing the well-received book on *Groupwork with Children and Adolescents* (Jessica Kingsley, 1993), *Therapeutic Use of Stories* (Routledge, 1997), and co-editing *Meeting the Needs of Ethnic Minority Children* (Jessica Kingsley, 1996), *Depression in Children and Adolescents* (Whurr, 1996) and *Management of Childhood Anxiety Disorders* (Arena, 1997). He is also interested in eastern, particularly Buddhist, approaches to mental health.

Dr David George was until recently Associate Director of Nene College, Northampton, the President of the National Association for Able Children in Education, and a member of the Executive Committee of the World Council of Gifted and Talented Children. He lectures both nationally and internationally on these subjects and is author of the books entitled *The Challenge of the Able Child* and *Enrichment Activities for the Able Children*.

Masud Hoghughi, FBPsS, CPsychol, is a Consultant Clinical and Forensic Psychologist. He has spent pretty well the whole of his professional life working with children and adolescents. For many years he was the Director of Europe's largest facility for seriously disordered adolescents.

Charmaine R. Kemps, DipFT, CQSW, has worked in the caring profession for nearly twenty-five years, with social work experience in residential child care, field work, families who had children with learning difficulties, and as a therapist in a child and family clinic. She is currently working in the Department of Child and Adolescent

Psychiatry, Milton Keynes, as a Family Therapist. She was born in Sri Lanka and emigrated to the UK with her parents and family when she was a child. She feels that the immigration process, transitional issues and acculturation process have also influenced her identity, and are part of her ongoing story.

Dr Sebastian Kraemer, BA, MBBS, MRCP, FRCPsych, after a first degree in philosophy studied medicine, specialising in paediatrics and later in psychiatry. Since 1980 he has been a consultant Child and Family Psychiatrist at the Tavistock Clinic and at the Whittington Hospital, London. His principal interests and publications are in family therapy and psychosomatic disorders, the training of child and adolescent psychiatrists, and the origins and roles of fatherhood. Besides clinical and academic work in the NHS he has written for, and consulted to, the media, children's charities, senior civil servants and politicians, on the clinical and research base for family policy, and the need for a political understanding of attachment through the life cycle. He is married, with two school-age sons.

Dr Ruchira Leisten, PhD, is a Research Fellow in the Social Policy Research Group at the Nene Centre for Research, Nene College. She is an experienced researcher in the fields of family health and community care. She is also the module coordinator for the research methods course on the MA in Policy Studies. She is married with two children aged 4 and 2.

Dr Paquita McMichael, MA, MEd, PhD, retired Head of Department of Social Science and Social Work at Moray House Institute of Education, Heriot-Watt University, for many years taught child development courses to social workers and teachers. A particular interest, stemming from her studies of young offenders and the unemployed, lay in the fathering role and the limitations gender stereotypes imposed on both men and women.

Peter Marsden-Allen is currently the Principal Social Worker at Northampton Child and Family Consultation Service. Before this he worked as the Manager of the Crescent Family Centre in Islington, London. He trained and worked as a community worker for fifteen years before becoming the training officer with the Association for Speech Impaired Children in London in 1980. After completing training as a social worker, together with research into parenting skills and further training as a family therapist; Peter practised both as a trainer, college lecturer and as a therapist in child and family guidance settings. Peter has researched and taught parenting skills to workers and trainees in family therapy.

Dr Shanthy Parameswaran, MBBS, DPM, MRCPsych, is based at the Paediatric Unit, Wexham Park Hospital, Slough, and works both in the hospital and the community settings. She had her initial training in psychiatry at the Middletown Hospital in New York State and later at St George's Hospital, London. She has been working as a Consultant Child and Adolescent Psychiatrist for the past fifteen years and has encouraged the issue of parenting as a fundamental problem in many cases. Her work as a consultant to Barnardos residential school and home has also provided deep insight into this problem.

Professor Gerda Siann, BSc, Msc, PhD, FBPsS, holds the NCR Chair in Gender Relations at the University of Dundee. Her research interests are focused on child development and gender issues and she has lectured and published widely in these fields. She is the author of *Gender, Sex and Sexuality*, published by Taylor & Francis in 1994.

FOREWORD

*Parents . . . are sometimes a bit of a disappointment to their
children. They don't fulfil the promise of their early years.*

(Anthony Powell, *A Buyer's Market*, 1952)

All parents want to do their best for their children. But sadly, some
parents do not even show the early promise to which Anthony Powell
refers. Despite every good intention, deficits in parenting often appear in
the first few days in the life of a new born.

As Dr Dwivedi writes in his Introduction, many believe that parenting
is a skill that comes naturally to all, or at any rate to most parents. It is
true that for those parents who have enjoyed a secure childhood
themselves, and especially those who have helped in the care of younger
brothers or sisters, nephews or nieces, much does come naturally. But
the fact that children, from the earliest days of life, differ in their
temperaments and require individualised care, means that often
experience with one child cannot necessarily be generalised to others.
Further, many parents have unfortunately not enjoyed good experiences
in their own childhoods and have no role models with whom to identify.

It is therefore essential that opportunities to discuss and learn about
parenting are made available at every stage of the life cycle—at school, in
the pre-conceptual period, during pregnancy, and in the early years of
parenting. It is amazing to me that there is so little discussion in our
society about the need to place parenting as a subject firmly within the
National Curriculum. Surely, this is just another example of the way we
under-value parenting. Until parenting is placed within the curriculum,
and child development, of which parenting is an essential part, is an
examinable subject, it is difficult to see how young parents, especially
those with poor early experiences themselves, can expect to enter
parenthood with confidence. The National Curriculum, some will say, is
already overcrowded. But try to think of a subject currently in the

curriculum that is of greater relevance to those three-quarters of our children who will one day be parents themselves.

In the meantime, parents frequently find themselves in need of professional help. It is important that professionals are well equipped for this task. Many professionals, especially child mental health professionals, educational psychologists, health visitors and family doctors, need relevant information and skills to enhance parenting in those who consult them. Such information is not readily available, and I hope this book, written, as it is, from so many different perspectives, will both fill a gap and stimulate discussion about this vitally important subject.

Philip Graham
Chairman, National Children's Bureau and
Emeritus Professor of Child Psychiatry,
Cambridge

PREFACE

When I started to piece together the story behind the book, I felt overwhelmingly amazed by the variety of strands intertwined with each other in so many different ways. I also began to appreciate the value of having had an intimate familiarity with parenting patterns in so many cultural contexts and the opportunity to work at the cutting edge of exploring and reshaping parenting practices in several communities, for example during late 1960s and early 1970s, through the Faculty of Preventive and Social Medicine at the Institute of Medical Sciences, Varanasi, and as an Assistant Professor in the Department of Social and Preventive Medicine in Simla. I am very grateful to Dr R. R. Dwivedi, Professor S. D. Gaur, Dr Goswami, Professor V. M. Gupta, Professor P. Kaur, Rama Khan, Professor S. M. Marwah (Tiwari, 1997), Dr Param Hans Rai (Dwivedi, 1997), Professor H. C. Saxena, Dr K. P. Shukla, Dr M. P. Singh, Kamala Singh, Professor O. N. Srivastava (Behere, 1997), Laxmi Chandra Srivastava, Professor H. C. Srivastava, Professor J. Tandan, Professor I. C. Tiwari (Marwah, 1996), A. K. Tripathi, the late Dr A. K. Varma, Dr K. L. Varma, Dr H. C. Varshney and many others for their help, support and guidance during various community projects.

I was also fortunate to have postgraduate psychiatric training during the mid-1970s at Cambridge where, in those days, most of the mental health services were organised around groupwork. Not only customers but also the providers utilised group processes for continuous growth and development (Clark, 1996; Law, 1994). The influences of the social therapeutic approaches of Dr David Clark, Dr Graham Petrie, Dr Ross Mitchell, Dr Bernard Zeitlin, Rev. Michael Law, John Lambert, the late Dr Rajan Pillai and many others still reverberate within us. The rich memories of those days in the trainees of that time (such as Roger Brittain, Punya Das, John Decartret, Tim Dyer, David Frost, Yionnis Missios, Vasilis Moutsos, Guru Nayani, Simon Oakeshott, Geremy Pfeffer, Geoff Pullan, Mike Shooter, Subhash Tandon, George Vistas and Julia Wilkinson, to name only a few) are still treasured as uniquely creative learning experiences. A recent television series 'The Pioneers' has attempted to capture the essence of that creativity as well. For me, those experiences greatly enriched and solidified the basic foundation for comprehending the Post-Modern concepts of auto-poeisis and co-construction of reality so relevant for the development of today's parenting programmes.

I am also grateful to the enormous influences of Dr Suryakant Bhate, Dr Sheila Pittock, Dr Bob Palmer, Professor Sidney Brandon, Dr Tom Burney, the late Dr Ivan Carter and many others during my higher training in child psychiatry at Leicester.

When I joined the Department of Child Mental Health in 1980 at Northampton as a Consultant, the Ken Stewart Family Centre, an essential limb of the Department, had already pioneered a unique programme in enhancing parenting skills. The idea of this day unit had been conceived by the late Dr Ken Stewart who had worked as the Consultant Child Psychiatrist and the Medical Director of the Child Guidance Clinic in Northampton. The programme had been designed to help families who were mainly at the margins with multiple and severe difficulties and at risk of further damage to their mental and physical health and welfare. The programme allowed several families to work together utilising the principles from [modified] therapeutic communities, group analysis, [multiple] family therapy and so on (Dwivedi *et al.*, 1984). Dr Amit Bhattacharyya, Trevor Chandler, Andy Howard, Mark Hook, Maggie Jones/McKechin, Stuart Lovett, Liz Shedden, Mike Travers and Eileen Woolley, to name just a few, had been intimately involved with the programme at different times. Personally for me, the opportunity to supervise and offer ongoing consultation to such a venture proved to be an extremely valuable learning experience.

Ironically the Centre was also threatened with closure for financial purposes and we remain deeply indebted to Dr Terry Lear, the then Chairman of the Division of Psychiatry, who managed to impress upon the Area Health Authority to prevent such a closure. The energy derived from these threats led to the development of a variety of other therapeutic groups mainly for children. Dr Lear also encouraged the fruitful development of these group-therapeutic activities at the Centre as he has been a leading group analyst of international fame and has served as the President of Group Analytic Society at one time. Locally he was heavily involved with the development of Midland and Warwick University courses in groupwork and family therapy.

I am also grateful to other members of the executive Committee of the Midland Course in Groupwork and Family Therapy, such as Dr Harry Tough, Dr Julie Roberts and Mr Patrick McGrath, among others. Patrick McGrath has also been of tremendous help in running our Groupwork with Children and Adolescent Courses which have become nationally attractive and have led to a publication of a well-received handbook with a Foreword by Robin Skynner (Dwivedi, 1993) and the formation of the Child and Adolescent Group Workers Association.

As a number of therapeutic groups for children evolved, in the framework of limited overall resources within the service, the time and resources for parenting programmes became less and less available. Originally each set of several families attended separate whole days every week which were popularly known as 'Family Days' but later these were reduced to only one day a week and eventually to a half day a week. Currently the programme is run with several modifications by Sarah Hogan, Vyvienne Tipler and others and focuses on parents of children up to 5 years of age. It contains a variety of psycho-educational components and also utilises experiential group processes.

The Systemic Training in Effective Parenting programme was brought to our service by Chris Hallam, who now works in Canada, but the programme has been well nurtured by and has thrived in the hands of Paul Sellwood.

Among a number of therapeutic groups for children at the Ken Stewart Family Centre, the group for children with encopresis also involves their parents in a number of groupwork activities. This was inspired by the treatment approaches at the Manor Hospital in Aylesbury. Eileen Woolley, Sue Bell, Kim Twigger, Jan Pawlikowski and many others have helped develop it further. A substantial number of children with such difficulties associated with shame, also experience emotional hostility from their parents. So, the components of the programme were developed to address these issues either directly or indirectly (Dwivedi & Bell, 1993). This programme is run by Jan Pawlikowski and Vyvienne Tipler. When the parents attending the group see the staff persevering in celebrating even the smallest achievements by the children, they too begin to practise such attitudes and responses themselves.

Since the Child Mental Health Service has joined to form the integrated Child Health Directorate of the Northampton General Hospital NHS Trust, health promotion and prevention with emphasis on positive parenting has acquired renewed vigour and enthusiasm. With the support of the Northampton Health Authority, particularly Dr Dorit Braun (who has also contributed a chapter in this volume) and that of Mel Parr from PIPPIN and the efforts of Dr Sheila Shribman, Dr Nick Griffin, Dr Cliona NiBhrolchain, Peter Harper, Vee Hales and Sarah Hogan, we have launched another parenting development initiative which has developed into an interesting research project with Margaret Wysling in a key role.

Yet another parenting development venture with which I have been associated (in the form of giving a keynote speech), started at a school in Earls Barton. Val Baily and David Billett organised a study day and invited the parents of children attending the school. The study day created an excellent opportunity for exploring various aspects of parenting and the potential for its enhancement. This led to the parents forming an association and organising further programmes by themselves.

Peter Marsden-Allen has recently joined our service as the Principal Social Worker. He brought with him an enormous wealth of experience in developing yet another powerful parenting enhancement programme. This programme synthesises the principles from solution-focused brief therapy, transactional analysis and the role of developing meta-perspectives for paradigm shifts. This is helped by creating opportunities for learning through group processes and playback of video-taped parenting experiences and role plays. Chapter 8 in this volume is contributed by Peter on the basis of his experience of running the programme in a family centre in London.

Since 1983 I have had the opportunity to Chair the Steering Committee of the Northampton Multidisciplinary Conferences almost annually. It has really been so fruitful to have the wealth of the experiences of various members on this Committee, such as Adrian Bell, Chris Handley, Peter Harper, Danielle Hill, James Linnell, Fred McLarren, Leon Owen, Simon Villett, Dr Malcolm Walley and others. One of the aims of these conferences has also been to promote respect and understanding between disciplines. It is the straitjacket of logic that encourages disciplines to minimise their similarities and magnify their differences so that an elephant is seen as very different from a mouse. These conferences have attempted to see a lot of the elephant in a mouse and a lot of the mouse in an elephant!

In 1995, the theme of the conference was rightly chosen to be Parenting Patterns. In the context of our having been involved in a variety of parenting enhancement programmes, the direct inspiration for this book arose in that conference. In fact, two of the contributors to this book (Dr Sebastian Kraemer and Masud Hoghughi) provided the keynote addresses. Other speakers included Roy Atkinson, Trevor Chandler, Les Pullan, Marianne Stone, Lee Tack and Margaret Wysling.

The proceedings were Chaired by Chief Superintendent Parry and Dr Jill Meara. In her introductory remarks Jill quoted her 6-year-old daughter Joanna's following poignant words 'defining' good parents.

Good mums are nice to thae chldrn and arent strit and fede the chldrn and love the chldrn thaey spend mouny on them and wst time on them. Good dads are prity much th same as good mums.

Dr David George, who has also contributed a chapter in this book, gave this as a keynote speech to the conference on Creative Practices in 1996.

The theme for yet another conference was violence. Vicky Kemp, the then Community Safety Officer for the County, became interested in, as we discussed further, the value of groupwork in helping children (with disorders of conduct and emotional disturbance) and their parents, with a view to community safety and crime prevention. She helped put together a bid for Single Regeneration Budget funding for a project. Together with Phil Davis, John Sleet, Pam Gillett and Brenda Briggs we launched this initiative with the help of two part-time groupworkers: Suresh Chauhan and Sue Edwards.

In spite of a number of recent official documents by, for example, the Health Advisory Service (1995) and the Department of Health (1995), highlighting the value of child mental health, these are still truly 'Cinderella' services. In such a climate, there is a pressing need for more powerful and enhancing parenting programmes. We are, therefore, immensely delighted with the timely manifestation of this volume.

I am also very grateful to my colleagues in the Child Health Directorate including the Child and Family Consultation Service and the Ken Stewart Family Centre, such as Fran Ackland, Husni Ahmad, Sally Beeken, Tony Brown, Bob Butcher, Jane Coles, Peter Daish, Sheila Dawson, Linda Flower, Jess Gordon, Linda Hall, John Hewertson, Frances Jones, Guru Nayani, Anthony Maister, Clare Marshall, Smita Pandit-Patil, Dienye Pepple, Alan Phillips, Tania Phillips, Ian Robertson, Timothy Sales, Karen Salter, Marcus Thomas, Fiona Thompson, Hannah Turner, Christine Walker and all others in addition to those whose names I have already mentioned in other contexts above and the administrative staff, such as Karen Amos, Brenda Baldwin, Mary Battison, Myrna Couttes, Jean Kurecki, Sharon Smith, Lynda Tyrer, Deviani Vyas and Angela Welsh. My special thanks to my secretary, Naina Sadrani, and also to the staff from the Princess Marina Hospital library, Carol Weller, Dorothy Stephen and Angela Concannon.

The warmth and support from my wife Radha, my sons Amitabh and Rajaneesh and my daughter-in-law Amrita, have been most invigorating for me in this project. All the excitement associated with the birth of our delightful grandson, Siddharth, has also coincided with the birth of this book. I am also grateful for the affection, help and support of my mother Kusum, brothers Amar, Arun, Arvind, Ved and Anand, sisters Savitri and Asha and also our long-standing family friends of more than three decades, such as Arun Kumar Dubey, Subhash Chakravarti, Manjeet Kumar Chaturvedi, Mahendra Singh Fauzdar, Surendra Mishra, Suresh Naubar, Prabhakar Shukla, Rajjan Shukla, Kamalakar Tripathi and many others.

Finally, I wish to thank all the authors of this book for the excellent quality of their contributions, to Comfort Jegede, Michael Coombs, Wendy Hudlass, Rachel Gillibrand, Mike Shardlow and others at John Wiley & Sons for their unfailing support and to all the readers for taking the trouble to read and make full use of this book.

Kedar Nath Dwivedi

REFERENCES

Behere, P. B. (1997) 'Professor Srivastava: an Appreciation.' In K.N. Dwivedi & V. P. Varma (Eds), *Depression in Children and Adolescents*, London: Whurr.

Clark, D. H. (1996) *The Story of a Mental Hospital: Fulbourn 1958–1983*. London: Process Press.

Department of Health (1995) *A Handbook on Child and Adolescent Mental Health*. London: HMSO.

Dwivedi, K. N. (Ed.) (1993) *Group Work with Children and Adolescents: A Handbook*. London: Jessica Kingsley.

Dwivedi, K. N. (Ed.) (1997) *Therapeutic Use of Stories*. London: Routledge.

Dwivedi, K. N. & Bell, S. (1993) 'Encopresis.' In K.N. Dwivedi (Ed.), *Group Work with Children and Adolescents*. London: Jessica Kingsley.

Dwivedi, K. N., Lovett, S. B., Jones, M. H., Wright, J. M. & Woolley, E. (1984) 'Family treatment on a day treatment basis: a case illustration.' *A.F.T. Newsletter*, August: 3–9.

Health Advisory Service (1995) *Child and Adolescent Mental Health Services*. London: HMSO.

Law, M. (1994) *In the Eye of the Storm*. Cambridge: Fulbourn Hospital.

Marwah, S. M. (1996) 'Fourth decade of Professor Ishwar Chandra Tiwari's contributions: an insight.' In K. N. Dwivedi & V. P. Varma (Eds), *Meeting the Needs of Ethnic Minority Children*. London: Jessica Kingsley.

Tiwari, I. C. (1997) 'Professor Marwah's inspiring contributions.' In K. N. Dwivedi & V. P. Varma (Eds), *A Handbook of Childhood Anxiety Management*. Aldershot: Arena Publishers.

INTRODUCTION

Kedar Nath Dwivedi

It is a real pleasure to have the opportunity to introduce this volume on enhancing parenting skills. Of all the tasks that any sentient being performs, parenting must, by far, be the most important. It is through parenting that we make societies and cultures that are altruistic, narcissistic or egocentric, shaping all the future that is going to be visited on this earth and beyond and creating heaven or hell for all the generations to come.

The essence of good parenting is the development of a taste for delight in the delight of others. It is built upon a foundation of empathy, through which one gets in touch with the fantasies, feelings and needs of the child within, and therefore of the child without. The whole process of parenting is, therefore, an extremely delicate and complex partnership with many dimensions.

Parenting also provides an opportunity to practise and improve one's ability to balance and harmonise. It is a little like pottery, where there is a need for balance between the hand inside and the hand outside the clay on the wheel. Similarly in parenting, one hand is concerned with intimate emotional care, support and nurturing while the other hand sets boundaries, promotes better emotional and behavioural management and offers discipline. Without the hand inside, the pot is likely to break. In the absence of the hand outside, it can assume a form that is very ugly.

Luckily a great deal of parenting just happens naturally. Also good or bad parenting has a tendency to breed itself. A piece of iron, for example, by being in contact with a magnet, becomes magnetised and in turn can

Enhancing Parenting Skills: A Guide Book for Professionals Working with Parents.
Edited by K. N. Dwivedi. © 1997 John Wiley & Sons Ltd.

magnetise another piece of iron. Similarly the qualities of parenting tend to be transmitted and flow like a river. Kendler (1996), exploring the genetic-epidemiologic perspective using the Parental Bonding Instrument in a study on a large number of twins, concluded that 'The provision of parenting is influenced by attitudes derived from the parent's family of origin as well as by genetically influenced parental temperamental characteristics. The elicitation of parenting is influenced by temperamental traits of the offspring that are, in turn, under partial genetic control' (p. 11.)

However, the difference between humans and other sentient beings lies in our enormous potential for continuous learning. Although it may be possible to train a dog to screw nut number 19, it is impossible to educate it to the level at which we educate human beings. Human beings can learn to grasp the framework behind processes and can contribute towards its improvement. Thus, not only can we be trained as good drivers, but we can also be educated in systemic thinking so that when our cars decide to have a massive tantrum, we can open the bonnet and, instead of being overwhelmed by the complexity of the contents underneath, we can use a framework, say for example, the electrical subsystem and so on, to make sense of what may be going wrong and what needs to be done.

It is with anticipation and excitement that most people enter parenthood, but the complexity and pressures of modern life can turn that event into an isolating and difficult experience. As family life has become so complex today, the context of parenting has also changed considerably. Parenthood, therefore, is no longer a simple thing but has many manifestations, motives and meanings.

Parenting is rightly attracting more political attention now than ever before. In the UK, an All-Party Parliamentary Group for Parenting, which includes members of both Houses and all political persuasions, has been recently established with a quasi-official status. A Parenting Forum has also been formed to highlight and campaign in favour of the importance of parenting education and support for parents and families along with the publication of its regular newsletter from the National Children's Bureau.

Parents wish to do their best for their children. However, they need the support of others to acquire the needed knowledge and skills, to choose what would be best for their children and also to turn for help when they need it. A variety of professionals are, therefore, now involved in contributing to the assessment of parenting skills and in planning, organising, coordinating and offering help to parents for enhancing their parenting skills. The importance of the professional–parent relationship cannot be overemphasised. It is, however, important to have the right balance between public support for parenting and the private responsibilities of parents.

Not only parents but professionals too are faced with challenges and are having to make decisions in the face of uncertainty and rapid changes in social processes and family life. Edwards (1955, p. 237) points out

> The concept of 'parenting skills' features large in professional, political and popular discourse on the role and responsibility of parents . . . It is clear however, that the service providers, predominantly women, formulate a role for themselves in the face of poverty and poor housing which they feel powerless to change.

Although there is a great deal of literature dealing with many aspects of parenting, there is a lack of a suitable and comprehensive books that would help professionals with their practical programmes.

This volume is aimed at meeting this important need. It begins by setting the parenting scene in historical, socio-economic, gender and ethno-cultural contexts. Thus, Chapter 1 on Parenting Yesterday, Today and Tomorrow by *Sebastian Kraemer*, Chapter 2 on Parenting at the Margins: Some Consequences of Inequality by *Masud Hoghughi*, Chapter 3 on Gender Issues in Parenting by *Paquita McMichael* and *Gerda Siann* and Chapter 4 on Approaches to Working with Ethnicity and Cultural Differences by *Charmaine Kemps* fully explore these perspectives. In Chapter 5 on Parenthood: Assessment of 'Good-enough Parenting' by *Shanthy Parameswaran*, the details of the parenting assessment prócess are clarified. The next three chapters—Chapter 6 on Parent Education Programmes by *Dorit Braun*, Chapter 7 on Group Work with Parents by *Harold Behr* and Chapter 8 on Developing Home-Based Parenting Skill Programmes, Supported by Group Sessions of Parenting Techniques by *Peter Marsden-Allen*—detail various practical aspects of setting up educational, therapeutic and psycho-educational parenting programmes. Certain specific contexts for parenting, such as hyperactivity, stepfamily, gifted and disabled children, are examined with a view to setting up programmes for enhancing parenting in such contexts. Thus, Chapter 9 on Helping Parents Cope with their Hyperactive Children by *Jo Douglas*, Chapter 10 on Stepfamilies by *Kathleen Cox*, Chapter 11 on Parenting of Gifted Children by *David George* and Chapter 12 on Parenting Learning Disabled Children: Realities and Practicalities by *Ruchira Leisten* focus on these specific issues.

I have been extremely fortunate in receiving a contribution of excellent quality from each of the authors. For me, it has been a privilege and great pleasure to put together the work of such an extraordinary group of multidisciplinary experts. I am sure it is going to be immensely useful to a large variety of professionals, such as general practitioners, social workers, psychologists, psychiatrists, health visitors, community psychiatric nurses, probation officers, education welfare officers, teachers, school doctors, school nurses, paediatricians and many other child care professionals interested in enhancing parenting skills. The book also has an important political message for the policy makers as regards the importance of investing in parenting and will also be of great interest to members of the legal profession.

REFERENCES

Edwards, J. (1995) '"Parenting skills": Views of community health and social service providers about the needs of their "Clients".' *Journal of Social Policy*, **24** (2), 237–259.

Kendler, K. (1996) 'Parenting: A genetic-epidemiologic perspective.' *American Journal of Psychiatry*, **153** (1), 11–20.

PARENTING YESTERDAY, TODAY AND TOMORROW

Sebastian Kraemer

INTRODUCTION

In the past few years, spurred on by increasing anxiety about child abuse, violent crime, delinquency and drug misuse, public debate about the contribution of parents has become more intense. It has always been tempting to blame parents for the bad behaviour of their children, but this is a more thoughtful discussion. Without blame, it is possible to see what effects different kinds of parenting have on the lives of children, even extending into their own adult lives in the next generation. An enormous number of books and articles, conferences and policy statements have appeared, to the extent that we can say there is a movement towards supporting parents in their task. It is only possible to do this now that we understand just how difficult and stressful the task is. Until recently there was little public or professional acknowledgement of the immensity of parental commitment, perhaps because much of it was carried out by women, mostly mothers, whose voices were not heard. Even now it is easy for busy adults to resist a serious exploration of children's needs, because to do so arouses poignant memories of one's own childhood, both happy and sad, nostalgic and painful.

In this chapter, I outline a story of parenthood, from past to future, seen through the lens of attachment theory. Those working closely with families, such as health visitors, social workers, child carers and parent supporters in the voluntary sector, need a coherent framework in which

Enhancing Parenting Skills: A Guide Book for Professionals Working with Parents.
Edited by K. N. Dwivedi. © 1997 John Wiley & Sons Ltd.

to understand family processes. They also need to know that their work cannot flourish in the absence of a coherent national policy on parenthood. The privatisation of children's care and needs is no longer an option.

WHAT IS NEW?

There is a paradox about parenting in that the core task does not change much, yet it is only in the past few decades that we have been able to spell out clearly what it is. Even thousands of years ago you might find children and parents doing similar things to what they do now. Babies are the same as they were then and so are their needs. The first thing a baby needs is to be held, and most of us instinctively feel this, even with other people's babies. We are programmed to be interested in tiny children, and are all familiar with the way in which babies in prams can hypnotise us with their big eyes. Even hyperactive teenagers are calmed for a moment by the experience.

If you go back far enough into prehistory, you would find no humans at all but creatures resembling us in many ways. The higher primates of today, such as chimpanzees or gorillas, probably represent something like our prehuman ancestors, and they look after their offspring in quite familiar ways. The popularity of zoos and nature programmes on TV has a lot to do with the fact that we can identify so readily with animals, particularly those that form attachments between adults and infants. The most obvious sign of this is the way the little one holds on to the adult; but, of course, you don't have to hold on to be attached. Any visit to the countryside in the spring will demonstrate the system at work. Lambs play around in the field, but as you approach they rush to the ewe and furiously suckle at her teat. (For some reason they also wag their tails vigorously). It's important that each lamb knows which ewe to go to, and this depends on quite early postnatal contact between the two. Farmers say that it is possible to get lambs adopted by sheep that have not given birth to them, but this has to be skilfully managed. The sea mammals, with neither fur nor limbs, show how attachment is principally a matter of proximity. I am always impressed by the way that dolphins swim together in parallel with an invisible bond between them.

Parenting is not simply a social activity. It is an essential biological process, without which our infants would not survive. Newborn humans are particularly fragile because they still have a lot of developing to do. They are nowhere near ready for any kind of independence. All they can do with any skill is to suck at a nipple or teat. Of course they are also well equipped with voice boxes to ensure that everyone knows when they need looking after, and within a few weeks are able to entrance their caretakers with smiles. None of this is new. It has been like that for tens of thousands of years.

JOHN BOWLBY AND ATTACHMENT THEORY

The originator of attachment theory, John Bowlby, died in 1990, aged 82. He was the son of an eminent surgeon and was brought up in Edwardian style (see Holmes, 1993). So what could such a man possibly understand about the intimacies of mother and child in the modern world? After the Second World War the reconstruction of society included some quite new observations about children. It became clear that food and clothing were necessary for them to thrive, but not sufficient. Some who had been evacuated had suffered terribly because they were taken away from their loved ones. It was also noted that children in institutional care did not thrive, and some even died, in the absence of love. It didn't have to be parental love, but it did have to be close and intimate. Bowlby said that such attentiveness was as important as vitamins. But because of the conventional segregations of husbands and wives of the time, it seemed obvious to everyone, including him of course, that this was about the child's tie to the mother (actually the title of one of his early papers). He noted that children who became delinquents in adolescence had suffered deprivation, or actual losses, in parental care, by which he meant maternal care. Women heard of Bowlby's work and believed that they were being told that unless they spent every minute of the day and night with their infants they would damage them for ever. No doubt some mothers did not realise how much their children needed adult human company—it was quite a common practice, for example, to leave babies in the pram outside to be 'aired' most of the day. But of course it was a terrible misunderstanding, not helped by prevailing custom and Bowlby's own limited social experience, to think that continuous care meant that only one person had to provide it.

The fact is, children needed looking after. What this actually means is becoming clearer now that research based on Bowlby's original work is showing how even quite subtle mismatches between parents and babies can lead to later social and learning problems for these children. Clinicians and researchers (e.g. Murray, Cooper & Stein, 1991) are beginning to see that a whole range of problems, many of which obviously have serious social consequences, are dependent to a considerable extent upon the quality of attachment in early life. We now know that those who have had good attachments to their parents have a far greater chance of passing on this good fortune to their own children (Steele, Steele & Fonagy, 1996). Without secure attachment, many of life's ordinary stresses become serious threats. The predictable hurdles of starting school, leaving home and becoming an adult with a sexual and (if lucky) a working life are all points of potential crisis. In addition, although most families still start off intact, as many as a half of all British children will experience the break-up of their parents' relationship (Clarke, 1992). Children and young people who are insecure are at greater risk of a whole host of problems provoked at times of change or loss, including delinquency and bullying, accidents, eating disorders, depression, chronic non-specific ill-health, addictions, and, of course, difficulties in intimate relationships. Secure children have greater confidence, are more generous and have greater capacity to deal with inevitable conflicts with peers. They are more curious about the world and therefore keener to learn (Sroufe, 1989). Love is not enough, however. The greatest stress for parents is dealing with feelings of rage and hatred, both in themselves and in their children. When children see that we can tolerate and survive such powerful emotions, without resorting to verbal or physical violence, they can learn to do the same.

Attachment is often misunderstood as a kind of instant bond, like superglue, as if one needed to get stuck to the parent and hold on for ever. It is really the opposite, more like a flexible gravitational force. Just as in the most common experience of gravity, the attachment mechanism is most easily observed when one of the participants is big and the other small. From the infant's perspective, the parental figure, usually but not necessarily the mother, seems gigantic and attractive, especially when the little one is tired, hungry, frightened or in pain. Then the child needs to be close to his caregiver, for the sake of protection. Of course the original function of this process was to protect the infant from predators and other life-threatening dangers. In humans such dangers are fewer, but the need for emotional protection is greater. A baby alone and in distress is subject to the most awful terrors, which we can barely imagine. (The threat of recalling such states from our own infancy or early childhood may even prevent us from taking the notion of attachment seriously.) Babies need adults to help them make sense of their own states of mind. Infants have very powerful feelings, both of pleasure and of pain, which are probably more embedded in the body than our adult experiences seem to be, but they cannot yet think about those feelings in a very organised way. Therefore, the adults who look after them, besides having to protect them from harm (in fact, from dying) and cleaning, feeding, clothing and putting them to sleep, have a fundamentally important task of helping them to understand their own minds. The notion of an infant having thoughts is quite novel, and arises out of early psychoanalytic work, including Bowlby's (see also Miller *et al.*, 1989). Just because we forget our early experiences does not mean that they did not occur, or that they were vague and meaningless as was often assumed in the not so distant past. But the capacity for thinking cannot develop in an emotional vacuum. Video studies of mother–infant interaction show how the two can attain a rhythm—like a dance—in which each responds to the other's cues. Topics of this kind are difficult to mention without putting some people off. It is rather like discussing sexual intercourse, in that the process is intimate, private, and rather disturbing to contemplate. They are, after all, lovers. What the mother–baby studies show is that when it goes well the baby is looked after not only physically, but also psychologically. The psychological health that results means, among other things, being able to understand both your own and other people's feelings. It also gives you more confidence in your own point of view, and more curiosity about the world around you, including other people's points of view. These are fundamental social skills, and most people have them in some degree.

It is important to note here that the attachment process probably determines not only emotional and social development, but also the stability of physiological variables. There is strong evidence from animal studies to show that an early separation from the mother, for example, has profoundly disturbing effects on the maintenance of body systems such as the circulation and pressure of the blood, immunity from infection, hormone levels, temperature control and so on (Hofer, 1995).

Even when they are past infancy small children cannot be left alone without an adult close by, but what is the point of this proximity? Is it just to prevent accidents? No, it is to be present, so that the child is conscious that someone is there. You might not have to say anything at all, though there will be inevitable bursts of chatter, laughter or tears. When, as a child, you start school you can probably dress yourself and wipe your bottom, but you still need someone to be available to manage all sorts of experiences, not just to help with doing up buttons. You need someone to look after you and somewhere familiar where this can take place. The important thing about being looked after is that it is done by someone who not only protects you from harm but also keeps you in mind, who thinks about you quite a lot of the time, even when you are not there—someone who is interested in you, who wants to know how you are, what you would like to eat, to play with, to take to bed when you go to sleep, someone who knows about how you began in life and, just as important as all the others, knows how to deal with you when you behave badly.

We can say similar things about teenagers, who also make enormous demands on the capacity of their parents to keep calm and not be swayed by powerful and contradictory emotions. But the point is simply that none of these requirements has changed significantly in thousands of years. What has changed is the knowledge we now have about these issues. Besides the brilliant research studies on infant attachment, there is also the intergenerational work that shows, as many people intuitively knew, that your attachment to your parents has a profound influence on your capacity to look after your own children. There is a strong correlation between one generation and the next, but the influences of father and mother are not necessarily related. So you can acquire different skills and different deficits from each parent. Although formal research has not yet reached that point, clinical and casework experience shows how significant other close attachments can be—with grandparents, step parents, foster parents, childminders, nannies, and so on.

A secure attachment is not a glue, but more an invisible bond. When all is well it can stretch and the offspring can move away to explore the world around. It is a condition for learning and being curious about other relationships and other things. The anxiously attached child cannot feel free like this (Bowlby, 1988), but has to cling to the parent, in case she gets unhappy or ill or even disappears. So the elastic is very tight, actually rather glue-like, and development is inhibited. If the parent is rejecting, the bond may lose its elasticity and the child may float freely, apparently without needs, be street wise and self-reliant, but actually desperate to be looked after. But of course attachment is lifelong; it is not only for children. Only adolescents routinely deny this truth, as many have to, in order to escape the gravitational field of home. The rest of us know how important it is to have someone close, somewhere to live and to belong to and something to do that makes sense. All these are attachments.

Many, though not all, of the ideas I have summarised here have become what might be regarded as the *official* view on parenting. That is to say, it is no longer possible to pretend that children can be treated badly and not suffer from it, even if they seem to forget about it. But we need to be careful now not to be too certain about what we think is right for children, as if there were no room for doubt. The truth is that there are no rules about childcare, but there are some principles that we can be fairly confident are universal. The most important of these is the primacy of protection—that is what attachment is about, and it means protection both from physical and emotional harm. Modern policy on families must be based on this primary goal, which is the promotion of secure attachments between parents and children.

In the past there were no policies at all. Children were loved, hated, abused, abandoned and killed. But the single most obvious difference between past and present is the fact that, until the twentieth century, children often died before their parents, indeed before their first birthdays (Kessen, 1965), and if they did not die they were often abandoned. The Paris hospice in the eighteenth century had a revolving door, rather like the device used in banks for taking and delivering cash, except without the window, so no one would see who had left the child. In London, Thomas Coram built the foundling hospital in 1740. You can still see in their little museum the pathetic trinkets left with the babies so that they could be identified by their parents, just in case they were able to retrieve them at a later date. It would be convenient to think that in such circumstances people would not get so attached to their children, to make it easier to lose them. There is little evidence for this view. Epitaphs for children who have died often demonstrate the agony of parental grief, even if it is tempered by the expectation that the child will be better off in heaven. Indeed, this may be so since the quality of childcare in past ages was probably on average far poorer than it is today. It is important to distinguish the love that parents have for children with the actual care they provide. They are not strictly correlated. (This, incidentally, is particularly true of fathers, including modern ones.) It is quite possible to be devastated by the death of a child whom one has loved and at the same time treated quite cruelly.

Lloyd de Mause's shocking text, 'The evolution of childhood', begins with the memorable words 'the history of childhood is a nightmare from which we have only recently begun to awaken' (1976, p. 1.) He outlines a series of stages in child rearing which suggest indeed that in ancient times the death of children was not only expected, but often willed. There were economic reasons for infanticide—it was the only reliable form of family planning in those days—but de Mause's thesis is that children are also the recipients of all sorts of projections put on them by parents. You can see how this might arise. A baby is a captive in your home who, however much he or she is loved, will tend to persecute you with the inevitable demands of a helpless person. The infant cannot wait, he or she is greedy and selfish. If seen this way it is not surprising that children have so often been identified as essentially evil beings. (Do you need to be reminded of the fact that your children can seem to be angels one minute and devils the next?) Even in the not very distant past of, say, two hundred years ago, children were often quite cruelly neglected before they were able to walk and talk, and then, if they managed to survive, were likely to be faced with quite active measures on the part of their caretakers to control their movements. The swaddling of babies with bandages was meant to prevent them from doing terrible things to themselves, as well as to limit their freedom. It was thought that crawling was bad for them because it is similar to the way animals move around. (And, of course, in those days it was an offence to human dignity to think that we could have anything to do with animals. Look at the trouble Charles Darwin had when he said that we are descended from wild creatures.) Except when they needed attention, small children were wrapped up for several months, and would be left lying around, or even hanging up, like articles of clothing or luggage. This was a widespread practice in Europe until the nineteenth century. We can be shocked by this now, because we have far better appreciation of children's actual needs. To the parents of past times such behaviour was not at all negligent. And it limited the demands of small children, though presumably not the noise they could make. A silent child was preferable: '. . . expressions of tenderness towards children occur most often when the child is non-demanding, especially when the child is either asleep or dead' (de Mause, 1976, p. 17).

Susanna Wesley, in a letter to her son John, the founder of Methodism, in the eighteenth century wrote:

> I insist on conquering the wills of children . . . the parent who studies to subdue self-will in his children, works together with God in the saving of a soul: the parent who indulges it does the devil's work . . . break their wills betimes . . . let a child from a year old be taught to fear the rod and cry softly . . . at all events from that age make him do as he is bid if you whip him ten times running to effect it. Let none persuade you that it is cruelty to do this; it is cruelty not to. (Cited by Newson & Newson, 1974)

The pressure to produce obedient children was justified by the fear that if they were to die untamed they would not go to heaven, but it is clear that there is an element of the projection that de Mause speaks of, and with which we are all familiar even now. And it is worth noting that the parent who is expected to enforce God's will is the father. It is also likely that the privilege of sexual abuse of his children was assumed by the same father, justified by all sorts of excuses such as the need to prepare his daughters for marriage. I do not dwell on adults' sexual contact with children in this chapter, but it should be clear that the extent of all child abuse was far greater in the past than it is now. The difference is that in the past it was either taken for granted, or just ignored.

The notion of parenting is a new one. In the past there were mothers and fathers, but also many others who took different roles in relation to children. Older siblings, particularly in large families, would have had some duties with younger ones, and the so-called extended family was more in evidence than now. I say so-called because there is a tendency nowadays to idealise this arrangement, as if it were in all ways better for children. We might imagine a peaceful rural scene in which all the uncles and aunts, grandparents and even great grandparents somehow live together, so that no one is ever alone, and no child is without somebody to care for him or her. There is some truth in this. People travelled far less than they do now in almost all past societies, so that surviving relatives were more likely to live nearby if not in the same house. Domestic architecture, furthermore, even in quite grand houses, which were often built without corridors, tended to allow little privacy. This is hardly ideal, however. Is it really so wonderful to have a crowd of people living with you all the time? Moments of intimacy, whether between adults or between adults and children, were probably rather rare. The exclusive relationship which all children crave from their parents will have been virtually unobtainable. Even in large modern families it is hard for any individual child to spend much time alone with one parent. We now know that the sort of relationships that lead to secure attachments will be few in number and all the attachment figures will be well known to the child. So the extended family, particularly when it is large, might well have diluted these intimate bonds. A little child could be cared for by up to a dozen different people in the day, or by none of them at all, since any one of them might reasonably assume that someone else was responsible. If a child wandered off from the household, who would check that he or she was gone? In this arrangement, parents were not necessarily the closest to their children, though they would most likely still feel the strongest interest in them over the child's lifespan. Even today fathers can have this kind of extended family link to their children. The children may not see him for days, or even weeks. He may not be a caretaker at all. Support for parents, the principal theme of this book, must not be organised in such a way as to obscure the answer to this simple question: *Who at this moment is primarily responsible for the care and protection of this child?*

In the past fifty years fashions in advice to mothers have changed very rapidly. The old idea of the child as a kind of enemy still survives but is no longer the official view. But even up to the time of the Second World War, the standard method of childrearing was built on this assumption. Something had changed, however. It was now thought that the early years of a child's life were indeed formative ones, and that it was therefore a public matter how children were brought up. 'The neglected toddler in everyone's way is the material which becomes the disgruntled agitator, while the happy contented child is the pillar of the state' said Gwen St Aubyn in a parenting manual published in 1935 (cited by Humphreys & Gordon, 1993). All this was in the context of enormous losses of men in the Great War and in South Africa, and an explicit concern that we needed to replenish stocks of obedient fighting men in case there was another war. It is important to note how parenthood is related to the prevailing moral code. In earlier times God's will was the driving force, but by the early twentieth century it was the survival of the nation that mattered most. The most influential expert of those days was Dr Frederic Truby King, originally based in New Zealand, who launched a successful movement to convert mothers to breast feeding. Besides this laudable aim, almost everything else he preached was quite horrific. The key to the Truby King method was to feed your baby boy by the clock every four hours and never at night. If you gave in to him he would become spoiled and spineless and, by implication, be no use as a soldier when he grew up. To toughen them up, babies were to spend much of the day on their own outside in the fresh air, and should not be cuddled or comforted even when in distress. Mothers were not encouraged to play with babies, because it would excite them too much. Toilet training began in the first year. Masturbation was a dangerous pastime that would lead to unmentionable problems later in life. Various devices, hardly different from the swaddles and splints of earlier times, were recommended to prevent it. Thumbsucking was almost as bad. Fathers had no role except earning money. Middle-class mothers were particularly taken by this method, in the expectation that they could produce perfect children, but it was heartbreaking. Only a decade later, but with a world war in between, Benjamin Spock published the first edition of *Baby and Child Care*. It was a breakthrough for parents, and sold millions of copies. He said you can trust your own judgement about what the child, particularly the baby, needs. He did not say that you could let children do anything that they liked. He said that you should know what the baby wants, which is not necessarily the same as doing what the baby wants.

> Children are proud to think that they can be truly useful and will rise to the challenge. This can begin very young. A baby of 9 months shouldn't be allowed to get the impression that it's alright to pull mother's hair or bite her cheek, but that he owes her respect. (Spock, 1968)

PARENTING TODAY

The revolution in social life that has occurred in the past twenty years will probably never be reversed. Women's work is no longer confined to the home. Furthermore, the nature of paid work has changed for both men and women, with women gaining and men losing. Most new jobs now go to women, and are part time. These are not always well paid, but they may be convenient. But for both sexes there is no security in work. You don't get a job 'for life' any more. The institution of marriage has changed in parallel with this. If present trends continue, a third or more of the next generation won't get a husband or wife, or a partner, for life any more, either. This has its impact on children. Whereas in Victorian times children would, if they survived, gain step parents through the death of biological ones, now the process is driven by separation and divorce. There is an enormous amount of panic about all this. The arguments about single parents have been painfully polarised, and readily hijacked by the media and politicians with their own agendas. The fact is that about three-quarters of families in Britain still contain both the original parents, and that many step and single parents manage to bring up their children well enough. In spite of the mental pain caused by family breakdown, and by the years of conflict that may precede it, it is often poverty that is the greatest enemy of single parents. But we do know from research that the greatest emotional damage comes from continued battles over the children between separated or divorced parents (Amato & Keith, 1991).

Another subject for ill-informed panic is the extent of child abuse. It was only in the 1960s that paediatricians realised that the strange patterns of fractures they were seeing on the X-rays of small sick babies were in fact multiple injuries, and the term 'battered baby' came into use. Over a decade later, a similar revelation dawned on child health professionals and social workers, which was that the disclosures by children of sexual abuse done to them in secret by adults were not lies. By now we are familiar with the sickening truth, which is that children are statistically at far greater danger from their parents and caregivers than from anyone else. We know that although parenthood is incredibly stressful, it is less likely to be abusive if the parents have been supported. The best support you can have is that provided by your own parents a generation earlier. But if you haven't had that, then it is even more important to obtain it from elsewhere. This is not something that can be left to chance; there are scattered signs that it is being recognised by those making or influencing policies in education, health and social services. But the way government departments are organised goes against any coordinated effort to promote secure attachments for the next generation. Simply advising social workers to give more support to families at risk is unlikely to make much difference, for example.

PARENTING TOMORROW

We have a choice: the nightmare or a better world. The nightmare is easy to describe—more homelessness, more hopeless adolescents getting caught up in drugs and prostitution, or having babies before they are ready to be parents. No employment for young people, not even for graduates. Lawless groups roam the streets. Some say we are returning to the Middle Ages, with the multinational companies taking the place of powerful and rivalrous City States, where the lucky few enjoy the privileges of wealth and happiness locked away in fortresses with armed guards. The vision of a better world is difficult to picture partly because after twenty years of decline, we are demoralised and defeated. It's not worth planning for change, we just have to plan for survival. We can do better than that, but it does require a leap of the imagination. We need a national policy that promotes parenthood and will put money into it.

When a baby is newly born he or she needs looking after by a very close circle of people. No one can do this task alone. Often grandmothers, friends or childminders will help, mostly women. In my view, fathers and stepfathers must be there too. There is considerable pressure from the European Commission to introduce proper levels of parental leave throughout the EU. Sweden, only recently a member, leads the way. Both parents have the right to paid leave from work intermittently over several years of the child's early life. This is just the first step in promoting parenthood, and it is important for children to be looked after by both mothers and fathers. Little children see women being effective both as parents and workers. Unless fathers are included in looking after children, how are the children going to see what men are like, and how can men find out what children are like? You may say that men should not be allowed near children in case they abuse them sexually. Possibly, but the evidence from systematic research is that men will rarely abuse their own children if they are involved in caring for them from the very start (Parker & Parker, 1986). Fathers are just as capable of devoted parental care as mothers, and there is no need to discriminate against their taking an equal share in the task if they are available to do so. Their role is not just to punish children; they are also needed to look after children, just as mothers do, which includes being both loving and firm as the occasion demands (Kraemer, 1995a). There has been an enormous change in the prevailing view of fatherhood, in that many men are now proud to say how much they do for their children, even if it is sometimes an exaggeration. Less than fifty years ago most men would have been puzzled by the very idea of participant fatherhood, but would have been keen to show that they provided for the mother and children by earning money. Being the breadwinner is no longer a male prerogative, however, and that notion should now be put to rest. The non-domestic world may still seem to be dominated by male values, but the fact is that men are increasingly marginalised. Without the opportunity to be useful parents, men will slide further into meaninglessness, as we are beginning to see in the suicide statistics.

The second step is a revolution in childcare, including support for parents who are not employed. New family centres, offering childcare facilities, are being set up which encourage participation of both mothers and fathers, and are used by families across the social spectrum. Yet these are pioneers in a virtual desert. At present there is little in the way of organised quality childcare in Britain. This also costs money, but possibly not as much as it would seem. If employers were to contribute to childcare costs, for example, they might well save on retraining new staff to replace those that have to leave. Some parents want to take longer breaks from work to be with their babies, others are keen to return. Either way they will need help. The future of parenthood depends on the task being shared with others. Whatever arrangements are made for non-parental childcare the people doing it have to be properly trained, and properly paid. It is not sufficient to leave these costs to the parents themselves. The privatisation of family life has been the policy of both the political left and right until now, and it will not do.

Because children's needs are now known to be so much greater, it is inconceivable that one or two people can successfully carry out the task unaided. If it is shared between skilled people, there is far less chance of neglect and abuse. Of course, if the caretakers are neither valued nor skilled, they may well abuse the most vulnerable children, as we have seen in numerous local authority scandals. Rather than talk of children's centres or nurseries, Penelope Leach in her most recent book *Children First* (1993) talks of 'child-places' where all sorts of child-related activities—formal and informal—might take place, with and without parental involvement. There is a role for child and adolescent mental health professionals in such a place. They were once collectively known as 'child guidance', which is easier to say but is now rather an out-of-date concept. The newer model of work involves assessment and therapy with children, young people and families as before (see, for example, Daws, 1989) but there are far too many children with serious problems to leave it at that. Health visitors, teachers, social workers, childcarers and others are in daily contact with children who are clearly disturbed or at risk of abuse and neglect. Calling a case conference may be necessary, as may a referral for specialist help, but often it is not clear what should be done and mental health specialists are increasingly being asked to give informal advice to front-line workers. Sometimes a brief consultation can be surprisingly helpful. Often it is possible to point out that the children in question are in far greater trouble than the worker thought, which helps to set in motion more appropriate action (Kraemer, 1995b).

The revolution has to go further than that. People need homes and jobs. We have seen the disastrous effects of high-rise housing. It's better to build neighbourhoods where children can play without being run over. (Although the total of road deaths in Britain is going down, the number of children injured or killed in the streets is going up.) Nobody expects full-time life-long employment, but the welfare and taxation systems are still locked into the idea that you either work or you don't. You can do both and, if you are a parent, some of the time that you are not working can be devoted to your children.

Finally, education. If parenthood were taken seriously it would be put on the National Curriculum from primary school onwards. Teachers would need to be specially trained to do this kind of work, which is different for didactic instruction. After leaving school there are opportunities to learn about caretaking. There is much talk nowadays about voluntary service for young people. Some, such as Michael Young (Young & Halsey, 1995), even say it should be compulsory! This could include supervised experience in looking after the elderly, people with disabilities, toddlers and infants. It could introduce, in a way that no other programme could, the realities of attachment and dependency to young people just becoming adults. It may even postpone their thoughts on parenthood for a while, which is no bad thing. Preparation for parenthood is obviously most in demand when the baby is either on the way or just born. Besides antenatal classes and parent support groups there is also a wide literature for parents to read, including the authoritative series from the Tavistock Clinic *Understanding your Child* (available from Rosendale Press, 10 Greycoat Place, London SW1P 1SB), published in separate books for each year of life from babyhood to the teens, and including a special edition for parents of disabled children.

CONCLUSION

Modern practice in enhancing parenthood must be based on a clear vision of the goal—secure attachment. Other contributions in this book will show some of the many approaches that can be adopted to achieve it. My intention here has been to outline a historical sequence to put the reader in context. The dawning recognition both of the importance and the burden of parenting is just one of the strands in the movement bringing the lives—the needs and rights—of children into the open. The care of young children particularly has remained until very recently largely a hidden activity, carried out informally, in cash or in kind, by women doing their best, with little public support or recognition.

REFERENCES

Amato, P. R & Keith, B. (1991) 'Parental divorce and the well-being of children: a meta-analysis.' *Psychological Bulletin*, **110** (1), 26–46.
Bowlby, J. (1988) *A Secure Base*. London: Routledge.
Clarke, L. (1992) 'Children's family circumstances: recent trends in Great Britain.'

European Journal of Population, **8**, 309–340.

Daws, D. (1989) *Through the Night: Helping Parents with Sleepless Infants*. London: Free Association Books.

de Mause, L. (1976) 'The evolution of childhood.' In L. de Mause (Ed.), *The History of Childhood*. London: Souvenir Press. [Republished as *The History of Childhood: The Untold Story of Child Abuse*, New York: Bedrick, 1988 and London: Bellew, 1991.]

Hofer, M. (1995) 'Hidden regulators: implications for a new understanding of attachment, separation, and loss.' In S. Goldberg, R. Muir & J. Kerr (Eds), *Attachment Theory: Social, Developmental and Clinical Perspectives*, Hillsdale, NJ: The Analytic Press.

Holmes, J. (1993) *John Bowlby and Attachment Theory*. London: Routledge.

Humphreys, S. & Gordon, P. (1993) *A Labour of Love: The Experience of Parenthood in Britain 1900–1950*, London: Sidgwick & Jackson, p. 49.

Kessen, W. (1965) *The Child*. New York: Wiley, p. 8.

Kraemer, S. (1995a) 'A man's place.' In C. Clulow (Ed.), *Women, Men and Marriage*. London: Sheldon Press.

Kraemer, S. (1995b) 'The liaison model: mental health services for children and adolescents.' *Psychiatric Bulletin*, **19**, 138–142.

Leach, P. (1993) *Children First*. London: Michael Joseph.

Miller, M., Rustin, M. E., Rustin, M. J. & Shuttleworth, J. (Eds) (1989) *Closely Observed Infants*. London: Duckworth.

Murray, L., Cooper, P. & Stein, A. (1991) 'Postnatal depression and infant development.' *British Medical Journal*, **302**, 978–979.

Newson, J. & Newson, E. (1974) 'Cultural aspects of childrearing in the English-speaking world.' in Richards, M. (Ed.), *The Integration of a Child into a Social World*. Cambridge: Cambridge University Press, p. 56.

Parker, H. & Parker S. (1986) 'Father–daughter sexual abuse: an emerging perspective.' *American Journal of Orthopsychiatry*, **56** (4), 531–549.

Spock, B. (1968) *Baby and Child Care*. London: New English Library, p. 29.

Sroufe, L. A. (1989) 'Relationships, self, and individual adaptation.' In A. Sameroff & R. Emde (Eds), *Relationships Disturbances in Early Childhood*. New York: Basic Books, p. 88.

Steele, M., Steele, H. & Fonagy, P. (1996) 'Associations among attachment classifications of mothers, fathers, and their infants: evidence for a relationship-specific perspective.' *Child Development*, **67**, 541–555.

Young, M. & Halsey, A. H. (1995) *Family and Community Socialism*. London: Institute for Public Policy Research.

Furthermore, in the course of lifespan development, the task of socialising children is shared between parents, teachers, authority figures, peers and the increasingly widening circle of people who from time to time undertake, with an individual child, tasks which in one much younger would be adopted by the biological parents. Because of these, it seems sensible to relate parenting to neither its *agents* (i.e. biological parents or their surrogates) nor the *end product*, which may be a competent and well-behaved or a handicapped and badly behaved child. Rather, parenting would be best regarded as a *process* which denotes certain attitudes, values and key purposes in the engagement between adults and children.

Despite the huge literature on parenting (over 30,000 references in the psychology and social science databases alone) there does not appear to be an adequate analysis and identification of the fundamental elements of parenting (Smith & Pugh, 1996). Close examination of the process suggests that the core elements of parenting are *care, control* and *development*. Each of these has a 'negative' aspect which denotes *safeguarding* or *freedom from* and a 'positive' one which suggests *promoting, fostering* and *encouraging* that particular area of activity.

Care

Care denotes the process of protecting the child from avoidable illness, harm, accident and abuse. On the positive side it encompasses looking after the child and meeting the child's needs for physical, emotional and social well-being (Pringle, 1986).

Protection from harm requires the parent to ensure that the child is not exposed to any unacceptable risks from accidents, animals or other human beings, and is free from illnesses and anything that causes pain or other distress. This demands that parents should, for the *sake of the child*, refrain from violence or other distressing forms of conflict in the home and also ensure that they and the child are not socially isolated. The child would receive enough stability, love and constancy to develop appropriate attachments (Bowlby, 1970; Erikson *et al.*, 1985; Fahlberg, 1991; Holmes, 1993) as a bulwark against subsequent experience of loss and difficulty.

The positive aspect of care goes beyond meeting the child's needs for survival, and concentrates on maximising its well-being physically, emotionally and socially. Here, the wider needs of the child (Erikson, 1968; Pringle, 1986) would be met in a manner that would equip it to meet positively and securely the challenges in the course of development from childhood into adolescence and beyond.

Control

Control is concerned with *setting and enforcing boundaries* for the child in the course of development. It starts with dos and don'ts of feeding, toilet training and exposure to risk and moves to the child's emotional and physical expressions of anger, distress and exuberance towards parents and a widening circle of others. Preventing the child from throwing food around, a stair guard to prevent the child from falling down the stairs, a fireguard and a playpen are all initial forms of physical boundary setting accompanied by verbal explanations, transmitted to the child until they become part of his or her internal control.

But the negative boundary setting is not enough to develop the child's social behaviour. Most parents, therefore, while prohibiting some behaviours, encourage others, which is why and how children eventually learn to keep themselves dry and to hold the banister when they walk up and down stairs.

Identifying boundaries is meaningless unless it is accompanied by relatively consistent enforcement. Most parents use a combination of talking and gentle physical intervention (such as stopping food being thrown about or seating the child on the potty) until the child learns what is required. In due course and, with parental encouragement, the behaviour becomes established and is sustained by natural reinforcers of parental praise, habit and social approval. The more conscientious and concerned the parents, the more they articulate general rules of behaviour (Aronfreed, 1968; Robinson, 1972) which, by virtue of their generality, make it easier for the child to learn how to behave properly under a variety of conditions.

Development

Development is concerned with 'gilding the lily'. Parental concern with doing the best is translated into ensuring that their children are not stunted or frustrated in realising their intellectual, physical, aesthetic and other potential. Most parents regard it as 'normal' and 'natural' to devote much of their time and resources to the positive development of their children's interests, abilities and potential (such as membership of clubs, learning to play an instrument, going on expeditions, etc.) rather than spending it on their own pleasure.

In the child's early years, parents are concerned mainly with care rather than control or development. As the child survives infancy and early childhood, while nurturance continues and deepens, greater prominence is given to issues of boundary setting and enforcement, particularly in the demanding environment of school, peer group relationships and use of free time. Once the norms in this area are established and the child behaves in an acceptable manner, so the emphasis moves on to development. This makes evolutionary sense, since without adequate care and control, no development is possible.

Continuity

It is important, therefore, to recognise that all three strands of parenting continue *throughout* the lifespan of an individual, with different elements emphasised at different stages, in part as a consequence of the particular relationship between the individual and those who undertake parenting. Thus, the state provides services for physical and psychological care of the population throughout the lifespan, friendships are formed in which parties look after each other's social needs, law enforcement agencies continue to demand observance of the laws of the country and opportunities are provided by many agencies for developmental activities. Biological parents' prominence in parenting gives way to peers, partners and employers and eventually the circle fully turns when children begin to take care of their parents. The basic process and elements of parenting remain the same.

Given the range of actions involved in parenting, it may help the development of a disciplined approach to recognise that almost all parenting activities focus on needs and problems in one or more of six areas of functioning: (1) physical; (2) intellectual/educational/ vocational; (3) home and family relationships; (4) skills for making and maintaining social relationsips; (5) anti-social behaviour; and (6) personal/clinical state (Hoghughi, 1978, 1992).

PREREQUISITES OF PARENTING

The major emphasis in the relevant literature is on discovering the role of parenting and identifying the main skills involved in order to use them for training (Fine, 1980, 1989; Harman & Brim, 1980; Neville *et al.*, 1995). It suggests that if parents had the appropriate skills, they would be able to bring up their children as good citizens. Yes, there is the occasional nod in the direction of parents requiring resources, but this is notably lacking in either parent education programmes or in government's and public commentators' hand wringing about how to improve parenting (Smith & Pugh, 1996).

As a task, parenting is conceptually no different from any other, though it is vastly more complex and demanding than most. As with any other task, it has four critical prerequisites of (1) knowledge and understanding, (2) motivation, (3) resources and (4) opportunity. To achieve good enough parenting, whether as parents or policy makers, we need to understand the task and *know* what to do, must *want* to do it, must have access to the appropriate *resources* and have the *opportunity* for carrying it out.

Knowledge

Knowledge covers the large complex of facts concerning the individual child in relation to other children; what the possible sources of harm may be, both in general and in relation to the particular child; how the child's physical, emotional and social care needs may be best met; what the necessary and sufficient rules of behaviour are and how best they may be enforced; what the child's developmental potential is and how action may be taken to promote it. Understanding goes beyond just factual knowledge. In this context, it presumes some insight regarding the dynamics and 'causes' of the child's needs, arising in the first instance from the natural and intense identification of parents with their children.

Because a child's development is dynamic, knowledge of what to do with the child needs to be constantly updated and applied to every stage and aspect of its life. It entails picking up basic signals from the child, interpreting them correctly and dealing adequately with them. So parents become quickly adept at picking up meanings of different forms of crying and facial expressions in their children. This is relatively easy at first because of the limited range of children's expressions, but becomes increasingly complex as the range widens and the child begins to exhibit expressions and modes of behaviour picked up from sources other than the home.

Knowledge of physical, emotional and social needs of children, of boundaries and how to enforce them, and of opportunities for development, is fundamentally shaped by personal experience of parenting. It is significantly augmented by learning from others in the course of growing up, teaching and inculcation at school, exposure to appropriate media and adequate support and instruction from professionals throughout the child's life.

It is clear that in a complex, 'multi-valued' society there is increasingly less certainty about what are facts and what are value-laden judgements, as seen in the debate surrounding whether it is good to cane troublesome children as a form of discipline (Wheen, 1996). We call our society 'multi-valued' precisely because there is wide diversity of opinion about 'facts', and how they are to be interpreted and used in practice. Increasing labour mobility and break-up of families deprive children of the benefits of 'traditional wisdom' available from parents and neighbours. More importantly, the media—which are the new moral exemplars and arbiters—present a wide range of parenting models. The models do not represent any coherent values or approaches to parenting. This is acceptable for the majority of parents who are part of an educated and articulate public which can make the appropriate distinctions and allowances in interpreting the material, but not those for whom diversity becomes a dilemma and choice a source of confusion.

Motivation

Motivation refers to 'wanting' to do something, either for gain or for avoidance of pain. We know a considerable amount about the physiology and psychological aspects of motivation and have some ideas of how to assess and enhance it (e.g. Ford, 1992; Werner, 1992). We even know from clinical practice ways of turning adversity to advantage by cognitive restructuring in order to create positive motivation. However, by comparison with other areas of practice, applied motivational theory remains the black hole of psychology. In a relatively liberal and humane society, we simply do not know how to motivate people to want to do something if our well-tried methods of either encouraging by reward or frightening at the prospect of unpleasant outcomes fail to deliver what we are after.

All mammals seem to have strong emotional and protective tendencies towards their offspring. In humans, this takes a complex form from one extreme of self-destruction to the other of infanticide. For the vast majority of parents, children are the most precious feature of their lives and they are prepared to sacrifice much for the sake of their children, including personal time, effort and resources.

However, parents' motivation is tied up with their wider personal state. As we know from extensive research, mentally unhealthy and otherwise stressed parents not only fail to give adequate parenting but inflict damage both by default and intentionally (Coyne *et al.*, 1987; Goldstein, 1988; Goldstein & Strachan, 1987). This is because parental motivation is limited by sense of self-worth, the ability to foresee the consequences of particular forms of parenting and being in a state to act 'correctly'.

Resources

Resources refer to what we need to be able to carry out any task. These usually mean money, goods and services. In the context of parenting, money is required to purchase basic necessities which meet children's need for food, shelter and warmth, as well as any 'luxuries' that may promote their well-being.

However, the most important resources for parenting are people who interact with and raise the child. These are chiefly the biological parents, but also include members of the extended family, neighbours, teachers and an increasing range of others. The 'people' element of parenting involves their number, qualities and skills and, as the child grows older, their total personality and circumstances.

'Number' has not been adequately explored in relating to parenting, although we know that children without fathers (normally through break-up) present a much wider range of troubles for the future (Dennis & Erdos, 1992; Wadsworth, 1979; West & Farrington, 1973) and those with close grandparents less. It appears, however, that the stability and quality of parenting processes are more important than the number or the gender of the available parent figures (Graham, 1989; West, 1982).

There is no simple answer to why two-parent families produce, on the whole, less troubled children. Factors such as better economic state, less stress due to loneliness, greater protection from others' predatory behaviour, must all play a part. But also, part of the answer must lie in simply the greater pool of qualities and skills that two people bring to parenting tasks. Qualities are inborn characteristics, such as intelligence, warmth, compassion, sensitivity and the like. Skills are developed and effective ways of doing things, acquired through instruction, observation, practice and other modes of skill acquisition.

Opportunity

Opportunity refers to parents having the time and space to bring up their children. This demands interaction between parents and children, consistently and over a long enough period for parenting processes to make the necessary impact.

HOW FAR ARE THESE PREREQUISITES OF PARENTING MET?

In general terms, we have a huge body of information about child development, needs of children, sources of harm and how damage to care, control and the development needs of children can best be avoided. This body of knowledge is constantly evolving, complex and diverse. Although it is possible to distil the essentials into a readily comprehensible form, the necessary codification work has not been done. Its accessibility is, therefore, significantly affected by social and economic circumstances of parents and how actively they seek out knowledge and understanding.

The majority of parents are, by definition, economically and socially adequately resourced. They acquire knowledge through their own 'good enough' experience of parenting, increasing interest in children's issues as they begin to approach child-bearing stage and pursuing further knowledge in order to provide their children with adequate care. If there should be problems about which they do not know, they have enough sense to seek that knowledge from whatever specialist sources may be available, such as GPs, antenatal clinics and publications.

By contrast, those at the margins are more likely to have come from poor and disadvantaged families where they themselves experienced poor parenting. Their school experience is too limited to equip them with the necessary knowledge. They often do not have close or appropriate family and social networks from whom to learn. Their exposure to benevolent people such as health visitors and specialists is often fragmented and chaotic and what they learn from diverse portrayals of parenting by the media is simply a source of confusion rather than enrichment.

These are the parents who cannot interpret their children's state well enough to protect them against avoidable harm, such as accidents, illness and abuse. They are themselves unsure about standards of acceptable behaviour and how to enforce them in the case of children who become increasingly impulsive, badly behaved and truculent. Their methods of boundary setting are inconsistent and inadequate, frequently exacerbating rather than remedying children's problem behaviour. Their lives are so fraught that the idea of developing their child's potential and, therefore, the necessary knowledge base for it, does not very often arise.

By the same token, their motivation to provide high-quality parenting for their children is disturbed and often stunted. Their own life experiences have not led them to develop a strong sense of self-love or self-respect and, therefore they find it difficult to extend these to and practise them with their children. Their life is a constant struggle for survival, physically, psychologically and socially. They live in the twilight zones of our towns and cities, with little sense of control over their destiny or hope of improving it (Hoghughi, 1993). In these circumstances, their motivation to engage in the complex and demanding tasks of parenting is severely undermined. They cannot love their children and promote their welfare any more than they can love themselves, and that is not very much.

Disadvantage and deprivation of material resources is what we know most about in relation to marginal families. The very definition of falling below half the average national income or being two standard deviations down from the average highlights the shortage of resources. We know that such families are poorer, have more people on social security benefits, suffer from disproportionate unemployment, illness and premature death, smoke and drink more of their income and suffer greater stress through the pressure of debts, cutting off of water, electricity, rent arrears and the like, than the rest of society (Blackburn, 1991). The disparity between their access to goods and services and that of the better off is complex, vast and apparently ever-increasing. (Church, 1985; Wilkinson, 1996)

What is less often talked about is that the *personal* resources of marginal parents are even more glaringly deficient than their material ones. We know from considerable research that they are less educated and articulate, less alert to their children's needs and, judging by their criminal careers, more lacking in fellow feeling, sensitivity and, by virtue of themselves being brutalised, less compassionate (Hoghughi, 1978, 1983, West, 1982). Their disproportionate representation in crimes against the person also bespeak of their aggressive tendencies as a way of solving problems. This is extended to the handling of their children in which punitive harshness alternates with collusion, bribing and disregard. They have the core characteristics of the 'multiply deprived'— the 'conglomeration of impairments' which include marital disruption, parental illness, poor domestic care of the child and home, dependency on social services, overcrowding and poor mothering (Kolvin *et al.*, 1990).

Given this endowment of their qualities, it is hardly surprising that they do not often have the opportunity to acquire and develop *skills* in caring for, controlling and developing their children. They cannot often accurately pick up cues regarding their children's state and take appropriate action, communicate adequately with them, express their affection or provide guidance in a consistent and supportive manner.

We know little about how much time marginal parents spend with their children. There is some circumstantial evidence, such as television viewing habits (Halloran *et al.*, 1970) which indicates that these parents spend little of their time together with the children conversing and sharing perspectives which may help guide the child in handling the environment. On the contrary, many seem not to be concerned with how much time the child spends in the home and do not bother to ask what he or she is doing outside, partly out of neglect but in part to reduce the inevitable conflict between them (Wilson, 1980, 1985). This does not, of course, take into account the disruption of contact with parents and opportunity to benefit from whatever parenting they offer, due to the children being taken into care, parents separating or going to prison, hospital and other reasons for absence.

CONSEQUENCES

As is evident from the above, significantly disadvantaged parents have major difficulties in acquiring and utilising the necessary knowledge and understanding, motivation, resources and opportunities for 'good enough' provision of care, control and development of their children. So what are the consequences of parenting at the margins?

1. Although the general level of health of all children in Western societies is improving, this is much less the case in those countries such as the UK where inequalities of income are greatest (Wilkinson, 1996). Furthermore, the health of children from marginal families is worse than their well-off counterparts, ranging from infant mortality to obesity and malnourishment, accidents and substance misuse (Dallison & Lobstein, 1995; Kolvin *et al.*, 1990; Kuh & Macleod, 1990; NCH, 1992; Townsend & Davidson, 1982; Wilkinson, 1996).

2. The mechanisms for transmission of parental adversity to children are complex and operate throughout the lifespan. These range from the effect of malnourishment, trauma and drug use on the brain and body of the developing foetus (Istvan, 1986; Porter *et al.*, 1984; Rutter & Rutter, 1993) to subsequent ability of parents to respond to their children's emerging needs, from prevention of harm to adequate provision of care (The Black Report, 1980; Jenkins & Smith, 1990; Kumar, 1993).

3. Family adversity is particularly evident in exposure to harmful drugs. There is by now well-established evidence that disadvantaged people are more likely to use and suffer from the effects of drugs of all sorts (e.g. West & Farrington, 1977). Indeed, drug use is itself an index of much other social adversity, used as a coping aid in response to inadequate diet, poor sleep, stress and lack of social support (Blackburn & Graham, 1991). Apart from the immediate health hazards from the antenatal stage onwards, smoking uses up to 20% of the disposable income of marginal families (Marsh & McKay, 1994). An estimated similar amount goes on drinking.

   Mothers who smoke are likely to produce underweight children who are more likely to be anaemic. This in turn affects their concentration and attention in the classroom and thence educational achievement. These factors taken together may, in part, account for the much higher levels of impulsivity and hyperactivity and poorer attention span seen in the children of such families, with dramatic long-term implications for antisocial behaviour (Klinteberg *et al.*, 1993; Satterfield, 1987).

4. Moreover, children from these families are themselves more likely to start early smoking, drinking and experimenting with illegal drugs. The first two have been well established by research (HEA, 1990). The third seems likely as the drug culture takes hold even in those countries like the United Kingdom which were in the past immune from it at least among poor people who did not have the money to buy drugs. There is also now evidence that drug pushing and offending to buy drugs is becoming a well-established pattern of criminal activity among adolescents (Hoghughi, 1996). This is associated with the use of weapons, the development of gangs where they did not previously exist, and rising stakes for gaining and protecting individual 'turfs'. Health education activities aimed at young people seem to be singularly ineffective and, if anything, raise the profile which feeds the stimulus-hungry and deviant imagination (Bell & Bell, 1993).

5. We know from extensive and long-standing research that children of marginal families are likely to do less well on intelligence tests and at school (Hoghughi, 1983, 1997a; West, 1982). Due to the downward social mobility of marginal families, the children may start off with a poorer genetic endowment. This is exacerbated by the impact of disadvantage which limits parents' ability to provide adequate resources for children's education, take interest in their education (Blatchford, 1985; Douglas, 1964; Hirschi & Hindenlang, 1977; Stattin & Klackenberg-Larsson, 1993) or know how to get the best out of school for them (Bernstein, 1971). The children, therefore, are more likely to truant, get excluded, drop out of school and leave without qualifications that would fit them for anything but dead-end jobs. Because of personal and familial reasons, young people from marginal families are less likely to benefit from training and support schemes. They are more likely to remain poor and continue in crime simply as a means of economic sustenance (Farrington & West, 1990). Whereas previously getting an unskilled job and earning money with which to pursue legitimate interests was a significant gateway out of a delinquent career, this has now been largely closed. The unemployment rate for such youngsters in some areas of the UK is as much as 85%.

6. The single most consistent finding on marginal families is that they engage in inadequate or deviant parenting practices, as a result of which they produce deviant children who grow up to produce another generation like or relatively worse than themselves, simply

because some effects of adversity become more concentrated from one generation to the next (Rutter & Madge, 1976; Wilkinson, 1996).

Setting aside poor income, housing and health, we also know that in all Western societies family break-up is on the increase but that it affects marginal families more dramatically than others. The rate is higher, the age of onset earlier and the number of recompositions greater. Poor parenting practices multiply as partners change. Children's anxiety at changes of home setting and maladaptive attempts at coping with them never get the opportunity to be corrected, eventually presenting as mental health problems. This is the daily experience of clinicians working with such young people.

An understandable preoccupation with meeting the needs of a new partner deflects the parent from meeting adequately the child's needs for secure attachment, unconditional love, time and tranquillity in which to communicate and careful attention to his or her evolving response to parent's and partner's state and demands. In these circumstances, not only do children fail to receive adequate parenting, but their difficulties in adapting to the frequent family conflict and distress result in a range of problems which undermine their very sense of a positive self and thus bedevil subsequent adjustment throughout the lifespan. There is some debate about the extent and the mechanisms, but little dispute about the adverse outcomes.

Although family discord is particularly damaging to temperamentally vulnerable children, being fatherless has even more serious consequences for boys. 'Families without fatherhood' deprive children of marginal families from adequate material and emotional care, boundary setting and enforcement, protection against other predatory people and opportunities for role modelling (Dennis & Erdos, 1992). The fact that mothers of such children have occasional partners exacerbates rather than alleviates the children's condition (Dunn & Kendrick, 1982). Mothers' backgrounds, amplified by disturbances of personal relationships and worries about almost everything else, account for the high prevalence of mental health problems among lone mothers (Burnell & Wadsworth, 1981).

When we consider that, in some parts of major cities, two-thirds of families are headed by a women and 85% of them are dependent on social security benefits, the extent of the problem of and for marginal families becomes apparent. Although the financial cost is high and increasing, the human and developmental costs for the children are much greater. The long-term consequence of fluid family structures is that the children are often rootless, without solid and secure social identities, vulnerable to stress from their mothers and similarly rootless peers. They are much more likely to drift into a range of maladaptive lifestyles, including delinquency, and stay there for want of a strong counter-pull.

Family break-up and disorganisation means that contact between the lone mother and grandparents and the rest of the family support network is attenuated. We know that good social relationships are important protectors against mental ill health (Blaxter, 1990) and that their absence is likely to trigger off depression and other clinical difficulties (Brown & Harris, 1978). Thus, particularly in urban areas, young people are becoming deprived of the benevolent influence of extended family members. To that extent the transmission of stabilising and protective factors is impeded and young people become more alienated from values underlying them. The apparent rise in the number of young people who, with others, have broken into the homes of, or otherwise victimised, their own family members is indicative of the outer edges of such alienation.

In the UK, particularly, we are highly sensitised to physical, emotional and sexual abuse of children. The evidence suggests that abuse is widespread, both within families and targeting of their members by outsiders. Given that such abuse is culturally so deviant, we would expect it to be more widespread in marginal families, and this is indeed what we find (Hoghughi, 1997; Parton, 1989). The reasons most frequently cited when registering children for child abuse are marital problems, debts and unemployment (Creighton, 1992).

7. It has been known for a long time that existence of social networks is an important aid to children's social development and major protective factor against mental ill health (Blaxter, 1990). Next to families, peer groups are the major influence on shaping child and adolescent behaviour. Appropriately assertive relationship with peers demands strong attachment to a close and supportive base, which are missing in marginal families. Poor peer relationships are strong predictors of both psychiatric disorder (Asher & Coie, 1990; Rutter *et al.*, 1970) and delinquency (Thornberry *et al.*, 1994).

   Even delinquent groups demand social skills from their members. An apparently continuing rise in solo delinquency indicates greater alienation from peer groups and greater propensity towards extreme forms of antisocial behaviour. This may be one of the consequences of fatherlessness and chronically unstable family life, depriving vulnerable youngsters of basic social skills.

8. Traditionally, antisocial behaviour by the young has been seen as the greatest and most visible consequence of parenting at the margins. There is high-quality and fairly consistent research evidence to suggest that almost all forms and facets of antisocial behaviour are

worsening both in quantity and quality. Although certain libertarian social commentators (mainly characterised by those who do not directly deal with adolescents) give other interpretations, the evidence is overwhelming (Farrington *et al.*, 1994; Farrington, 1996). There is more disruption by young people in social gatherings; defiance of adult authority; running away from schools, home and other placements; significant increase in verbal and physical aggression towards adults and each other; and more offences against person and property, particularly of grave crimes in the UK. The incidence of sexual offending by young people is increasing and this has had to be recognised in new legislation. There is evidence of greater and more deliberate challenge to authority structures. Young people are more ready to express hostility to services such as fire brigades and ambulances which are called to assistance, and agents of law enforcement, such as the police. They are now responsible for between a quarter to a half of all offences committed in Western countries, the proportions varying according to a number of demographic and social circumstances (Farrington, 1996; Hoghughi, 1983, 1997; Marshall, 1996; Utting *et al.*, 1993).

The liberal policies of the past three decades aimed at diversion and treatment seem to be increasingly giving way to harsh forms of social control without any corresponding attempt at ameliorating the conditions which underlie persistent delinquent behaviour. This is most evident in the United States, which usually precedes Europe by about a decade, where capital punishment of juveniles has been reintroduced in a number of states. In the United Kingdom, recent policy has been towards significantly greater punitiveness towards juveniles and reduced tendency to show lenience to their age or social circumstances. Given the weight of adversities experienced by such young people and their families, there is some consensus that this new approach will exacerbate their condition and that, therefore, extent and quality of offending will continue significantly to deteriorate.

9. Family stability and harmony are essential prerequisites of psychological health, unless other exceptionally protective factors are active. That is why there is such well-established connection between family pathology and psychological difficulties among young people (Wahler & Dumas, 1987). The effects of home difficulties are amplified by developmental processes (Feldman & Elliott, 1990; Rutter & Rutter, 1993), particularly when children come from multi-problem families (HAS, 1995).

Of all clinical problems, conduct disorders which combine deviant attitudes, inappropriate emotional responses and antisocial behaviour are the most prominent consequence of inadequate and deviant parenting (Herbert, 1987; Kazdin, 1987; Loeber, 1990; Marshall, 1996; Robins, 1966; Rutter & Smith, 1995). The prominence of conduct disorders arises from their visibility and social impact. However, no less insidious and damaging but less visible are the affective disorders—anxiety, depression, related suicide and deliberate self harm, which are associated with adverse childhood experiences (Bifulco *et al.*, 1987, 1992; Kreitman 1976, Rutter *et al.*, 1986; Rutter & Rutter, 1993). Children from marginal families make up a disproportionately large segment of 10–25% of all children, particularly in inner city areas, who present significant mental health problems (Wallace *et al.*, 1995).

The children of such parents also grow up with a fatalistic view of the world, in which events are perceived as being controlled by external forces (Hoghughi, 1993) which they cannot hope to influence. Being fundamentally shaped by capricious adversity, they adopt a pain-avoidance, pleasure-seeking approach to life, geared to momentary pleasures and short-term gain, even at the expense of longer term well-being, as seen in substance use, truancy, stealing cars and general offending.

Paradoxically, as global economic competition creates leaner and more efficient economies, as in the UK, so it produces human casualties of marginal families. Being weighed down by poor personal condition, inadequate job-related training and insufficient stability to seek and hold employment, they drift in and out of shadows, unable to establish a firm foothold for moving out of their state. However well motivated, they are inadequately resourced to fulfil their children's needs, alleviate their difficulties or seek and sustain external help.

The new competitive market and outcome-driven health, education and social services, are contributing to this by excluding those youngsters who are unable to respond to the increasingly rationed and focused resources for helping those in need.

Parenting has always been difficult. After all, the demands of physical, emotional and social nurture and the willingness to set and enforce boundaries, put pressure on parents—and not always in proportion to their abilities and resources. However, the complexity of rapidly changing societies, the relative decrease in parents' resources matched by increase of pressures on their children to behave in a deviant manner, have created new stresses which parents find difficult to manage. Parental conflict and rejection and resulting drift for the children, are the consequence.

More importantly, the factors associated with deficient and deviant behaviour in the young, well established through research and outlined above, are seen to be gathering weight under the influence of massive economic pressure and political shift to the right. As a result, there are more youngsters at the margins and their behaviour at the edges more outlandish. The increase in established vulnerability is matched by a decrease in protective factors. Given the momentum in social and economic changes, the deterioration in children's condition is likely to continue.

This is a gloomy and pessimistic view of the prospects for young people being brought up by parents at the margins. What of solutions? I believe we need to recognise explicitly and as *the* core element of social policy, the importance of *parenting as the vehicle for social development*. Shaping, constantly monitoring and benevolently supporting it to achieve the core tasks of care, control and development, should become the central plank of *all* social policies.

Indeed, I believe that the idea of a *parenting society* should become the organising principle of all we do. The whole function of government in providing care services, creating laws that define boundaries of action and structure for enhancing the country's potential can be seen as variants of core parenting tasks of care, control and development. In such a society, we would each, irrespective of our other differentiating roles, adopt a fundamentally *parenting attitude* to each other and thence to the marginal parents and their vulnerable young. Without re-inventing extended families or the 'social contract', we must recognise the heavy price to be paid if we do not adopt a mutually supportive role and immense gains in social *and* economic wealth if we do. This does not mean a 'nanny' or 'welfare dependent' society but one in which we recognise that, even on purely economic grounds, it pays us to prevent further damage and integrate marginal families into mainstream society. We are neither short of good ideas nor of adequate resources. What we need is a collective vision of a less inequal society which we are prepared to make real.

REFERENCES

Aronfreed, J. (1968) *Conduct and Conscience.* New York: Academic Press.

Asher, S. & Coie, J. D. (Eds) (1990) *Peer Rejection in Childhood.* New York: Cambridge University Press.

Bell, N. J. & Bell, R. L. (Eds) (1993) *Adolescent Risk Taking.* Newbury Park: Sage.

Bernstein, B. (1961) 'Social Structure, language and learning.' *Educational Research*, **3**, 163–176.

Bernstein, B. (1971) *Class, Codes and Control.* London: Routledge.

Bifulco, A. T., Brown, G. W. & Harris, T. O. (1987) 'Childhood loss of parent, lack of adequate parental care and adult depression: a replication.' *Journal of Affective Disorders*, **12**, 115–128.

Bifulco, A. T., Harris, T. O. & Brown, G. W. (1992) 'Mourning or early inadequate care? Re-examining the relationship of maternal loss in childhood with adult depression and anxiety.' *Development & Psychopathology*, **4**, 433–449.

The Black Report (1980) 'Report of the working group on inequalities in health.' In *Inequalities in Health: The Black Report and the Health Divide*. London: Penguin.

Blackburn, C. (1991) *Poverty & Health*. Milton Keynes: Open University Press.

Blackburn, C. & Graham, H. (1991) *Smoking among Working Class Mothers*. Coventry, University of Warwick, Dept. of Applied Social Studies.

Blatchford, P. (1985) 'Educational achievement in the infant school: the influence of ethnic origin, gender and home on entry skills.' *Educational Research*, **27** (1), 52–60.

Blaxter, M. (1990) *Mental Health and Lifestyles*. London: Routledge.

Bowlby, J. (1970) *Attachment and Loss, Vol. I–III*. New York, Basic Books.

Brown, G. & Harris, T. (1978) *The Social Origin of Depression: a Study of Psychiatric Disorder in Women*. London: Tavistock.

Burnell, I. & Wadsworth, J. (1981) *Children in One Parent Families*. University of Bristol.

Church, J. (Ed.) (1995) *Social Trends*. London: Central Statistical Office, HMSO.

Coyne, J. C., Kahn, J. & Gotlib, I. H. (1987) 'Depression.' In T. Jacob (Ed.), *Family Interaction & Psychopathology: Theories, Methods and Findings*. New York: Plenum Press.

Creighton, S. J. (1992) *Child Abuse Trends in England and Wales (1988–1990) and an Overview from 1973–1990*. London: NSPCC.

Dallison, J. & Lobstein, T. (1995) *Poor Expectations—Poverty and Undernourishment in Pregnancy*. London: NCH & Maternity Alliance

Dennis, N. & Erdos, G. (1992) *Families without Fatherhood*. London: IEA Health & Welfare Unit.

Douglas, J. W. B. (1964) *The Home and the School*. London: McGibbon & Kee.

Dunn, J. & Kendrick, C. (1982) *Siblings: Love, Envy and Understanding*. Cambridge, Mass.: Harvard University Press.

Erikson, E. (1968) *Identity, Youth & Crisis*. New York: Norton.

Erikson, M. F., Sroufe, L. & Egeland, B. (1985) 'The relationship between quality of attachment and behavior problems in preschool in a high risk sample'. In I. Bretherton & E. Waters (Eds), *Growing Points of Attachment Theory and Research*. Monographs of The Society for Research in Child Development, Serial No. 209, Vol. 50, Nos. 1–2, pp. 147–166.

Fahlberg, V. I. (1991) *A Child's Journey through Placements*. London: BAAF.

Farrington, D. P. (1996) *Understanding and Preventing Youth Crime*. York: Joseph Rowntree Foundation.

Farrington, D. P. & West, D. J. (1990) 'The Cambridge study in delinquent development: a long term follow up of 411 London males.' In G. Kaiser & H. J. Kerner (Eds), *Criminality: Personality, Behaviour, Life History*. Berlin: Springer Verlag.

Farrington, D. P., Laugran, P. A. & Wikstrom, P.-O. H. (1994) 'Changes in crime and punishment in America, England and Sweden between the 1980s and the 1990s'. *Studies in Crime and Crime Prevention*, **3**, 104–131.

Feldman, S. S. & Elliott, G. R. (Eds) (1990) *At the Threshold: The Developing Adolescent*. Cambridge, Mass.: Harvard University Press.

Fine, M. (Ed.) (1980) *The Handbook on Parent Education*. New York: Academic Press.

Fine, M. (1989) *The Second Handbook on Parent Education*. New York: Academic Press.

Ford, M. (1992) *Motivating Humans: Goals, Emotions and Personal Agency Beliefs.* Newbury Park: Sage.

Goldstein, M. J. (1988) 'The family and psychopathology.' *Annual Review of Psychology*, **39**, 283–299.

Goldstein, M. J. & Strachan, A. M. (1987) 'The family and schizophrenia' In T. Jaboc (Ed.), *Family Interaction & Psychopathology: Theories, Methods and Findings.* New York: Plenum Press.

Graham, J. (1989) *Families, Parenting Skills and Delinquency.* Home Office Research Bulletin.

Halloran, J. D., Brown, R. L. & Chaney, D. C. (1970) *Television and Delinquency.* Leicester: Leicester University Press.

Harman, D. & Brim, O. (1980) *Learning to be Parents: Principles, Programmes and Methods.* London: Sage.

Health Advisory Service (HAS) *Child and Adolescent Mental Health Services: Together we Stand.* London: HMSO.

Health Education Authority (HEA) *Young People's Health & Lifestyles.* London: HEA.

Herbert, M. (1987) *Conduct Disorders of Childhood and Adolescence: A Social Learning Perspective*, (revised edn), Chichester: John Wiley.

Hirschi, T. & Hindenlang, M. J. (1977) 'Intelligence and delinquency: A revisionist review'. *American Sociological Review*, **42**, 571–587.

Hoghughi, M. S. (1978) *Troubled and Troublesome: Coping with Severely Disordered Children.* London: Burnett Books/Andre Deutsch

Hoghughi, M. S. (1983) *The Delinquent: Directions for Social Control.* London: Burnett Books.

Hoghughi, M. S. (1992) *Assessing Child and Adolescent Disorders—A Practice Manual.* London: Sage.

Hoghughi, M. S. (1993) *Youth at the Margins.* Aycliffe: Centre for Adolescent Studies.

Hoghughi, M. S. (1997a) *Adolescent Criminals: Surviving at the Margins.* Oxford: Bowerdean (in press).

Hoghughi, M. S. (1997b) 'What is sexually abusive behaviour?' In M. S. Hoghughi, S. R. Bhate & F. Graham (Eds), *Working with Sexually Abusive Adolescents.* London: Sage.

Holmes, J. (1993) *John Bowlby and Attachment Theory.* London: Routledge.

Istvan, J. (1986) 'Stress, anxiety and birth outcomes: a critical review of the evidence.' *Psychology Bulletin*, **100**, 331–348.

Jenkins, J. M. & Smith, M. A. (1990) 'Factors protecting children living in disharmonious homes.' *Journal of the American Academy of Child & Adolescent Psychiatry*, 29, 60–69.

Kazdin, A. E. (1987) *Conduct Disorders in Childhood and Adolescence.* Newbury Park: Sage.

Klinteberg, B. A., Andersson, T., Magnusson, D. & Stattin, H. (1993) 'Hyperactive behaviour in childhood as related to subsequent alcohol problems and violent offending: a longitudinal study of male subjects.' *Personality and Individual Differences*, **15**, 381–388.

Kolvin, I., Miller, F. J., Scott, D. M., Gatzanis, S. R. M. & Fleeting, M. (1990) Continuities of deprivation: the Newcastle 1000 Family Study. *ESRC/DHSS Studies in Deprivation and Disadvantage.* Aldershot: Avebury.

Kreitman, N. (1976) 'The coal gas story: UK suicide rates 1960–71.' *British Journal of Preventive and Social Medicine*, **30**, 86–93.

Kuh, D. & Mcleod, M. (1990) 'Women's childhood experience of parental separation and their subsequent health and socioeconomic status in childhood.' *Journal of Biosocial Science*, **22**, 121–135.

Kumar, D. (1993) *Poverty & Inequality in the UK—the Effects on Children*. London: National Children's Bureau.

Leach, P. (1994) *Children First*. London: Michael Joseph.

Loeber, R. (1990) 'Development and risk factors of juvenile anti-social behaviour and delinquency.' *Clinical Psychology Review*, **10**, 1–41.

Marsh, A. & McKay, S. (1994) *Poor Smokers*. London: Policy Studies Institute.

Marshall, L. (1996) 'Do experiences in childhood cause psychopathy?' *Forensic Update*, **45**, 3–9.

Murray, C. (1990) *The Emerging Underclass*. London: Institute of Economic Affairs.

NCH (1992) *Children in Britain in 1992*. London: National Children's Home

National Institute of Mental Health (NIMH) (1995) 'Family processes and social networks.' In *Basic Behavioural Sciences Research for Mental Health*. Washington: US Dept. of Health & Human Services.

Neville, D., King, L. & Beak, D. (1995) *Promoting Positive Parenting*. Aldershot: Arena Publications.

Parton, N. (1989) 'Child abuse.' In B. Kahan (Ed.), *Child Care Research, Policy and Practice*. London: Hodder & Stoughton.

Porter, R., O'Connor, M. & Whelan, J. (Eds) (1984) *Mechanisms of Alcohol Damage in Lifers*. London: Pitman.

Pringle, M. K. (1986) *The Needs of Children*, 3rd edn. London: Hutchinson.

Robins, L. (1966) *Deviant Children Grown Up*. Baltimore: Williams & Wilkins.

Robinson, W. P. (1972) *Language and Social Behaviour*. Harmondsworth: Penguin Education.

Rutter, M. & Giller, H. (1983) *Juvenile Delinquency: Trends and Perspectives*. London: Penguin.

Rutter, M. & Madge, N. (1976) *Cycles of Disadvantage: A Review of Research*. London: Heinemann.

Rutter, M., Izard, J. & Read, P. (Eds) (1986) *Depression in Young People: Clinical & Developmental Perspectives*. New York: Guilford.

Rutter, M., Izard, J. & Whitmore, K. (Eds) (1970) *Education, Health and Behaviour*. London: Longman.

Rutter, M. & Rutter, M. (1993) *Developing Minds: Challenge and Continuity across the Life Span*. London: Penguin.

Rutter, M. & Smith, D. (1995) *Psychosocial Disorders of Childhood: Time Corrections*. Lexington, MA: Lexington Books.

Satterfield, J. H. (1987) 'Childhood diagnostic and neurophysiological predictors of teenage arrest rates: an 8 year prospective study.' In S. A. Mednick, T. E. Moffitt & S. A. Stack (Eds), *The Causes of Crime: New Biological Approaches*. Cambridge: Cambridge University Press.

Smith, C. & Pugh, G. (1996) *Learning to be a Parent: A Survey of Group-based Parenting Programmes*. London: NCB.

Stattin, H. & Klackenberg-Larsson, I. (1993) 'Early language and intelligence development and their relationship to future criminal behaviour.' *Journal of Abnormal Psychology*, **102**, 369–378.

Thornberry, T. P., Lizotte, A. J. & Krohn M. D. (1994) 'Delinquent peers, beliefs and delinquent behaviour: a longitudinal test of interaction theory.' *Criminology*, **32**, 47–83.

Townsend, P. & Davidson, N. (1982) *Inequalities in Health — the Black Report*. Harmondsworth: Penguin.

Utting, D., Bright, J. & Henricson, C. (1993) *Crime and the Family*. London: Family Policy Studies Centre.

Wadsworth, M. (1979) *The Roots of Delinquency*. London: Martin Robertson.

Wahler, R. G. & Dumas, J. E. (1987) 'Family factors in childhood psychology.' In T. Jacob, (Ed.), Family Interaction and Psychopathology. New York: Plenum.

Wallace, S. A., Crown, J. M., Cox, A. D. & Berger, M. (1995) *Epidemiologically Needs Based Assessment: Child and Adolescent Mental Health*. London: Department of Health.

Wallace, S., Crown, J., Cox, A. & Berger, M. (1976) *Health Care Needs Assessment: Child & Adolescent Mental Health*. London: Dept of Health.

Warr, M. (1993) 'Parents, peers and delinquency.' *Social Forces*, **72**, 247–264.

Werner, B. (1992) *Human Motivation*. Newbury Park: Sage.

West, D. J. (1982) *Delinquency: Its Roots, Careers and Prospects*. London: Heinemann.

West, D. J. & Farrington, D. P. (1973) *Who Becomes Delinquent?* London: Heinemann.

West, D. J. & Farrington, D. P. (1977) *The Delinquent Way of Life*. London: Heinemann.

Wheen, F. (1996) 'Swish of the big stick.' *The Guardian*, 31 October.

Wilkinson, R. (1996) *Unhealthy Societies—The Afflictions of Inequality*. London. Routledge.

Wilson, H. (1980) 'Parental supervision: a neglected aspect of delinquency.' *British Journal of Criminology*, **20** (3), 203–235.

Wilson, H. (1985) 'Parental supervision re-examined.' *British Journal of Criminology*, **27** (3), 275–301.

3

GENDER ISSUES IN PARENTING

Paquita McMichael and Gerda Siann

INTRODUCTION

Until the mid-1980s, a British teacher welcoming 5-year-olds on their first day of school could confidently assume that the great majority of her new class would be living with two parents in a family in which the child's father was the chief breadwinner and the child's mother the chief caretaker. This assumption would be based both on demographic data (for example, in 1991, 94% of children lived in two-parent families), and on a cultural consensus that polarised parenting into two relatively fixed but different sex roles—the mother's and the father's. In the late 1990s, however, such an assumption would not be tenable. As many as one in five children now live in single-parent families (Muncie *et al.*, 1995) and for a sizeable proportion of those who live in two-parent families the father will be unemployed. Perhaps more importantly, from the viewpoint of this chapter, teachers are now aware that, in the population as a whole, cultural values concerning the interaction of gender with parenting have become less consensual. In particular, younger parents are less likely than their elders to endorse the traditional and relatively fixed identification of fatherhood with economic obligations and motherhood with pastoral ones.

Attitudes to, and values about, gender and sex roles have undergone a radical shift, particularly for those who fall into what Helen Wilkinson (1994) has called the 'post-equality' generation. She uses this term not to

Enhancing Parenting Skills: A Guide Book for Professionals Working with Parents.
Edited by K. N. Dwivedi. © 1997 John Wiley & Sons Ltd.

indicate that sexual inequalities have been eliminated but to encapsulate the findings, both from her own research and from other studies, which show a tendency for gender convergence on social issues among young people, notably on issues relating to family values.

In Britain, this post-equality generation has grown up in a period which saw a strong female prime minister as well as a number of other formidable female politicians. They can take for granted, in a way that their parents and grandparents could not, that women can head major corporations and can reach the upper echelons of the public service even if women, in general, still earn less than men, and even if the glass ceiling still remains in operation in many institutions and companies. Furthermore, while it could be argued that the media sometimes projects very sex stereotyped images, there is no doubt that there have been massive changes in the way women are portrayed in advertisements, in situation comedies, in documentaries (frequently produced and presented by women), and in the use of women presenters and journalists for hard news reporting and as experts in fields ranging through finance, economics, law and medicine to the arts.

Women, including mothers with young children, are also far more likely to be in employment now than in the past. Indeed, it has been estimated that by the end of the century more women than men will be in employment, albeit that many will be working part time (Edley & Wetherell, 1995). Furthermore, while most mothers who work do so out of economic necessity, research indicates that the majority of these, including those with young children, would prefer to have a paid job even if they did not need to work (Thomson, 1995).

There have, of course, been accompanying social and interpersonal shifts in social attitudes to the role of men. Perhaps the chief of these has been the implicit public acceptance that there is a plurality in social representations of masculinity. This is evident in the broad spectrum of magazines that are now directed to men, ranging from the unreconstructed sexism of *Mayfair*, through the celebration of laddishness of *Loaded* to the emphasis on the interpersonal in *Maxim* and on style and consumerism in *GQ*. Accompanying this growing acceptance that masculinity is far less circumscribed than it was in the past, there is also an increasing public preoccupation with what has sometimes been termed 'the crisis of masculinity'. This term is used to refer to the belief that, as more women move into the workforce and as jobs in the employment sectors traditionally dominated by men have declined, men are losing out more than women and are consequently less confident and more unsure not only about their employment prospects but also about their social roles.

There is little doubt that these social changes have impacted on attitudes to, and values about gender and family life. The impact can be seen very clearly in feature films such as, *Kramer vs Kramer, Three Men and a Baby* and *Mrs Doubtfire* which focused on men's love for children, even if the men were initially portrayed as inept (Coltrane, 1995). In the USA Carter (1992) has pointed out that dual career families express an intellectual commitment to gender equality in the sharing of household tasks and that in the early years of family life there is a relatively equitable division of family tasks. With the advent of children, there is frequently a shift in this division towards more traditional sex-role patterns, but this shift occurs largely for pragmatic reasons as the female partner moves towards part-time or flexi-working and the endorsement of egalitarianism as a goal remains.

This commitment, on the part of both sexes, to an egalitarian approach to working mothers, childcare tasks and childcare is also evident in the responses to a questionnaire dealing with these issues which we have recently administered to over 4000 students at a Scottish University (though it was noticeable that the endorsement of egalitarian responses was consistently more marked for women than for men). For example, only 23% of men and 14% of women agreed with the statement that 'all in all family life suffers when the woman has a full-time job' and only 28% of men and 18% of women disagreed with the statement that 'a working mother can establish just as warm and secure a relationship with her children as a woman who does not work'.

These movements away from traditional views of gender differences and towards a relative blurring of sex roles coincide and interact with rapidly changing patterns of family structure in the UK. Heterosexual couples living together, including those with children, are less likely to be married, the divorce rate continues to rise rapidly and the number of 'reconstituted' families continues to increase. Furthermore, an increasing number of young women, particularly those working in the professions, are electing not to have children or to defer having them till they are in their mid-thirties and then, when they do have children, choosing to bring them up on their own (Siann, 1994).

As a consequence of these psychological, social, economic and demographic changes, it is not surprising that increasingly fewer younger parents adhere to the circumscribed, if relatively secure, stereotypes of parenting referred to at the beginning of this chapter. Men are now increasingly likely to endorse pastoral and caring roles in parenting and both men and women are increasingly likely to endorse the notion of women working even when their children are young. Nevertheless, as the following sections of this chapter will show, these more egalitarian values about shared childcare are less likely to be put into practice than they are to be verbally endorsed. Before moving on to practice, however, we consider whether there are 'essential' differences between the sexes which predispose parents of either sex to 'parent' more successfully in some areas than in others. The term *essential* is used in this context to refer to a basic belief that there are major innate psychological differences between the sexes and that consequently men and women differ in their natures.

ARE THERE 'ESSENTIAL' DIFFERENCES IN MOTHERING AND FATHERING?

Is there Evidence for Unique Nurturing Capacities in Mothers?

The belief in distinct parental roles tends to focus particularly on what has been called 'nurturing'. This term is used to refer to the behaviour that is associated with the care of the infant. Adherents of an essentialist position, for example the feminist writer Alice Rossi (1975), argue that because women bear the babies and breastfeed them, the bond between the mother and her infant is, of necessity, stronger than the bond between the infant and its father. However, the biological base for different capacities in parenting children, particularly nurturing, is called into question by primate studies which indicate that in the case of gorillas, baboons and chimpanzees, males as well as females are able to undertake the care of infants. Whether the male capacity to nurture is called upon seems to depend both on the animals' environments and on their temperaments (Silverstein, 1996). Further evidence of plasticity, rather than sex-typed nurturing, comes from a study of rhesus monkeys in which, when the mother was removed from the cage, the male was found to be perfectly able to care for their infant (Silverstein, 1996).

We can also turn to different cultural contexts from our own to show that nurturing skills are equally available to men and women. For example, a study of Aka pygmies, a hunter-gatherer people from Central Africa, demonstrates that males may be expected to care for young children, including infants, for sustained periods of time while both fathers and mothers work together, caterpillar collecting and net hunting. The men share responsibilities for caretaking with their wives just as they share the subsistence activities (Hwang, 1987).

However, despite such comparative data and the fact that in Western societies there are numerous instances of men caring for their children on their own, current ideology is apt to define the relationship fathers have with their children in the context of their bond with their wives or partners and their role as supporters of mothering (Buss, 1995).

Are Parenting Skills Inherently Gender Biased?

By examining some of the constituents of caretaking we might find another way to determine whether mothers and fathers can perform equally well (provided they are not hampered by their own beliefs in specific gendered parenting roles). Consequently, we now turn our attention to a number of household tasks and childcare tasks, splitting these into practical and relationship activities.

Household tasks for the family consist of *practical* activities such as shopping, preparing food, cleaning, washing and planning family activities. Most studies show that, in two-parent families with children, these tasks are usually not only carried out by women, but have until recently been regarded as appropriately associated with mothers. Childcare is, of course, typically undertaken by mothers, particularly for infants whom the mother tends to feed, bath, put to sleep, attend to at night, play with and look after when ill. It is also mothers who tend to read to and play with older children.

In general then, studies indicate the close association of mothers with the practical tasks relating to cleaning, cooking and childcare, including the recreational aspects of childcare. One exception to this is the association of fathers with a particular recreational activity—rough and tumble play (Lamb, 1987). It has been suggested that the fact that studies show fathers are more likely than mothers to engage in robust and energetic play with children results from innately determined sex differences in aggression and dominance. This essentialist view of the father's role in such play has, however, been challenged by studies such as those of Hewlett (1991) who has shown that in cross-cultural contexts where men have a great deal of contact with their children they are no more likely to engage in rough play than women.

In general then, women are associated with most *practical* domestic and childcare tasks. Women are even more likely, however, to be associated with tasks relating to *relationships* with children. Indeed, the set of family tasks concerned with relationships that follow are typically assigned to mothers. They are: listening and attending, showing and receiving affection, giving and receiving feedback, setting reasonable limits, negotiating sensible compromises, managing and resolving conflict, care and protection. The only relationship activities associated with men are teaching and exercising discipline (Herbert, 1988).

It is, of course, not surprising that within an historical tradition which located women in the home there are such strong associations between women and most aspects of childcare. Nor is it surprising that men are associated with those aspects of childcare that are directly related to traditional masculine attributes and masculine sex roles, i.e. robust play, discipline and teaching. We need to ask, however, which, if any, among these has a gender-ordained requirement.

With respect to the *practical* tasks listed, theorists have not argued, nor have research studies demonstrated, that women are innately more able than men to do housework and carry out the practical components of childcare. With respect to relationships, there is less consensus. Some theorists, ranging from feminists such as Alice Rossi (1975) to sociobiologists such as E. O. Wilson (1975, 1978), who hold essentialist views of sex differences, have argued that there is evidence that women are, by nature, more sociable and more sensitive in personal interaction than men and that men are, by nature, more aggressive and dominant than women. They ascribe these differences to evolutionary processes and claim that because early men hunted while early women remained at home occupied in childcare, sex differences were important in natural selection. Hence, they would contend that the association of women with most interpersonal aspects of childcare and men with robust play, teaching and exercising discipline, is rooted in evolutionarily determined genetic causes. Other theorists reject the determinism of such essentialist views. This rejection is particularly marked in the case of 'social constructionists' such as Judith Lorber (1994). Lorber argues that the association of women with pastoral qualities and men with qualities associated with the exercise of power is rooted both in socialisation practices and in the economic and social forces that traditionally located women in the domestic sphere and provided men with social and economic power.

Although we endorse the social constructionist viewpoint, we accept that a number of other biological, and social scientists do not. Instead they would argue for a more essentialist viewpoint. Nevertheless, we contend that even the most fervent adherent of essentialist positions would have to accept two sets of evidence challenging the essentialist contention that central aspects of childcare are innately determined. First, within our own society, studies have demonstrated that men, given the opportunity to respond sensitively, can learn to carry out the relationship aspects of parenting as sensitively as women (Marsiglio, 1995). Second, anthropological studies indicate that in many non-Western societies fathers care for their children in a manner that in the West has been traditionally associated with mothers.

WHAT HAPPENS TODAY? MOVES TOWARDS SHARED OR EGALITARIAN PARENTING

Assuming then that both men and women *can* carry out most parenting tasks, let us look at what actually happens. How great a hold today has 'traditional' compared to 'egalitarian' parenting? 'Traditional' parenting ascribes to the father a dominant role as a breadwinner and decision maker concerned to bring up his children as moral members of society. His involvement with his children is largely through play and the exercise of discipline, but he may often 'help' his wife. The alternative 'egalitarian' model of parenthood expects either a high level of involvement by the father in all aspects of parenting or shared parenting with both parents dividing the role of parent between them. British research—reported by Lewis in 1986 and by Ferri and Smith (1996) which shows that as women increase their participation in the labour force men participate more in domestic tasks and childcare—suggests that there is a move towards more egalitarian parenting.

The Ferri and Smith study utilised interviews and self-completion questionnaires with a representative sample of 3137 British parents living in two-parent relationships who had been born in 1958. Their results showed that, in comparison to fathers, the mothers tended to occupy lower status jobs which were often part time and in some cases could be undertaken at times when their husbands were available for care—early in the morning or in the evening. Furthermore, as fathers' working hours increased to fifty or more a week, their participation decreased, even though their wives might also be working.

This study indicated that in Britain, despite the move towards egalitarian parenting, it still tends to be the mothers who take the main responsibility for the repetitive and time-consuming tasks while fathers are more apt to participate in play and recreation. In general, fathers' involvement is less likely to be through direct contact than through 'accessibility', i.e. they were available, perhaps reading a newspaper or watching television, but not necessarily actively engaged. The strongest element of egalitarian parenting in the Ferri and Smith survey was in respect to discipline or 'teaching children good behaviour', in which a large majority of parents felt they shared equally.

American studies stress that fathers' involvement in childcare varies considerably with social class and ethnicity (Coltrane, 1995) and that men are most likely to be involved heavily in childcare in dual career families. There is also evidence, however, that a substantial number of American women in dual career families still opt for part-time working when their children are young and that, as a consequence, such women tend to lose out in the career stakes. (This pattern is often referred to as the 'Mommy Track'.) Men, in such families, provide a higher proportion of the family income and hence take on less housework and caregiving. This may involve something of a loss to the men who cannot, as a result, develop and maintain parenting skills. It may, however, accord with notions of being 'the good provider' and reflect the father's continuing commitment to the family through increased efforts to earn.

There is no doubt that for working parents of both sexes, providing committed and dedicated parenting is fraught both with ideological and practical difficulties. The exigencies of the employment market, particularly in Britain, have resulted in employees working longer hours. Consequently, most working parents will, at some stage, have to balance the need to provide evidence of their dedication to their work to their superiors with the need to leave themselves sufficient emotional and physical resources for parenting. These conflicting demands tend to be exacerbated in Britain by the lack, in comparison to the USA and most other European countries, of affordable childcare provision (Muncie *et al.*, 1995).

In general, it is clear that large numbers of young British parents show a genuine commitment to shared parenting which overcomes the traditional strong maternal and paternal role expectations and the fact that working hours may be both long and demanding. However, despite intentions to 'help' their partners more, especially if they are working, many young fathers in Britain operate within a belief system, bolstered by economics and legislation, that stands in the way of egalitarian parenting.

Problems for Fathers in Shared Parenting

Lewis has (1986) observed that shared parenting may be a difficult option for fathers because:

- fathers will more often have longer working hours;
- fathers may easily feel marginalised in baby care, partly because of the greater emphasis on breastfeeding;
- mothers may guard their own areas of expertise and resist encroachment through the fathers' full involvement, preferring instead for fathers to 'help';
- men who wish to be fully involved may be seen as 'uncommitted' to work (if, for example, they leave work early to collect children from school if their wife is ill);
- men who care for children on their own are often isolated and without support networks;
- men have to assume a new identity in enlarging their parenting role and are not necessarily happier in doing so.

Positive Benefits to Shared House and Childcare

Lest it seem that fathers have everything to lose and little to gain we need also to take into account a comprehensive review of five studies of fatherhood carried out by Lamb *et al.*, (1987). This showed that as they contributed more to childcare they became more confident as parents, more satisfied in the role and increased their self-esteem. Coltrane (1989) goes further, observing that fathers who shared tasks equally became more aware of their children's needs and developed a 'maternal sense'. For mothers, Hoffman (1989) has suggested that shared care is the crucial factor in decreasing stress for those who work. Moreover, for both men and women (Ferri & Smith, 1996) paternal involvement appears to be a key factor in life satisfaction.

The Mesh between Maternal and Parental Parenting Ideologies

Although egalitarian parenting may be held up by social scientists as a desirable goal it may not be so in practice for individual couples. For example, in some couples, women may share with their husband a commitment to traditional patterns of parenting, and, as a result, such women may prefer fathers to 'help' rather than to participate equally. Indeed, Ferri and Smith showed that the most contented families were those where there was a single earner with the father employed. Together with contentment such parents were more often in agreement over child rearing than parents in other family types. However, such single-earner families were closely followed in levels of contentment and agreement by dual-career families. Families where there was no earner or where the mother was the sole earner reported the lowest levels of contentment and agreement. From this and similar surveys it might be concluded that a shared ideology of parenting as well as agreement over allocation of practical and emotional demands seems to underpin favourable family environments.

This brings us back to the question of whether parenting is necessarily gender based. It would seem that it need not be, but that the cultural context, the employment demands and the ideological stance of parents seriously affects whether gender free or egalitarian parenting can be practised.

PARENTS, GENDER AND SEX-ROLE DEVELOPMENT

In the next two sections of this chapter we look at research and theory bearing directly on gender aspects of child development, when parenting is carried out by a single parent or by two parents of the same sex.

Gender Issues in Single-Parent Families

The extent to which lone parenthood is regarded as a social issue varies in Europe (Song, 1996). In Britain (and more particularly with the emphasis since the early 1990s on 'family values'), lone parent families tend to be singled out as a cause for concern. In the Nordic countries, however, in terms of social policy, single-parent families tend to be grouped together with other family formations. As other chapters in this book indicate, in Britain there is a complex set of interactions resulting from this marginalisation of single-parent families and from the fact that in Britain single-parent families tend to be considerably poorer than their two-parent counterparts. These financial difficulties in Britain tend to be exacerbated because the lack of appropriate childcare provision for single parents makes it very difficult for such parents to work. In the next sections, we focus on one aspect of single-parent families—the implications for children of being reared by a parent (or parents) of a single gender. In doing so, however, we bear in mind that for most single parents in Britain, parenting will present a multitude of difficulties that are associated with lack of financial resources and, in the case of a large number of mothers who fall into the 'never married' category, social stigmatisation.

The media frequently suggest that children brought up in single parent families face two main disadvantages in the area of gender. The *first* of these is concerned with what social scientists have tended to term 'gender-role identification' (Williams, 1987). The mass media do not of course utilise this terminology. Instead, drawing on popular appropriations of social science jargon they ask: 'How can boys learn to be men, or girls to be women, if there is no appropriate "role model" in the family?' The *second* disadvantage concerns the extent to which children can develop optimally if there is either no female figure to nurture them or no male figure to discipline them. In posing these questions, the media draw, of course, on traditional discourses of gender which polarise the attributes of the sexes, both in terms of sexuality— 'feminine' women and 'masculine' men—and in terms of personal attributes—women are skilled at caring and men at controlling.

Gender Role Identification

Turning to the first of these issues, gender role identification, it is clear that all theories on gender development agree on a central tenet which is that the very great majority of adults, whatever their sexuality, identify unproblematically with either the male or female gender (Siann, 1994).

There is no such agreement, however, on how this identification occurs. Nevertheless, in general it is useful to regard theories of gender identification as either 'essentialist' or 'social'.

As we indicated earlier, *'essentialist'* theories assume that there are clearly differentiated attributes, psychological and social, for the sexes. In general, the pivotal differences tend to be polarised along the following lines: men are dominant, active, aggressive, analytical and adventurous, while women are caring, compassionate, empathic and intuitive.

For essentialist theorists who are *sociobiological* in approach, single-parent families should pose no problem in gender identification in that masculine and feminine attributes are regarded as 'hard-wired', that is they are inborn.

However, for other essentialist theories, notably those with a psychoanalytic orientation, single-parent families pose very specific problems for gender development. Psychoanalytic theories are regarded as 'essentialist' because psychoanalysts argue that, by the age of 3 or 4, masculinity and femininity are so deeply entrenched that they are effectively part of human nature. They regard the manner in which this happens as dependent, in the main, on the interpersonal dynamics of same and opposite sex interactions and consequently for such theorists single sex parenting may pose particular difficulties for gender identification. (See Williams, 1987, for a discussion of psychoanalytic approaches to gender identification.)

In contrast to essentialist theorists, social learning and social constructionist theorists view gender identification as dependent on the social context, but they tend to differ in their views on the implications of this for gender development. On the one hand, *social learning* theorists regard single sex parenting as problematic for gender identification because there is no role model in the home from whom the child can learn. They often see this problem as exacerbated in the case of boys being brought up by mothers in that most primary teachers are also female. *Social constructionists*, however, do not regard single sex parenting as problematic for gender identification. This is partly because they do not regard the polarisation of gender identification as desirable and partly because they regard gender divisions and gender polarities as so endemic in social life that whether or not a child is exposed to a member of the same sex in the home is relatively unimportant in that he or she lives in a social world that is permeated by gender polarisation (Lorber, 1994).

Moving from theory to empirical studies, there is a great deal of demographic evidence that gender role identification is seldom affected by being brought up in a single-parent family. For example, large numbers of boys who were born in Britain during the 1914–1918 war were brought up in mother-only families and theirs was certainly not a generation noticeable for deviating from sex role stereotypes. Similarly, there is no evidence that young men brought up in what has been termed the 'matrifocal' (single-parent families headed by mothers) families in the Caribbean have problems in their gender identification. On the other hand, there is some evidence (Wallerstein & Kelly, 1980) that in the middle years of this century in the USA, girls growing up in single-parent families resulting from divorce had initial difficulties in relating to boys when they started dating but these problems tended to be short lived and centred on interpersonal behaviour rather than gender identification.

In the initial sections of this chapter we suggested that both males and females can parent in the manner stereotypically associated with the other sex. Men can nurture and women can be firm and authoritative. But at this stage, in the context of this discussion on one-parent families, it is perhaps worth developing one particular aspect of this discussion. This is the extent to which adolescent boys may be adversely affected in the absence of a male parent if their mothers are experiencing major financial and social problems and if they are living in areas of social deprivation. Attention has been focused on this by the media who frequently ascribe criminal behaviour in such young men to the fact that many come from broken or 'never married' homes headed by mothers. While it is possible that firm parenting from a loving but authoritative father may have saved some of these young men from their deviant ways, research suggests that the alleviation of social deprivation and the provision of employment opportunities may contribute as much, if not more, to the prevention of antisocial behaviour (Siann, 1985).

Gender Issues in Gay and Lesbian Families

In general, research on parenting in gay and lesbian families indicates that the major problems such parents experience are associated with homophobia in general and in particular with the stereotypes the public holds about the impossibility of growing up heterosexual in a gay family (Silverstein, 1996).

In many cases gay and lesbian parents have children by previous heterosexual relationships and, as a result, may be particularly anxious not to be seen by their ex-partners as influencing the sexuality of such children. For this reason, and also because most gay men and lesbian women are deeply aware of how important and personal discovering one's own sexuality is to the young person, it is particularly unlikely that as parents they would wish to influence their children's sexuality. Indeed there is little evidence to support the fear expressed by many heterosexual members of the public that gay and lesbian parents seek to influence their children's sexuality.

As this chapter, and other chapters in this book, indicate, although parental attitudes and values are important, children are powerfully influenced by social norms and media discourses and consequently, given the extent to which the educational system and the media endorse hetero- rather than homosexuality, it is not surprising that, with respect to their sexuality, children do not simply follow in their parents' footsteps. The very great majority of gay men and lesbian women were reared by heterosexual parents and, similarly, the children of most gay and lesbian parents are themselves heterosexual (Patterson & Chan, 1996).

GENDER, SEXUALITY AND AWARENESS OF DANGER

The media report scandal after scandal on child abuse, whether it be in parental homes, residential homes for children or among the priesthood. In these cases of direct or substitute parenting all the adults have responsibilities as guardians and protectors of children in their care. It would take a naive viewer of television or reader of the press to be unaware of these scandals and the repeated reporting of parental and professional negligence. Does this awareness affect the ways in which adults relate to children?

Little is known about the way fathers and stepfathers (or mothers) have been affected by the media and by the reporting of distressing cases of sexual abuse. We suspect that many contemporary parents, and especially step-parents, unlike previous generations, are now conscious of their own and their children's sexuality. Whether they are wary as well as aware and take precautions not to arouse the slightest suspicion, however unjustified, we cannot tell. However, there is at least the evidence provided by institutions engaged in training residential care workers. Awareness and wariness are frequent topics of anxious discussion among both experienced and inexperienced staff.

As yet, we have not come across any studies that have investigated these issues within the home but it may be possible to generalise from findings such as those of Murray (1996) who showed the extent to which men working in childcare centres in the USA felt that men caring for children who are not their own natural offspring 'just need to be ultracareful' (p. 383). There would seem little doubt that such a need to be cautious is felt by stepfathers as well as by male childcare workers. Such caution may also be felt by stepmothers for, although men may be more conscious of their vulnerability in caring and educational situations, women too are increasingly aware that on occasion behaviour that has typically been regarded as feminine—comforting and even cuddling those in need of affection and security—may be liable to misinterpretation if the child concerned is not their own.

Since we have argued that both men and women can meet the needs of children, though they may make different use of their opportunities, it is saddening that normal nurturing responses may be inhibited in both sexes for fear of appearing abusive.

RECOMMENDATIONS

We have taken a generally optimistic view of gender issues in parenting and end with a number of observations for professional workers to bear in mind when working with families. In general, we regard it as essential to take account of the complexity of family situations and resist easy categories and expectations.

- There is little in parenting that is gender assigned: men can nurture and women can exercise discipline.
- Although there may be a move from traditional to egalitarian parenting, the extent of this change varies with employment, social class, and family structure.
- Families may have different levels of commitment to egalitarian domestic and parenting practices.
- Children's needs can be met despite diverse patterns of parenting.
- Agreement between parents on gender allocated patterns of parenting contributes to family contentment.
- In schools and in youth clubs parenting and social education classes should cover gender issues.

In conclusion, we draw attention to the context created not only by social class and employment but by the images the media present of gender roles within the family. Professional workers may need to explore the expectations created by television and the press to understand the true impact of gender.

REFERENCES

Buss, D. M. (1995) 'Psychological sex differences: origins through sexual selction.' *American Psychologist*, **50**, 164–168.

Carter, B. (1992) 'Stonewalling feminism.' *Family Therapy Networker*, **16**, 64–69.

Coltrane, S. (1989) 'Household labor and the routine production of gender.' *Social Problems*, **36**, 473–490.

Coltrane, S. (1995) 'The future of fatherhood.' In W. Marsiglio (Ed.), *Fatherhood: Contemporary Theory, Research, and Social Policy*. London: Sage, pp. 255–274.

Edley, N. & Wetherell, M. (1995) *Men in Perspective: Practice, Power and Identity*. Hemel Hempstead: Prentice Hall.

Ferri, F. & Smith, K. (1996) *Parenting in the 1990s*. London: Family Policy Studies Centre.

Herbert, M. (1988) *Working with Children and their Families*. London: Routledge.

Hewlett, B. S. (1991) *Intimate Fathers*. Ann Arbor, MI: University of Michigan Press.

Hoffman, L. W. (1989) 'Effects of maternal employment in the two-parent family.' *American Psychologist*, **44**, 283–292.

Hwang, C. P. (1987) 'The changing role of Swedish fathers.' In M. Lamb (Ed.), *The Father's Role: Cross-cultural Perspectives*. Hillsdale, NJ: Lawrence Erlbaum, pp. 115–138.

Lamb, M. (Ed.) (1987) *The Father's Role: Cross-cultural Perspectives*. Hillsdale, NJ: Lawrence Erlbaum.

Lamb, M., Pleck, J. & Levine, R. (1987) 'Effects of increased paternal involvement on fathers and mothers.' In C. Lewis & M. O'Brien (Eds), *Reassessing Fatherhood*. London: Sage, pp. 108–125.

Lewis, C. (1986) *Becoming a Father*. Milton Keynes: Open University Press.

Lorber, J. (1994) *Paradoxes of Gender*. London: Yale University Press.

Marsiglio, W. (Ed.) (1995) *Fatherhood: Contemporary Theory: Research, and Social Policy*. London: Sage.

Muncie, J., Wetherell, M., Dallos, R. & Cochrane, A. (Eds) (1995) *Understanding the Family*. London: Sage.

Murray, S. B. (1996) '"We all love Charles": men in child care and the social construction of gender.' *Gender & Society*, **10** (4), 368–385.

Patterson, C. J. & Chan, R. W. (1996) 'Gay fathers' In M. Lamb (Ed.), *The Role of the Father in Child Development*. New York: Wiley.

Rossi, A. (1975) 'A biosocial perspective on parenting.' *Daedalus*, **106** (2), 1–31.

Siann, G. (1985) *Accounting for Aggression*. London: Allen & Unwin.

Siann, G. (1994) *Gender, Sex and Sexuality*. London: Taylor & Francis.

Silverstein, L. B. (1996) 'Fathering is a feminist issue.' *Psychology of Women Quarterly*, **20**, 3–37.

Song, M. (1996) 'Changing conceptualization of lone parenthood in Britain: lone parents or single mums?' *The European Journal of Women's Studies*, **3** (4), 377–398.

Thomson, K. (1995) 'Working mothers: choice or circumstance?' In R. Jowell et al. (Eds), *British Social Attitudes: the 12th report*. Aldershot: Dartmouth, pp. 69–90.

Wallerstein, J. S. & Kelly, J. B. (1980) *Surviving the Breakup: How Children and Parents Cope with Divorce*. New York: Basic.

Wilkinson, H. (1994) *No Turning Back: Generations and the Genderquake*. London: Demos.

Williams, J. H. (1987) *The Psychology of Women: Behaviour in a Biosocial Context*. London: Norton.

Wilson, E. O. (1975) *Sociobiology: The New Synthesis*. Cambridge, Mass.: Harvard University Press.

Wilson, E. O. (1978) *On Human Nature*. London: Harvard University Press.

4

APPROACHES TO WORKING WITH ETHNICITY AND CULTURAL DIFFERENCES

Charmaine R. Kemps

INTRODUCTION

To be thinking about enhancing parenting skills, presumes a legitimised professional or personal position, which is able to privilege power and authority. This position permits entry into the private domain of family life of ordinary citizens whatever their cultural and ethnic origins and authorises intervention as if there is some better knowledge or greater good to be gained.

Who is the judge of this better knowledge or greater good? Professional judgement is NOT objective. In this chapter I assume a Social Constructivist (Maturana, 1978) position, which asserts that persons are 'structure determined', and construct meanings according to what 'fits' with their own world view. This includes the professional. Therefore all meanings are subjective, and not 'true'. 'Observations' speak of our own preferences, values and prejudices, and professional training, which are viewed through our own cultural and ethnic filters (and no one is exempt from this construction of realities). The best service a professional can offer, in my opinion, springs from a conscious ethical position, in the humbling knowledge that there is no 'truth', only

Enhancing Parenting Skills: A Guide Book for Professionals Working with Parents. Edited by K. N. Dwivedi. © 1997 John Wiley & Sons Ltd.

preferred ways of being and thinking which are organised by dominant cultural values.

I assume that culture and ethnicity are part of the heritage of all human beings, be they of the dominant or minority cultures. For our purposes, I will draw attention to some of the complex issues faced by families from cultural and ethnic minority groups. I have avoided mentioning specific groups in the hope that the professionals reading this will relate the ideas, principles and frameworks to their own practices, whatever status they may be, or with whatever origin or state of acculturation their client/patient may be.

DISPELLING A MYTH

In the context of ethnicity and cultural issues, some myths need dispelling. One is an artificial distinction about difference in the ways that people respond to state 'intervention'. Families from the dominant culture are often no different to parents in families of 'ethnic' and 'cultural' minorities when it comes to accepting 'help' from public agencies. Family life is a private affair!

Broadly speaking, both are likely to feel indignity, and vulnerable. They may view professionals who want to tell them 'what, how and when' to do with their children with suspicion, as powerful, intrusive, stigmatising and threatening. Some may resort to avoidant behaviours, i.e. not opening doors, being out when we call, first-order change signified by superficial compliance. Others may protest by confronting the system. Still others may discover and respond to the helpfulness in the professionals' approach which might overcome the concerns about state intervention.

PARENTHOOD

Parenthood is organised by personal and cultural beliefs, histories and social environments, which may or may not be conducive to becoming good enough parents to their children. There is no definitive description of good enough parenting, but in the United Kingdom, the Children Act 1989 (1 : 4) treats the child's welfare as its paramount consideration; (2 : 1) retained the concept of parenthood as guardianship; (2 : 2) introduced the construct 'parental responsibility' to include previous legal terminology, of 'parental rights, and duties or powers and duties or rights and authority'. This is a relatively new construct and many families, including those from ethnic minority groups, probably live with the idea of parental rights, duties and authority rather than parental responsibility.

If this is the case, the idea of responsibility has to be nurtured by culturally sensitive practitioners. No one is perfect, so 'good enough parenting' in one person's eyes may not be so in another's. At what point do professionals decide, in their observations, that other people's parenting is not good enough and needs to change?

CHANGE

There are many theories of what effects 'change'. The Social Constructivist position (Maturana, 1978) asserts the belief that 'change' cannot be imposed or 'instructed', since human beings are determined by their own structure. Instead 'change' occurs as it is triggered by perturbations which occur in the drift of life, as it 'bumps' against various stimuli, including professionals. The 'type' of change is dependent on the recipient of this perturbation.

How to trigger helpful rather than hindering changes depends on our skills and competence in finding a sensitive 'fit' with those with whom we are working, as well as with those through whom (interpreters) we have to work. Our efforts are best directed at attempting to provide a human context for nurturing and growth. Within this context, our respectful presence in and for the system, care, advice, questions, material and emotional support, may introduce perturbations which will hopefully trigger an appropriate response.

TOWARDS A MORE CONSTRUCTIVE PRACTICE

To this end, 'Enhancing parenting skills' is a respectful and non-pathologising construct which observes areas of competencies and ability and ways of dissolving the problem (Anderson & Goolishian, 1992). To 'enhance' is to 'heighten or intensify (qualities, powers, value, etc.); improve (something already of good quality)' (*The Concise Oxford Dictionary*, 1990). It should respect cultural differences in parenting practices, expectations and rules, as long as the child's welfare is paramount.

Here we are on shifting sand as the professionals' observations are bound to have a bias. If the observations are based on what I call a deficit model, the problem becomes the professionals' observation and their organisation's power over the family system, as the family will be constructed in negative or pathological terms. To counteract this, I suggest that the professionals should become aware of some of the pitfalls, to avoid falling into them!

THE PURPOSE OF BECOMING AWARE OF ETHNIC AND CULTURAL ISSUES

Liddle (Liddle *et al.*, 1988, pp. 336–337) suggests seven objectives for training purposes, which I think can act as a useful set of premises for assessing what particular parenting skills we should seek to influence.

1. Avoid focusing on the interior of the family's functioning or dysfunctioning, and instead place assessments within the larger socio-cultural context.
2. Differentiate between universal, transcultural, culture-specific, and idiosyncratic family behaviours.
3. Differentiate between family situations in which cultural issues may have clinical relevance and those which are peripheral.
4. Attain a culturally relativistic framework for assessment and intervention, and an understanding of ethnocentric biases.
5. Avoid use of positive and negative stereotypes, which simplify the complexities within individuals and families, and create errors in assessments which stem from ethnocentric views.
6. Allow for validation of alternative value systems, which have their strengths and weaknesses.
7. Develop an 'exploratory, sensitive, and respectful attitude toward the client's cultural identity which is integrated with joining, defining a problem, and selecting interventions' (Liddle *et al.*, 1988, p. 337).

ETHNICITY AND CULTURE: WHAT MEANING DO THEY HAVE FOR THE INDIVIDUAL?

The constructs 'ethnicity and culture' have passed through several political phases and have somehow, in the main, been reduced to 'black and whiteness'. They may be politically correct, but are simplistic, 'colour' oriented and ignore and marginalise diverse minorities who do not fit into these categories. Think of all those tones of whiteness and blackness, and people who are 'white' but have black family members or ancestors, etc.!

Ethnicity is a complex construct, which characterises an aspect of 'identity'. It is traditionally acquired at birth, from parents' origins, and/or country of origin. Intermarriage between different ethnic groups has added complexity to this identity. Migration, leading to second, third or fourth generations establishing their lives in the adopted country, and migrating for a second, third, or fourth time has created a different complexity. 'Naturalisation', e.g. becoming British or American, means that it is no longer a simple matter of labelling particular societies as 'ethnic entities'.

ETHNICITY, CULTURE AND RELIGION: WHAT MEANING DO THEY GIVE TO LIVING?

It seems that 'ethnicity' and 'cultural identity' is context dependent. In the country of origin they are the 'norm' and are given no particular emphasis, but they derive different meanings and emphasis in the context of a contrasting host culture. Maintaining the subtleties between ethnicity, culture and religion seems a necessary part of respecting diversity in our society.

Ethnicity can be viewed as a

> concept of a group's 'peoplehood', based on a combination of race, religion, and cultural history. Ethnicity patterns our thinking and feeling in both obvious and subtle ways. It plays a major role in determining what we eat, how we work, how we relate, how we celebrate our holidays and rituals, and how we feel about life, death and illness. (McGoldrick, 1989, p. 69)

Falicov (1988, p. 336) defines culture as

> those shared sets of world views and adaptive behaviours derived from simultaneous membership in a variety of contexts, such as ecological setting (rural, urban, suburban), religious background, nationality and ethnicity, social, class, gender-related experience, minority status, occupation, political leanings, migratory patterns and stage of acculturation, or values derived from the same generation, partaking of a single historical moment, or particular ideologies.

Religion still plays a major role in determining identity, lifestyle and cultural patterns of many ethnic groups. Respecting and understanding the association between observable behaviour and to what extent parenting practices are organised by religious rituals, rules and traditions are of great importance to joining the family where they are. Ignoring this factor speaks more about the observer's ignorance, and it may hinder the work that needs to be effected by the professional.

In a multi-ethnic context, 'ascriptive identity works at multiple levels and is maintained by external stimuli, which crystallises around symbols and cues, e.g. language, behavioural traits or visual ones.' (Horowitz, 1975, p. 19).

ETHNICITY AND CULTURE ISSUES FOR PATIENTS/CLIENTS

Transition

Migration to a foreign country creates a passage of time, which is commonly constructed as a 'transitional' period. It is a dislocating experience in which the migration process has its own crisis period, labelled 'decompensation' by Sluzki (1979). During this period of 'decompensation', the task for the family is in 'reshaping its new reality, maximising both the family's continuity in terms of identity, and its compatibility with its new environment' (Sluzki, 1979, p. 384).

Factors which affect this transition (McGoldrick, 1989; Landau, 1982) depend on the reason for migration, and whether the original expectations can be fulfilled or not. For example, a voluntary move to join an already established family or friendship group will be different to fleeing from dictatorships or being of refugee status. The stress of migration is partly determined by the degree of harmony between the culture in the country of origin and the country and culture of adoption. For example, how alike or different are they?

Extended Family or Community Support

The availability of substitute community and support systems, in the absence of extended family and community of origins, determines how easily each family might resolve its difficulties. If the family has moved away from a traditional extended family structure, into a culture which values the 'nuclear family', normal family stress may become distress. The lack of extended family support when it is needed for the purpose of taking over, or maintaining rules, may leave gaps in the hierarchical structure that add unbearable stress to managing relationships during this transition. This dislocating experience can create alienation from the family of origin, particularly if a death of a significant elder occurs in the meantime (Ross & Phipps, 1986). The lack of a common language such as English, creates a complex barrier to adjustment in this transitional stage.

Confronting the New and Old Value Systems

Family members in transition have their own value and cultural system confronted at different rates, depending on how exposed they are to outside influences. Parents who wish to protect and preserve their former ways of being and doing, may be under pressure to change, e.g. by the influence of: working environments; friendships across cultural boundaries; teenagers who want to go to pubs; freedom of choice in, for example, supermarkets; T.V.; children who are bringing back different ideals and 'wants' as a result of their social and educational experience. If their lifestyles and person-hood are severely threatened they may become insular and/or transform religion and culture into fundamentalist issues which organise their community. This can often be a time of confusion and conflict as members of the family acculturate at different rates and begin to reconstruct a new world view which fits with their environment, but does not fit with their original view.

This conflict of ideals and values can be compounded if and when the country of origin is revisited and family and friends construct changes as too permissive, immoral, or at least, however mildly or strongly, label noticeable changes—e.g. language, accents, behaviour of the revisiting family—as 'foreign' or affected.

ETHNICITY AND CULTURE: ISSUES FOR PROFESSIONALS

The issues that arise for professionals are many and various depending on the context and task in hand. In a multi-ethnic society, professionals who are from ethnic minority groups, may coincidentally be experiencing similar processes to their patients/clients, which may or may not be a helpful connection. If it is to be helpful, identification with these processes might be a point of empathy and understanding, but it may be unhelpful and misguided if it leads to 'over-identification'. For professionals who originate from the dominant cultural group, their cultural norms and values may be applied to families from ethnic and cultural minority groups, as if they are 'right' and others are 'wrong'.

The juxtaposed relationship between the professional from either the dominant or minority culture and the patient's/client's culture brings together two or more world views, which are set in the context of a power differential. These complex levels influence perception, e.g. professionals are viewed as figures of 'authority' in many countries. The authority of a 'professional' from a similar culture to the patient/client may be viewed with suspicion and even contempt, while the response to the one from a dominant culture may be submissive and accepting. The professionals need to be sensitive to the effects of the multidimensional, powerful circular patterns of interactions which may develop in their working relationships. Responses and reactions will either contribute to a therapeutic conversation, or become a pattern that is anti-therapeutic and counter-productive.

The Language Problem

The lack of a common language such as English, frequently presents a barrier to communication. The tension of communicating difficult issues, either through official or family interpreters, may feel threatening to the family and problematic to the professional. Many professionals recount stories about frustrations and feelings of being misrepresented, mistranslated, and even peripheral to the conversation that can take over between interpreter and client. But research by Elsherbini (1996) suggests that there is no need to lower expectations when working with non-English-speaking families, using family, community, or official interpreters. She suggests that 'the use of interpreters of whatever kind makes it possible to be seriously effective' (p. 42). This research is useful in promoting more hopeful efforts. It also begs a less controlling stance, in the belief that perturbing the system by our presence and influence will trigger enough change, whatever that might look like.

Professional Status

Traditionally, families resolve practical and emotional difficulties within family boundaries. Having a status as a professional does not necessarily assure us a position in gaining a workable relationship with those whom we wish to influence. However, 'being professional'—i.e. skilful and competent, showing respect and allowing time for courtesies—may gain more credibility and is likely to be vital in demonstrating our desire to be helpful, rather than interfering or powerful or like colonisers who forced their values onto the systems they subjugated. Bear in mind that 'assessment' is multidirectional. They are observing and assessing us, our attitudes, age, gender-related status, etc., as much as we are observing them (Kantor & Kupferman, 1985).

In the circumstances, being authoritative (not authoritarian) and respectful of their cultural practices on entering the household is vital. There may be a clear hierarchical structure within the family group, which demands a respect for elders to be demonstrated prior to speaking with the family members concerned. Identifying and acknowledging that difficulties are present in relationships or that there are struggles with transitional issues—e.g. alienation, loneliness, sadness, depression, or grieving over the loss of their homeland, or missing parents or family members—are unlikely to be transmitted to outsiders as they would be private and family business. Yet, it might be these very issues which need to be addressed to enable and enhance the parenting skills.

CONCEPT OF FAMILY

As the concept of 'Family' has undergone many changes in recent times in the West, particularly since the Second World War, so has the need to redefine what we label as 'family'. In the USA and many Western European countries it has come to mean a 'nuclear' family consisting of parents and children, living autonomously. In some other countries, 'family' includes parents, children, grandparents, aunts, uncles, cousins, all of whom remain interconnected throughout the phases of the life cycle. In some, 'family' includes all the above-mentioned as well as friends and community, to the point where everyone it seems becomes an 'uncle' or 'aunt' to someone. In some, 'family' includes all relations including ancestors who are revered and seen as part of the present.

In many Western societies, 'successful' families are signified by the presence of dominant cultural values of independence, autonomy, self-determination, separation, individuation, self-expression, self-sufficiency, assertiveness and competition, clear and direct verbal communication (Dwivedi & Varma, 1996; Lau, 1996). In other societies, i.e. Eastern Europe, the East and Far East, these values would be an anathema and run counter to moral and religious values. Instead, family life stresses loyalty, interdependence, harmony, cooperation and non-verbal and indirect communication through the use of symbols (Lau, 1996). As mentioned earlier, professionals observe through their own cultural filters, and therefore should be attentive as to how and why they need to influence the skills of parents with whom they have become involved.

FRAMEWORKS FOR THINKING ABOUT ENHANCING PARENTING SKILLS

In the following section, I will outline some general principles and frameworks which can be used across ethnic and cultural boundaries, and are useful for organising our thinking and attitudes towards this work.

Ethnicity and the Family Life Cycle

The family life cycle is not intended as a fixed and static concept. It is a fluid, conceptual framework for the benefit of professionals who need to

Table 4.1: Ethnicity and the family life cycle

Life cycle stage	Emotional process of transition	Changes in family status
The unattached young adult	Individuation requires coming to terms with ethnicity, and families of origin	Differentiation of self from family—does not necessarily mean separation from family.
The young couple Commitment to couple as	Definition of sex roles. separate partners or as merged identity	Depends on cultural attitudes—re-alignment of relationships, e.g. as separate to original families/female recruited into male line/conformity to social norms of group.
Transition to parenthood	Observing the rituals of birth-giving, e.g. at home, hospital; with/without partner/family. Accepting new members into that system.	Adjusting to marital status to make space for children. Taking responsibility for parenting. May be shared with extended members of the family.
Families with adolescents	Increasing flexibility of boundaries. Contending with separation and openness to new values.	Parent–child relationships need to open possibilties for adolescents moving in and out of system. Cultural attitudes may create conflict between parent–child over different levels of freedom for female and male children.
Launching children and moving on	Accepting variety of exits from and entries to family system.	Dependent on cultural context and stage of migration. Expectations of success, financial support for family, loyalty to-wards family. Re-negotiation of marital relationship/inclusion of in-laws and children. Dealing with disabilities and death of parents.
The family in later life	Accepting the shift of generational roles.	Maintaining own/couple functioning. Supporting older generation. Dealing with loss of spouse, siblings, peers.

(Adapted from Carter & McGoldrick, 1989, p. 15)

make a holistic assessment of the stage the family has reached in the life cycle (see Table 4.1). It facilitates consideration of what tasks need to be achieved between parents and children, during and between stages, paying due respect to the ethnic and cultural expectations and norms; and what may be hindering the move through the passage of time from one stage to another.

Families from different ethnic and cultural backgrounds will emphasise different stages, e.g. some will place the emphasis on reaching young adulthood while others will place it in later life. McGoldrick (1989, p. 89) suggests that 'Every life cycle transition is an opportunity to repair cut-offs and reinforce continuities of the family. It is important to encourage families to use their life cycle transitions to strengthen individual, family and cultural identities.'

ISSUES WHICH INTERSECT WITH THE FAMILY LIFE CYCLE

Immigration

McGoldrick (1989, p. 83) states that 'immigration is so disruptive in itself that we could say it adds an entire stage to the life cycle for those families who have to negotiate it'. The implications of this knowledge for professionals is in understanding the stage at which the parents and children were at the time of immigration. Was the journey made as an extended family group; as adults, young adults, and/or children who immigrated at different periods of time and joined each other at different stages? Is this a first, second, or third generation issue? What part of their ethnicity is reflected in the cultural and religious beliefs and parenting practices? Or is it more a condition of human nature common to all human beings, which makes it necessary to intervene?

To assess the difference, the professionals need to 'know' themselves, and where they are coming from, their own ethnic, cultural, and religious prejudices and preferences. I refer the reader to the work by Pearce and Cronen (1980) and Cronen *et al.* (1982) on multiple levels of meaning, mentioned later in this chapter (see Figure 4.1).

Arranged Marriages

Arranged marriages (in contrast to individuals finding their own partners) is common practice across migratory borders, e.g. a marriage may be arranged for a woman in England with a family-chosen man from her homeland. This marriage is likely to encounter its own transitional crisis, as it steers its way through the clashes of the family's (or chosen man's) traditional beliefs about marriage, the role of men and women, and child rearing, versus the acculturated views of the woman. Family members are likely to involve themselves in trying to resolve the conflicts. Parenting may be inconsistent, and children born into this environment may become partisan to the conflict as parents struggle with their own marital issues.

Intermarriage

The likelihood of intermarriage increases as immigration has made it possible for people of different ethnic and cultural backgrounds to interact and socialise through work or leisure and religious association. The greater the difference between the couple in their religious and cultural belief systems, the more likely it is that value systems will be in conflict, which in turn would feed conflict in their beliefs about child-rearing practices, and therefore their ideas about parenting. The question is: How can professionals involve themselves in such conflictual situations without being disrespectful and interfering in the family's process?

Some communities have their own organised cultural and religious networks for managing the needs of their members. There is, I think, a dilemma about the extent to which public agencies should be involved, if such networks exist. It is preferable to respect the natural ecosystemic balance of such systems and find ways of working through them. This is influenced by my belief that, in addition to the authority and power invested in us to protect children and enhance patterns of parental care, we should extend our caring towards parents and the relationships between children and parents. This provides the context for change.

A CONCEPTUAL SCHEMA FOR WORKING WITH FAMILIES IN CULTURAL TRANSITION

Some cultures maintain a clear boundary between what is, and what is not, permissible for adults to talk about in the presence of the children. Cultural sensitivity is needed when asking questions, which may embarrass parents in front of their children. If necessary, make time to create a respectful private space. However, respect for the boundaries of personal space and privacy of family life need to be balanced with the professional's task, which should be based on the child's welfare.

A general conceptual schema and operational principles (Landau, 1982; Lau, 1996) for working with families in cultural transition can be used skilfully and appropriately in many circumstances and contexts where professionals wish to develop a working relationhip to establish ways of improving parenting skills.

Liddle's seven objectives (mentioned earlier in this chapter) act as a useful set of premises for this schema. This schema firstly assumes the need to be informed, through direct or interpreted conversation, about current parenting practices, before being able to take parents onwards. What beliefs, values or religious traditions influence the role of parenting? What are the formal structures for decision making in the family? Who does the family regard as its relevant family network? What is the life-cycle stage, and tasks to be performed?

The second stage ('Transitional Mapping') attempts to establish which phase of migration the family is currently in, and how it dealt with previous phases. What, if any, transitional issues and stresses may be undermining the particular skills of the parent that the professional believes requires enhancing? The task is a very delicate one and professionals would need to be aware of taking unnecessary detailed medical-type histories which might seem insensitive, inquisitive and irrelevant to the reason for their involvement.

If the family is not open to professional involvement, it may be useful to move to a third stage which is to recruit a 'link-therapist' (Landau, 1982). This would be a person who is acceptable to the family, e.g. in a patriarchal system, a man of some seniority may be most acceptable. Landau (1982) warns against using the most acculturated member of the family whose lifestyle and values resemble those of the therapist. Instead she suggests that the 'most effective link-therapist is a family member, whose position has not been resolved; one who, caught up in the system's transitional conflict, is himself in the process of the cultural transition. This is generally not the complainant, and may even be a peripheral member of the family' (p. 562). In this model, discussion and supervision between therapist and link-therapist are kept as simple as possible. A balance should be struck between supervising and authorising the link-therapist to make a difference.

Systemic Principles

Systems theory underpins most models of family therapy. It views individual family members (which includes transgenerations) as parts of a whole connected system. The principle is that individual actions and behaviour can only be understood in the context of the interactions (i.e.

language, and verbal and non-verbal behaviour) between them as a whole, and not as separately acting entities. Within this context all behaviour makes 'sense', and creates a circular pattern of interactions between family members. It is this pattern of interaction which creates the nature of relationships. If there are difficulties, it is considered to be 'interactional' rather than 'intrapsychic'. When dealing with parents from diverse ethnic and cultural backgrounds, the principle remains the same, adding the religious, cultural and family patterns into the picture.

In practice, the professional needs to devote time to understanding these patterns before imposing any changes. These patterns of interactions would be elicited in conversational style, by asking questions (not telling them) about their perceptions, beliefs, behaviour; ideas for the future, and present, etc. This would form the basis of information which could be used to advise, guide or model better parenting practices appropriate to the age and stage of the children.

NEUTRALITY

The concept of Neutrality (Ceccin, 1987) can be a helpful stance for the professional. It opens space for being with an individual or family and owning a non-judgemental stance in difficult circumstances. It opens therapeutic space for clients who may perceive the professional as 'multi-partial', i.e. on everyone's side, rather than partial or impartial. Being non-judgemental towards the person makes it possible to respect the family's cultural and personal histories, which account for their current practices, e.g. smacking, which may be acceptable in their own cultural tradition, but is unacceptable in Western child care practice.

CURIOSITY

Adopting a position of 'curiosity' (Ceccin, 1987) opens space for open-minded interest on the part of the professional, in the thinking and behaviour of every member of the family. It guards against thinking one 'knows', in the knowledge that there is always more to know that might make a difference.

COORDINATED MANAGEMENT OF MEANING (CMM THEORY)

This theory (Pearce & Cronen, 1980; Cronen et al., 1982) helps to situate ourselves in our communication with others and provides a framework for thinking about the communication between those whom we seek to influence and ourselves, our histories. It may explain how and why communication may be skewed for better or worse.

Communication is said to consist of multiple levels or meaning (Figure 4.1) which are hierarchically structured (Pearce & Cronen, 1980; Cronen et al., 1982). Each level is a context which acts like a springboard for making meaning of the language and nuances human beings use to communicate with each other, at any one moment in time. The relationship between these meanings influence each other in circular patterns.

The upward force influences the meaning of a conversation by 'implying' meaning to a higher context, as it is reminded and connects with previous memory senses and conversations. The downward force brings 'past contexts' to bear on one another, thus influencing the meanings of conversations in the present. This framework enables the professionals to be thoughtful about the content and language of their own statements, values and prejudices, and the influence of these on their patients/clients, as well as the influence of their patients' communication upon themselves. It introduces a sensitive perspective on communication which takes account of language and communication which has traditionally and culturally determined assumptions and meanings.

Example: Figure 4.1 defines each context in this framework. A breakdown of an example of a statement of a father to a child may be

'Do as I tell you, or I will beat you.'

Professionals, hearing this may interact with this communication at different levels, depending on their own history. For example, if in childhood they had been threatened with physical punishment, it could lead to identification with the child at point (E); it could remind them of their own parents' punitive attitudes, at point (B), even though point (B) and point (A) may have a very different ethnic and cultural meaning. This might recursively lead them to relate to the parents as they did to their own parents. This may reduce their authority as professionals who, in this role, need to care for parents as well as for children. In this example, bias towards the child without due attention to the parents' needs may alienate parents from children, and vice versa. This skew is not conducive to enhancing the parents' skill. To avoid blame and judgement on the parents, professionals need to be highly sensitive to their own life stories, and watch out for contexts which overlap with their clients/patients, and therefore the miscommunications which may occur.

Multiple levels of meaning

For example, statement to illustrate complexities in meanings:

'Do as I tell you or I will beat you.'

(A) CULTURAL PATTERN (Value beliefs of family system) Context: Family belief that fathers have the right to discipline their children to maintain order in society.
(B) LIFE SCRIPT (of an individual) Context: Recent immigration and acculturating processes.
(C) EPISODE (whole social encounter) Context: Parents disagreeing about the rules for going out and coming in.
(D) SPEECH ACT (utterance as a whole) Context: An argument about going out with friends.
(E) CONTENT (of a statement) 'Do as I tell you or I will beat you.' (Father threatens child with physical punishment if he or she is disobedient.)

Figure 4.1:   Multiple levels of meaning.

CONCLUSION

In this chapter I have attempted to draw attention to some of the broad and complex issues faced by families from diverse ethnic and cultural minority groups, and for the professionals dealing with them. The intention of presenting ideas, principles and frameworks, rather than examples of individual cases from specific ethnic and cultural groups, is to enable the professionals to pick and choose what is most helpful to their working context.

I believe that entry into the private domain of family life should always be undertaken humbly, no less with parents from ethnic minority groups. These parents are not only engaged in the 'normal' struggles of parenthood but, in addition, with the struggle to protect their traditions and culture which may have hitherto provided an unchallenged identity. Caring for them is likely to bring forth caring for their children.

Acknowledgements: My thanks to the health visitors and social workers in Milton Keynes who willingly shared some of the issues with which they contend in this aspect of their work with families.

REFERENCES

Anderson, H. & Goolishian, H. (1992) 'The client is the expert.' In S. McNamee & K. J. Gergen (Eds), *Therapy as Social Construction*. Sage Publications.

Carter, B. & McGoldrick, M. (1989) *The Changing Family Life Cycle: A Framework for Family Therapy*. Allyn & Bacon.

Ceccin, G. (1987) 'Hypothesizing, circularity, and neutrality revisited: an invitation to curiosity.' *Family Process*, **26**, 405–413.

Cronen, V. E., Johnson, K. M. & Lannaman, J. W. (1982) 'Paradoxes, double binds, reflexive loops: an alternative theoretical perspective.' *Family Process*, **21**, 91–112.

Dwivedi, K. N. & Varma, V. P. (Eds) (1996) *Meeting the Needs of Ethnic Minority Children*. London and Bristol, PA: Jessica Kingsley.

Elsherbini, M. (1996) 'Working with non-English-speaking families: can we be effective?' *Context*, **29**, 40–42. AFT Publishing Company.

Falicov, C. J. (1988) 'Learning to think culturally.' In H. A. Liddle, D. C. Breunlin & R. C. Schwartz (Eds), *Handbook of Family Therapy and Supervision*. New York, London: Guilford Press.

Glazer, N. & Moynihan, D. P. (Eds) (1975) *Ethnicity Theory and Practice*. Cambridge, Mass.: Harvard University Press.

Horowitz, D. (1975) 'Ethnic identity.' In N. Glazer & D. P. Moynihan (Eds), *Ethnicity Theory and Practice*. Cambridge, Mass.: Harvard University Press.

Kantor, D. & Kupferman, W. (1985) 'The clients view of the therapist.' *Journal of Marital and Family Therapy*, **3**, 225–244.

Landau, J. (1982) 'Therapy with families in cultural transition.' In M. McGoldrick, J. K. Pearce & J. Giordiano (Eds), *Ethnicity and Family Therapy*. New York, London: Guilford Press.

Lau, A. (1996) 'Family therapy and ethnic minorities.' In K. N. Dwivedi & V. P. Varma (Eds), *Meeting the Needs of Ethnic Minority Children*. London and Bristol, PA: Jessica Kingsley.

Liddle, H. A., Breunlin, D. C. & Schwartz, R. C. (Eds) (1988) *Handbook of Family Therapy and Supervision*. New York, London: Guilford Press.

Maturana, H. R. (1978) 'Biology of language: the epistemology of reality.' In G. Millar (Ed.), *Psychology and the Biology of Language and Thought*. Academic Press.

McGoldrick, M. (1989) 'Ethnicity and the family life cycle.' In B. Carter & M.

McGoldrick (Eds), *The Changing Family Life Cycle: A Framework for Family Therapy.* Allyn & Bacon.

McGoldrick, M., Pearce, J. K. & Giordiano, J. (Eds) (1982) *Ethnicity and Family Therapy.* New York, London: Guilford Press.

Pearce, W. B. & Cronen, V. E. (1980) *Communication Action and Meaning.* New York: Praeger.

Ross, J. L. & Phipps, E. J. (1986) 'Understanding the family in multiple cultural contexts: avoiding therapeutic traps.' *Contemporary Family Therapy,* **8** (4), 255–263. Human Science Press.

Sluzki, C. (1979) 'Migration and family conflict.' *Family Process,* **18** (4), 379–390.

White, R., Carr, P. & Lowe, N. (1990) *The Guide to the Children Act 1989.* London: Butterworth.

5

PARENTHOOD: ASSESSMENT OF 'GOOD ENOUGH PARENTING'

Shanthy Parameswaran

Many professionals working with children, adolescents and their familes are being increasingly required to assess 'parenting capacity'. In the forum of child protection it would be commissioned by the Child Protection Conference as part of the Child Protection Plan and members of different disciplines will be involved. It is essential that all professionals involved with the case liaise together. Good communication facilitates further understanding of the case and what is exactly being asked.

Maslow and Dias-Guerrero (as quoted in Skynner, 1986, p. 306) have given a clear but traditional account of maternal and paternal functions:

> We postulate that the major task of the mother, qua mother, is to love unconditionally, to gratify, to heal and comfort and smooth over; and that the major task of a father, qua father, is to support and protect, to mediate between the family and reality (the world), and to prepare his children to live in the extra-familial world by discipline, toughening, instruction, reward and punishment, judging, differential valuing, reason and logic (rather than by unconditional love), and by being able to say 'No' when necessary.

D. W. Winnicott (1960), the paediatrician and psychoanalyst, coined the phrase 'good enough parenting'. The term was used to denote a mother's ability to recognise and respond to her child's needs without having to be a perfect mother all the time.

Enhancing Parenting Skills: A Guide Book for Professionals Working with Parents. Edited by K. N. Dwivedi. © 1997 John Wiley & Sons Ltd.

WHAT IS 'GOOD ENOUGH PARENTING'?
DIMENSIONS OF PARENTING

The child has a need for:

- basic physical care—security and safety
- affection and approval
- discipline and control—which are consistent and age appropriate
- teaching and stimulation
- provision of normal life experiences
- encouragement of appropriate levels of independence
- response to its chaning needs and awareness that these needs have precedence over the parent's needs
- positive role models—'children are educated by what the grown up *is* and not by what he says' (Jung, 1968).

The supportive parent knows how to follow the child, rather than always leading him. Concerns over parenting usually rise in connection with all forms of child abuse, neglect, abandonment, parental mental illness or handicap, parental lifestyle, etc., and the assessment will vary according to the circumstances and the presenting problem. Black *et al.* (1991) list 18 likely situations where assessment of parenting may be called for, most of which fall into the following categories:

- The child's development or behaviour is abnormal or delayed and the extent of the parental contribution to the problem needs evaluation.
- The child is well, and currently not showing an abnormality, but the parents' ability to care for the child is of concern.
- Assessment of prospective adoptive parents or other carers.
- Planning is necessary for a child's future—e.g. consideration of rehabilitation or fostering.

Within the legal context (Section 31, Children Act 1989) the court may need to know that the child concerned is suffering or likely to suffer *significant harm* and that the harm, or likelihood of harm, is attributable to: the care given to the child, or likely to be given to him if that order were not made, not being what it would be reasonable to expect a parent to give to him; or the child being beyond parental control. Harm has to be at a significant level to reach the threshold criteria. When making a judgement of significant harm it is necessary to compare the health or development of the child in question with that which could be expected of a similar child. Harm has to be shown to arise from the failure to provide a reasonable standard of parental care. The question of significant harm is well discussed from a practitioner's point of view by Bentovim (1991).

THE ASSESSMENT PROCESS
General Considerations

Depending on the age and circumstances of the child, information should be obtained from the professionals listed below as recommended in the report from the Professional Practices Subcommittee of the Northamptonshire Child Protection Committee (Brown *et al.*, 1996).

- Midwife, health visitor, school nurse: This should include details of development, general health and specific health needs.
- Nursery or school staff: This information should include details of educational progress, quality of relationships with peers and adults, significant behaviours and identified special needs.
- Substitute carers: This should follow the same pattern as the information gathered from parents.

In addition the following professionals may be involved in the assessment and their reports need to be requested.

- Educational/clinical psychologists
- Psychotherapists
- Social workers
- Guardian *ad litem*
- Medical practitioners: General practitioners, paediatricians, psychiatrists.

However, an independent assessor needs to be objective about judgemental comments in other agencies' reports as opinions are often coloured by the social and moral values of the authors. In addition, he or she needs to form an opinion about the appropriateness of previous interventions and in particular consider that parents may have to cope with problems in the child caused by the impact of separation previously advocated.

Cultural and Class Perspective

Assessment must also take into account the family's cultural and racial characteristics. What one cultural group may consider as 'good enough' may be thought by another as barbaric, e.g. the initiation practices in tribal cultures may be viewed as abusive by Western society. Even within the same culture there are differences. For example, the use of physical punishment is considered acceptable by a certain class of people within the same culture. It is important to remember that culture affects all aspects of a child's life; how they use non-verbal communication, including play, their perception of the world, their experience of racism and their self-image. If these factors are not considered, misjudgement in the assessment may occur. However, what needs to be considered is whether or not the practices prevent the child's growth and development and leaves the child feeling worthless, with low self-esteem and low self-image. Within the Social Services Department the choice of person undertaking the assessment may take into account the race, gender, culture, sexuality and any other special needs of the child or family.

Who is seen and with whom and where will vary according to the circumstances and the presenting problem, but should include:

- Interview with the child alone.
- Interview with both parents (even though they may live apart).
- Interview with all other relevant adults and children separately and in various combinations to observe the interactions between the various members.

Each case will vary and call for different permutations. In multi-disciplinary settings two or more people may be involved jointly or individually in the assessment process. Joint assessment is advantageous, particularly when family interactions and relationships are being observed.

Assessment of the family in their own home should be considered but the majority of the sessions should take place away from the home as this emphasises the gravity of the process to the family. It also avoids distractions by visitors, telephone calls, television, etc. In addition, at the clinic video recordings may be available for later study. An assessment at the home would reveal household deficiencies in the areas of hygiene, provision for play, observation of mealtimes, bedtime routine, discipline, etc.

Timescale

Three to four months for completion of the assessment and report is usually needed. Too long a timescale may lead to therapeutic work. It is therefore important that the reasons for assessment with details of the concern be made explicit to the family from the outset. An explanation of the process, with appointment dates (including timescale in which report will be made available), should be made clear from the beginning. Trust and cooperation from the family is more likely when this happens.

Nevertheless, there are cases in which interventions need to be considered, attempted and monitored before the final decision about placement of the child can be made. During this *prolonged* assessment a parent's capacity to benefit from treatment may become apparent. Therapeutic assessment takes more time, around twelve months to complete. Prolonged therapeutic assessments may be considered for young parents with immature personalities who have the capacity to change and work with professionals. They need to have a more flexible attitude (*not* the attitude, 'if you leave us alone we will be all right') to learn new parenting skills (Fitzpatrick, 1995).

Supervision

Certain disciplines offer regular supervision to those undertaking the assessment. In these circumstances the supervisors should be aware of *professional dangerousness*. Professional dangerousness is the process by which individual workers or agencies can, unknowingly, act in such a way as to collude with, maintain or increase the dangerous dynamics of the family. This process is further discussed by Reder *et al.* (1993) and Dale *et al.* (1986).

PROCESS OF INFORMATION GATHERING

Members of the different disciplines and agencies have their own methods and styles of carrying out these assessments. The differences reflect their different training and clinical practices. The Department of Health (1988) publication *Protecting Children: A Guide for Social Workers undertaking a Comprehensive Assessment* offers a format of questions divided into eight sections under which the information gathered is to be reported. Bentovim and Bingley (1985) consider seven main dimensions of family interaction when observing family functioning in the context of assessing parenting capacity. Belsky (1984) groups the factors involved in parenting capacity under three main headings: characteristics of the parents; characteristics of the child; and sources of stress and support in the wider social environment. Reder and Lucey (1995) advise an interactional model to *understand* parenting capacity and suggest a number of themes arranged under five headings.

As there seems to be little disagreement about what constitutes good parenting, a starting point in parenting assessment would be to identify whether or not these needs, i.e. *Dimensions of Parenting*, are being met. The assessment should identify whether or not parents are able to provide for the essential needs of their child, whether they can accept the responsibility of being parents and their attitudes towards parenting. In general, the process should identify the strengths and weaknesses in the protective and nurturing processes.

It is possible to group the other factors concerned under the following headings.

Factors within the Parent

Physical/mental health of parents

Here the effect of the presence of a formal psychiatric disorder or substance misuse (alcohol or drugs) on the parenting capacity needs to be addressed. Some of the issues to be considered are: What is the nature of the psychiatric disorder? Is it treatable? What is the long-term outcome? What is the effect on the child of repeated parental hospitalisation? Does the child feel responsibile for his parents mental illness? Has the child been involved in the parent's delusional system? What is the danger of risk to the child? What is the effect of substance misuse on the parental mental state? Does the procurement of drugs or alcohol by the parents interfere with the provision for the child's basic needs? How does the substance misuse or psychiatric disorder affect parental cognitive state and judgement?

The psychiatric disorder needs to be assessed by an adult psychiatrist and treated accordingly. The parenting capacity can only be assessed by other professionals when the psychiatric condition is under control. Some parents can provide excellent care of their children when not intoxicated or when their disorder is under control with treatment. Repeated admissions and non-cooperation with treatment does not allow continuity and consistency in parenting.

Chronic physical illness in parents may affect the care parents may provide for their child. However such parents may provide for their child, with support from a partner, family, or outside agencies with whose aid these 'handicaps' can be overcome. If the physical problem affects the emotional state of the parent or disturb the caring environment of the child in any way, these effects need to be evaluated in the usual manner.

There is no evidence to suggest that mild learning disability in a parent prevents 'good enough parenting' (Gath, 1988). Homosexuality per se is no longer judged an impediment to satisfactory parenting. Gay men and lesbian women can provide effective parenting and there is no evidence that social, emotional or sexual development of children raised by them is affected in any major way (King, 1995).

In all these instances it is the individual child's compatibility with the parent that needs to be assessed.

Parents' internal working models

Recent studies and research findings mainly by Main and her colleagues (1991) into parents' internal working models of attachment and parenting behaviour suggest links between parents' narrative accounts of their own attachment history and their infants' behavioural response. When parents present a coherent singular model of their attachment history, the infant is considered secure. These parents may have had either a secure experience in childhood or a negative experience in childhood which they have satisfactorily worked through. In contrast, when parents present an incoherent and multiple models of their attachment history it suggests an inability to respond appropriately to their infant's needs and the child is thought to be insecure. Main and her colleagues have developed the Adult Attachment Interview (AAI) schedule. This is used to assess an adult's internal working model. It is a standardised semi-structured interview. Further research is needed to make the AAI more user friendly in clinical situations and to enable professionals to determine the parents' potential to respond to psychological treatments.

Factors within the Child

Age of the child

At different ages the child needs different types of care and control from his parents. Sensitive parenting keeps pace with the child's abilities and needs as he grows and faces the various developmental tasks (Belsky, 1984) and these vary at different ages. The parents must be flexible in their approach and gradually increase the child's responsibility and social involvement giving the child the message 'you are growing up' (Apley, 1982).

Temperament of the child

Children differ in temperament and this may determine the way in which they respond to a particular stress. Key factors include temperamental attributes such as activity level, social responsiveness and adaptability (Garmezy, 1984). Therefore, comments on the strengths and weaknesses of the child will be useful in the evaluation of the problem. The child's temperament can also contribute to the problem.

An ill child with sleep problems will need special skills from carers. Some children's temperament can trigger unresolved residues of adverse childhood experiences in their parents which, in turn, will interfere with their parenting.

Number of children in the household

Parents, particularly those with some form of handicap, e.g. learning disability, may be able to parent one or two children satisfactorily. However, the arrival of a third or fourth child may stretch their parenting capacity to the limit and lead to the failure of their parenting.

Physical and mental health of the child

A child with a physical handicap, e.g. poor eyesight or cerebral palsy, will demand different and more parenting skills. When a formal psychiatric disorder is present in the child its cause, course and prognosis should be evaluated. A child with a strong family history of schizophrenia will need a more stable environment with less stressful life events than a child with a lower genetic predisposition (Nuechterlein, 1986).

Children's internal working models

The internal working models of the child are considered to have developed on the basis of the child's true relationship with his early attachment figures. The feelings and thoughts that the child develops about himself and to his attachment figures influence the way he relates to his carers. This is discussed in detail by Jenner and McCarthy (1995).

In 1978 Ainsworth and her colleagues developed a procedure called the Ainsworth Strange Situation to assess infants' and toddlers' attachments to their caregivers. Four categories were identified: secure; insecure–avoidant; insecure–ambivalent; and insecure–disorganised.

A secure child is able to explore his environment with his mother as a secure base. He returns to her from time to time. He becomes disturbed when she is absent and is glad when she returns. The parents of a secure infant are able to read their child's signals and respond to them appropriately with warmth. On the other hand, an infant showing insecure–avoidant explores his surroundings with little reference to his mother and shows little distress to her absence or pleasure at her return. He may even ignore her. This type of attachment to the mother is associated with maternal insensitivity to the child's signals and maternal rejection. An insecure–ambivalent infant is greatly distressed by his mother's absence and is not easily pacified by his mother's return. This is associated with maternal insensitivity and unpredictability. An insecure–disorganised child freezes or exhibits stereotype movements in his parents' presence and is the most worrying type of behaviour. It is often associated with more serious parental behaviour such as child abuse, parental pathology such as maternal depression or a history of loss of significant figures in childhood with unresolved grief.

Factors within Family Relationships

Parent–child relationship

Here the aim is to observe the parent–child interaction. The parents' feelings towards the child and their ability to empathise with their child are examined. Particular attention is paid to negative attitudes such as coercive interventions, blaming, belittling and rejection of the child. A certain child may be favoured, scapegoated or made to assume a parenting role to the younger children. The latter has been recently observed in large Asian families where the oldest girl is forced to take on parental duties to the detriment of her academic and social development. Sometimes the birth of the child may coincide with a major life event and this may then influence the parent–child interaction.

The couple relationship is viewed as the most crucial element. In 1986, Dale *et al.* stated that 'if the spouse relationship is not viable in a family where serious child abuse has occurred, then neither is the family'. Here the parents' ability to sustain a supportive relationship with a partner, the qualities of the spouse, the extent to which child rearing is shared and satisfaction and achievements apart from parenting are examined. It may be necessary to explore past relationships in order to understand repetitive patterns of behaviour. Multiple partners or unrealistic expectations from the partner may suggest an inability to form deep and meaningful relationships. Often when the couple feel their emotional needs are not being met by the other, they may turn to the child for this or blame the child for the failure of their relationship; then the child becomes over-involved in the family's discordant relationships.

The key aspects of *family interaction* (Bentovim & Bingley, 1985) include the affective status, communication, boundaries, alliances, stability and adaptability, and family competence. These terms are familiar to family therapists. *Affective status* refers principally to the family atmosphere. It includes observations of the predominant mood and the circumstances in which family moods change markedly. *Communication* relates to how messages are given and received by the various members of the family. It also refers to the verbal and non-verbal messages and the agreement between them. The clarity of the messages and how much listening members do without interruptions are also observed. *Boundaries* pertains to the degree of emotional involvement of the family members and the degree of individual autonomy. The generation boundaries, whether they are rigid, flexible or diffuse, are noted. *Alliances* refers to the quality and pattern of different relationships within the family. Sometimes two or more members gang up against another or there may be a particular member being scapegoated. *Stability* refers to the senses of continuity of a family and *adaptability* to the ability of the family system to show appropriate responses to different situations. *Family competence* relates to the capacity of the family to deal effectively with problems.

Other family relationships

Here the relationships with siblings, grandparents and other relatives are explored. The aim is primarily to look at generational and current family influences shaping the relationship between parent and child.

Factors within the Environment

The role of the extended family, friends and neighbours and their influence need consideration. Parents who lack secure support are more vulnerable to stressful life events which may lead to parenting breakdown and mental health problems (Brown & Harris, 1978). In many cases the quality of parenting improves dramatically when a strong social support network is provided (Hetherington *et al.*, 1978). The greater the social isolation the more likely that parental handicaps will affect the parenting capacity. Many abusive families are socially isolated. The role in child care of any other adults who live at home should be considered along with the parents' relationship to professional workers.

Capacity for Change

The following are some of the factors that need to be considered: the willingness of the parent to admit there is a problem and to accept responsibility for it; motivation to work towards change and an ability to ask for help from relatives, professionals or voluntary agencies. Previous improvement may suggest that appropriate help may again be beneficial.

Physical growth and development. Examination of the child is usually sought in cases of non-accidental injury and in cases of emotional abuse that is seen to affect the physical development of the child. The physical examination is usually carried out by a paediatrician. Measurement of physical development (height, weight and head circumference) in young children is a good indicator of satisfactory or unsatisfactory progress. Height is a sensitive indicator of a child's physical health. Failure to thrive due to non-organic causes is now well recognised, and it appears to affect more boys than girls (Rudolf & Hochberh, 1990). However, the medical practitioner must be familiar with the environmental variables that will influence growth, e.g. social class of parents, family size, overcrowding, ethnicity, parental height, etc. A child's growth will normally follow a given centile throughout the growing period. Growth velocity measures the rate of growth. A significant change in growth velocity—say, an increase in a child removed from the parental home and placed in care—would be indicative of the quality of parenting prior to the removal (King & Taitz, 1985). The rate of growth and development under different conditions is an important part of the assessment. Further information on physical findings and their significance as presented to the court has been well recorded by Stone (1992).

Developmental assessment tests

The developmental assessment test commonly used is the Ruth Griffiths scale. This test should be carried out by specialists who have had the necessary training. It is most helpful for a child under the age of 3. Developmental scores are obtained in five areas: gross motor, personal-social, hearing and speech, eye–hand coordination, and performance. If speech and language are considered to be affected a more detailed assessment may be indicated, e.g. by a speech therapist. Language development is sensitive to the effects of an abusive and neglectful environment. Rapid and marked improvement in a child with speech delay when placed in a different home or following positive changes in the original environment is indicative of the quality of care prior to the change. Mary Sheridan's chart (1960, revised 1975)—illustrating the developmental progress of infants and young children in the motor areas, hearing, speech, visual and social behaviour—is also useful in the assessment process. It is still considered to be one of the most reliable descriptions of normal human development in the early years. Child development schemata covering a number of developmental areas and the state of attachments to significant figures have been described by Fahlberg (1985). Professional workers will be able to make reference to these charts when a child's development is thought to be delayed or interrupted. Any delay in cognitive development and learning capacity with poor concentration and short attention span may need a psychometric assessment by an educational or clinical psychologist.

EVALUATING THE RESULTS OF THE ASSESSMENT

At the end of the assessment process, some method of evaluation is necessary to pull all the pieces together. Kinston and Bentovim (1982) describe the concept of family focus as a way of organising and making sense of the vast amount of information collected. The focal hypothesis connects and explains the problem observed to the family's characteristic pattern of interaction. The manner in which significant events in the family of origin or procreation have been addressed and the meaning of such events to the family will determine the family's characteristic pattern of interaction. For example, some families will recreate and repeat past events; some will avoid or reverse them; yet others will find scapegoats to 'deposit' them.

It is advisable not to be too dogmatic in the process of evaluation given the wide variation of the factors involved. The aim is not to give specific weight to each of the factors but to consider how these factors affect the parenting of the individual child, how incapacitating it is to the process of parenting and how remediable and liable to change it is and by what means (Swadi, 1994). The evaluation will include a degree of subjectivity based on clinical experience. The final opinion will be a balancing out of many issues and will be determined by professional judgements about the relative weighting of the several groups of factors.

WRITING THE REPORT AND RECOMMENDATIONS

The following points may need consideration:

- Professionals from the various disciplines who are called upon to carry out assessments and provide reports, have their own guidelines, usually recommended by their professional bodies.
- The reports from social workers, health visitors and teachers deal with children and parents over time and their long-term observation is essential in forming an opinion.
- A one-off assessment by a paediatrician or a psychiatrist which may take place over a short span of time must be supplemented by the longer time observation of the others.

In the court the judge would refer to the welfare checklist in the Children

Act 1989 in determining any question with respect to a child's upbringing. It would therefore be prudent when writing the report to bear the list in mind. The court in effect will go through the list, in cases where a local authority seeks a care or supervision order.

The welfare checklist

This includes the following:

(a) the ascertainable wishes and feelings of the child concerned (considered in the light of his age and understanding)
(b) his physical, emotional and educational needs
(c) the likely effect on him of any change in his circumstances
(d) his age, sex, background and any characteristics of his which the court considers relevant
(e) any harm which he has suffered or is at risk of suffering
(f) how capable each of his parents, and any other person in relation to whom the court considers the question to be relevant, is of meeting his needs
(g) the range of powers available to the court under this Act in the proceedings in question.

Department of Health, 1989, p. 18)

A child is not just an object of care. A child is a human being with a voice worth listening to. It is therefore no surprise that the child's voice is first on the checklist. Ascertaining the wishes and feelings of the child is vital for the court. As Lord Scarman states in the case of Gillick v West Norfolk and Wisbech Health Authority in 1985 'Parental right yields to the child's right to make his own decisions when he reaches a sufficient understanding and intelligence to be capable of making up his own mind on the matter requiring decision.' Where a guardian *ad litem* has been appointed this task falls mainly on that professional person. It is important to separate the wishes and feelings of the child into a section on its own in the written report. However, recent judgements in courts have thrown doubt on whether or not children can 'truly' consent or dissent to treatment or for that matter any intervention that has impact on their lives. The effect of these decisions from the angle of medicine, ethics and the law are examined by Devereux *et al.* (1993).

The Children Act (Section 1{5}) also states that where a court is considering whether or not to make one or more orders under the Act with respect to a child, it shall not make the order or any of the orders unless it considers that doing so would be better for the child than making no order at all. This non-intervention principle needs consideration when making recommendations to the court as the court will not interfere unless it is satisfied that its interference will do good.

The new Act also implies that the child is best cared within the family and expects professionals to work in collaboration with the parents for the welfare of the child.

Ingrained in the Children Act is the principle that the welfare of the child is paramount. When conflicts arise between the needs of the child and the needs of the parent the child's interests must be placed first: *'The child must never be used as a therapeutic tool for the parents'* (Jones *et al.*, 1987, p. 107). A parent's physical and mental state may worsen if it is decided permanently to remove the child from the parent's care but it is the welfare of the child that must be considered. A child must not be seen as therapy for parents.

If it is decided that the parents are unable permanently to care for the child, the young child must not be allowed to remain in limbo. Permanent carers must be found as early as possible. The disadvantages arising from multiple carers and moves must be clearly stated so as to be avoided in the best interests of the child and prevent the child from being in long-term care. The Children Act (Secion 1{2}) states clearly that the court must pay due regard to the principle that any delay is likely to prejudice the welfare of the child. In some instances with treatment or with the passage of time a parent's physical and mental health may improve, but this time factor must be taken into account. A young child may not be able to wait for the improvement to occur. The younger the child the more critical is the time factor to enable the child to make satisfactory attachments to caring adults.

When treatment is recommended the parents' and family's willingness to accept treatment should be noted. Last minute cooperation with treatment when the parents had from the start refused it, must also be recorded. Sometimes a change of mind occurs when lawyers recommend parents to accept treatment as it will improve their chances of keeping the child. In recommending treatment, consideration should also be given to features within parents which will indicate a positive outcome, e.g. ability to be reflective, to accept blame and not to blame the children, etc. Interventions that may be helpful and resources available to achieve this change should be clearly stated. Sometimes rehabilitation may have been undertaken and failed or not been possible at all and, if so, this information must also be included in the report.

The court will often like to know the time limit to achieve rehabilitation and this needs to be stated. Rehabilitation can normally take around 12–18 months. No parents can be perfect but with professional help they can become 'good enough' parents for their child. The aim is to provide the child with a more favourable environment within a short space of time. When treatment is recommended there should be arrangements in place to monitor it.

The court also finds it useful if the assessor could predict the various courses of actions recommended and discuss the advantages and disadvantages of alternative care or care of one parent versus another. Sometimes the problem lies in the difficulty of the parent who has custody to tolerate the other parent's contact with the child. This question of continuing contact with parents and siblings should be addressed and the ability and tolerance of those caring for the child to accept and cope with the contact should be considered. The Children Act embodies an assumption that continued contact between a child, parents and the family should be promoted.

Foster parents, too, sometimes become over-possessive about the child in their care and this may influence their attitude towards the parents. Nevertheless the parents' ability to look after the child may not be the only factor when the court is considering whether or not to return the child to its parents. The court may consider the attachment ties which the child has formed with its alternative carers, particularly if the child has been placed with them for a long period from a very young age.

A CASE EXAMPLE

A 20-year-old mother, Ms D, was referred with two children, aged 3 years and 9 months, by Social Services as they felt Ms D was unable to provide a standard of adequate care for her elder son. Previously Ms D had asked her child to be taken into care as he had both an eating and sleeping problem and was losing weight. Following placement in care, a proper sleeping and eating routine was soon established and the child gained weight. The child was then returned to his mother but within four weeks he lost weight and his mother requested that the child be taken into care again.

The Social Services drew up a rehabilitation programme and offered intensive help for the mother with her two children. It was noted that the child in care became anxious soon and after contact with his mother and expressed his anxiety by wetting, vomiting and refusing to leave the foster home. Ms D later asked for her child to be returned to her care claiming she had a stable partner. She also claimed that she had been depressed following the birth of her second child, but her mood improved with time. She had not sought or had treatment for her depression.

Some of the behavioural problems that the child exhibited could be understood on the basis of difficulties a child shows following separation from his mother. The impact of the separation cannot be overlooked.

Appointments were offered at the clinic to see Ms D with her children, with her partner, the child on his own and with the foster carer. Soon after the appointments were made Ms D broke off her relationship with her partner following an argument. The partner refused to take any part in the assessment procedure.

The observation of the child with his mother and foster carer and the interview of Ms D on her own which formed part of the assessment for the court is summarised here and illustrates some of the points discussed above. A joint assessment was carried out with the co-therapist behind a one-way mirror.

Observation of the Child and Mother

M is a bright, independent boy, who has a good vocabulary. He is naturally curious and explores with interest. Ms D demonstrates that she has 'learnt' to play. She talks to her son, allows him to explore toys and asks him questions. Ms D also makes use of the different materials on offer. However, the play was mostly adult led and directive, rather than child centred. It appeared that Ms D became very involved in the play herself—as if she had never learned or been allowed to play herself—so that she was more interested in what she was doing rather than following M's play. At times, she found it hard to tolerate his interventions, telling him he was 'messing it up' while making a cake in the sandpit. In many ways it was like observing two young children engaged in 'parallel play'. Ms D offered little physical contact or praise to her son and he did not approach her.

Observation of M while Ms D was engaged In talking

M is an able boy who enjoyed the opportunity to play in the sessions. He remembered the setting from one session to the next despite three weeks in between and made straight for the sandpit, on the second occasion asking his mother to pull up his sleeves.

M demonstrated imaginative play and good vocabulary. He talked to himself about his games and sang songs and made car noises appropriately. M became more excitable when playing with the dolls' house, pushing large animals in the upstairs windows. This caught the attention of his mother who dramatised the play and M responded by becoming more excitable and noisy. However, M can tolerate long periods of playing on his own, demonstrating his independent character. He rarely sought adult attention in this time. M tolerated this separation from his mother with no complaint.

Ms D, while talking, remained watchful of her young son, often turning to see what he was doing. However, there was little verbal or physical interaction as M did not seek her attention and she did not approach him. On one occasion when the therapist intervened to prevent sand going everywhere, M became very upset. Ms D said 'come here' but did not go to him even when he began to sob. M eventually came to his mother and allowed her to comfort and cuddle him saying all the time that he wanted his foster carer. Ms D can calm him but has difficulty allowing his expression of real sorrow and despair and asking him continually to calm down because she could not understand him.

Boundaries

M is a high-spirited determined little boy as demonstrated in his need for very clear structured boundaries over routines such as eating and sleeping.

Two occasions were observed when M refused to cooperate—tidying up and leaving the room. Ms D found this behaviour difficult to manage: her voice rose in irritation and she remarked on her own needs, i.e. hunger, and threatened to leave without M. M was able to delay the departure by persuading his mother to return to the game which allowed a protracted and noisy exit. M also demonstrated inappropriate boundaries by hugging both therapists on his way out.

Observations of M with his Foster Carer

M again demonstrated his high level of independent play but appeared quieter and less excitable in the presence of his foster carer. He also checked with her and approached her for help in contrast with his relative lack of contact with his mother. The foster carer responded by going up to M and assisting him: remarking on his play, praise and encouragement. Not surprisingly, his attachment behaviour to his foster carer is of a different order to that towards his mother and the only noisy play is when his foster carer talked of her imminent departure to Australia.

M's relationship with his mother points to an insecure–avoidant attachment, shown by his ability to tolerate her attention being elsewhere for long periods and seeking little solace from her, as noted during the observation sessions. This may, of course, be better understood by the fact that he has now lived apart from his mother for one-third of his life.

Interview with Ms D

At the interview with Ms D on her own the therapists endeavoured to get some idea of Ms D's own early attachment patterns. Her choice of adjectives to describe her relationship with her mother were: separate, hidden, a laugh. Ms D has no memory of her early childhood and her period in care for failure to thrive. She has no story to account for this as it has never been discussed in the family. There was no warmth in the relationship with her mother: no physical contact or emotional closeness. Ms D does remember her mother making funny faces and having a laugh with the children, however. Descriptions of her relationship with her stepfather were: glare, social, stubborn. She could not find any polite words to describe her relationship with her natural father.

It appears that a look from her stepfather was enough to reduce her to tears. While her stepfather is a sociable person, his contact is with friends not with family and Ms D would not talk to her father about worries. There are some discrepancies in the account too. While a distant stepfather, there is a sense of intrusiveness and overprotection. This theme is repeated in Ms D not feeling protected by her parents during frightening incidents in her adolescence and a feeling of being to blame.

While Ms D was thoughtful in her responses to the questions and painted a coherent picture of a family where secrets, poor communication and coldness are the norm, there are gaps and inconsistencies in the story which point to insecure attachment patterns. The evidence is recollection of her early childhood—most of her memories date from about ten years onwards; she describes being put down, laughed at (about relationships with boys), unprotected and violated. Ms D has had to learn to rely on her own resources without seeking or accepting help, which makes her current situation difficult for her to accept or tolerate.

Ms D acknowledges that her 'victim' role had led her to make poor choices in her relationships with men and to continue repeating the learnt patterns of childhood. Once in a relationship she finds it hard to extricate herself.

Ms D describes herself as very committed to her children and of being determined not to replicate her cheerless childhood for them. She appreciates that they need a more 'sociable life' than she experienced and says she is also making new friends.

While complying with the demands for treatment stipulated by the Social Services Department, Ms D's attitude to help remains defensive and dismissive. She has a long history of surviving on her own and it is difficult for her to accept that there may be other ways. This may mean that while she can appreciate the concerns Social Services have about her parenting, she does not always understand the need for change, nor would she necessarily predict or manage her children's changing needs in the future. She has no blueprint to follow.

(Outcome: A full care order was made on M and he was freed for adoption.)

CONCLUSION

Parenting is a complex process. It is multiply determined by a number of factors within the child, parent, family and environment. Parenting consists of specific tasks which require specific skills. Every parent has the right not to be perfect. So the question 'When does good enough parenting become bad parenting?' is difficult to assess.

The changing attitudes in our society means that the criteria for acceptable and non-acceptable levels of care and control by parents keep changing. The focus at present is not on parental rights but on parental duties. The child's wishes are listened to and the child's welfare is considered paramount.

The basic problem in deficient parenting appears to lie in the conflict between care and control. The demand for care in these parents seems to provoke anxiety, frustration and anger while the demand for control generates aggression and the need to dominate. These parents view the help given to them as a way others exert control over them, hence they dismiss and reject any help offered.

Bruno Bettelheim (1987) used the phrase, 'love is not enough'. All children have the right to survival, protection and development. There is no such thing as the *perfect* parent but a *good enough* parent which Dr Bettelheim promises is all we need to be.

REFERENCES

Ainsworth, M. D. S., Blehar, M. C., Waters, E. & Wall, S. (1978) *Patterns of Attachment: Psychological Study in the Strange Situation*. Hillsdale, NJ: Erlbaum.

Apley, J. (1982) 'One child.' In J. Apley and C. Oustend (Eds), *One Child*. London: Spastics International Medical Publications.

Belsky, J. (1984) 'The determinants of parenting: a process model.' *Child Development*, **55**, 83–96.

Bentovim, A. (1991) 'What is significant harm? A clinical viewpoint.' In *Proceedings of the Children Act 1989 Course* 7/8 May 1991. The Royal College of Psychiatrists, pp. 42–46.

Bentovim, A. & Bingley, L. (1985) 'Parenting and parenting failure; some guide lines for the assessment of the child, his parents and the family.' In M. Adcock and R. White (Eds), *Good-enough Parenting*. BAAF, pp. 45–57.

Bettelheim, B. (1987) *A Good Enough Parent*. London: Thames & Hudson.

Black, D., Wolkind, S. & Hendriks, J. H. (1991) *Child Psychiatry and the Law*. London: Gaskell, Royal College of Psychiatrists, pp. 31–35.

Brown, E., Campbell, P., Fanthorpe, C., Hales, V., Kenny, P., McCleod, B., Smart, D. & Wheeler, B. (1996) *Report form Comprehensive Assessments Working Group*, unpublished. Northamptonshire Child Protection Committee.

Brown, G. W. & Harris, T. (1978) *Social Origins of Depression: A Study of Psychiatric Disorder in Women*. London: Tavistock.

Dale, P., Davies, M., Morrison, T. & Waters, J. (1986) *Dangerous Families*. London: Tavistock Publications, pp. 33–37.

Department of Health (1988) *Protecting Children: A Guide for Social Workers Undertaking a Comprehensive Assessment*. London: HMSO.

Department of Health (1989) *An Introduction to the Children Act 1989*. London: HMSO.

Devereux, J. A., Jones, D. P. & Dickenson, D. L. (1993) 'Can children withhold consent to treatment?' *British Medical Journal*, **306** (6890: 29 May), pp. 1459–1461.

Dunn, J. & Kendrick, C. (1982) *Temperamental Differences in Infants and Young Children*. CIBA Foundation Symposium 89. London: Pitman.

Fahlberg, V. (1985) *Attachment and Separation*. London: BAAF (British Agencies for Adoption and Fostering), pp. 91–95.

Fitzpatrick, G. (1995) 'Assessing treatability.' In P. Reder & C. Lucey (Eds), *Assessment of Parenting*. London and New York: Routledge, pp. 102–117.

Fonagy, P., Steele, M., Steele, H., Higgitt, A. & Target, M. (1994) 'The theory and practice of reseliance.' *Journal of Child Psychology and Pyschiatry*, **35**, 241–257.

Garmezy, N. (1984) 'Stress-resistant children: the search for protective factors.' In J. E. Stevenson (Ed.), *Recent Research in Developmental Psychopathology*. New York: Pergamon Press.

Gath, A. (1988) 'Mentally handicapped people as parents. Is mental retardation a bar to adequate parenting?' *Journal of Child Psychology and Psychiatry*, **29**, 739–744.

Golombok, S., Spencer, A. & Rutter, M. (1983) 'Children in lesbian and single parent households: psychosexual and psychiatric appraisal.' *Journal of Child Psychology and Psychiatry*, **24**, 551–572.

Green, R. (1978) 'Sexual identity of 37 children raised by homosexual or transexual parents.' *American Journal of Psychiatry*, **135**, 692–697.

Hetherington, E. M., Cox, M. & Cox, R. (1978) 'Effects of development on parents and children.' In M. E. Lamb (Ed.), *Non Traditional Families*. Hillsdale, NJ: Erlbaum.

Jenner, S. & McCarthy, G. (1995) 'Quantitative measures of parenting: a clinical-developmental perspective.' In P. Reder and C. Lucey (Eds), *Assessment of Parenting*. London and New York: Routledge, pp. 136–150.

Jones, D., Pickett, J., Oates, M. & Barbor, P. (1987) *Understanding Child Abuse*. London: Macmillan Education.

Jung, C. G. (1968) *The Collected works of Carl G. Jung*. Vol. 9. London: Routledge & Kegan Paul.

King, J. M. & Taitz, L. S. (1985) 'Catch up growth following abuse.' *Archives of Disease in Children*, **60**, 1152–1154.

King, M. B. (1995) 'Parents who are gay or lesbian.' In P. Reder and C. Lucey (Eds), *Assessment of Parenting*. London and New York: Routledge, pp. 204–218.

Kingston, W. & Bentovim, A. (1982) 'Constucting a focal formulation and hypothesis in family therapy.' *Australian Journal of Family Therapy*, **41**, 37–50.

Main, M. (1991) 'Metacognitive knowledge, metacognitive monitoring and singular (coherent) vs multiple (incoherent) model of attachment.' In C. M. Parkes, J. Stevenson-Hinde & P. Marris (Eds), *Attachment Across the Life Cycle*. London: Routledge, pp. 127–159.

Nuechterlein, K. H. (1986) 'Childhood precursors of adult schizophrenia.' *Journal of Child Psychology and Psychiatry*, **27**, 133–144.

Reder, P., Duncan, S. & Gray, M. (1993) *Beyond Blame: Child Abuse Tragedies Revisited*. London: Routledge.

Reder, P. & Lucey, C. (1995) 'Significant issues in the assessment of parenting.' In P. Reder, & C. Lucey (Eds), *Assessment of Parenting*. London and New York: Routledge, pp. 3–17.

Royal College of Psychiatrists (1982) 'Definitions of emotional abuse.' *Bulletin of the Royal College of Psychiatrists*, May, pp. 85–88.

Rudolph, M. C. J. & Hochberh, Z. (1990) 'Are boys more vulnerable to psychosocial growth retardation?' (Annotation). *Developmental Medicine and Child Neurology*, **32**, 1022–1025.

Sheridan, M. (1960; revised 1975) Reports on Public Health and Medical Subjects No. 102. The Developmental Progress of Infants and Young Children.

Skynner, R. (1986) *One Flesh Separate Persons: Principles of Family and Marital Psychotherapy*. London: Constable.

Stone, A. (1992) In V. Biggs & J. Robson (Eds), *Developing your Court Skills*. London: BAAF, pp. 32–41.

Swadi, H. (1994) 'Parenting capacity and substance misuse: an assessment scheme.' *ACPP Review Newsletter*, **16** (5), 237–244.

Waterhouse, S. (1992) 'The role of the guardian *ad litem* in preparing a child for family proceedings.' In V. Biggs & J. Robson (Eds), *Developing your Court Skills*. London: BAAF, pp. 58–67.

Winnicott, D. W. (1960) *The Maturational Processes and the Facilitative Environment*. London: Hogarth.

| 6 |

PARENT EDUCATION PROGRAMMES

Dorit Braun

This chapter will suggest that there are many existing opportunities in primary care settings for parent education programmes, which can be used to enhance parents' skills, knowledge and confidence in their role as parents, provided that programmes are planned and deliberate. I will argue that planned interventions are of benefit to parents, children and professionals, and will consider ways that programmes can be organised for maximum impact. Practical ways to set up and target parents education programmes will be suggested. Some comments on the skills needed by practitioners, and on the support required of managers will also be discussed.

WHAT ARE PARENT EDUCATION PROGRAMMES?

For the purpose of this chapter, parent education programmes are defined as any planned intervention which aims to educate parents about their role as parents. Such programmes include: parent education groups and classes, for example antenatal classes or groups set up to explore specific aspects of parenting such as children's behaviour or accident prevention; one-to-one work with parents at clinics or at their own home, for example when pregnancy is confirmed or when a postnatal visit occurs; and more informal interventions which occur at clinics and other settings where parents and children visit to receive

Enhancing Parenting Skills: A Guide Book for Professionals Working with Parents.
Edited by K. N. Dwivedi. © 1997 John Wiley & Sons Ltd.

advice and information about their child, including pharmacies and community-based projects. Parent education programmes can take place in an opportunistic sense—responding to parents where they are seen, and can also be structured—inviting parents to attend specific groups or events.

However, unless the practitioner undertaking the programme has a clear sense of what he or she is trying to achieve with each intervention, success may be limited or random. Many practitioners working in primary care have few opportunities to learn about or reflect on the purpose of parent education, or indeed to reflect on methods of education. Most practitioners know a great deal about aspects of parenting, but may know very little about education, having had few if any opportunities to consider a variety of educational approaches and their benefits. As a result, most practitioners use their own experience of having been educated to design and run parent education programmes. (See Combes & Schonveld, 1992, for a review of parent education and the work of health professionals.) This experience is likely to have been formal—lectures or talks—essentially about imparting information. Yet for all parents the experience of parenting is a complex mesh of feelings, emotions, experiences and aspirations. Parent education programmes have to engage with this emotional dimension of parenting if they are to have any real impact on what parents actually do with their children. It is relatively easy to give or receive information and advice; changing or modifying one's practice as a parent is much harder. As with any other intervention which attempts to influence what people do—how they behave—parent education programmes must be rather more sophisticated than the straightforward imparting of information.

WHY THE NEED FOR PARENT EDUCATION?

From the perspective of practitioners in primary care, there are a variety of reasons for running parent education programmes (see Combes & Schonveld, 1992; Rowe & Mahoney, 1993; Pugh et al., 1994). These include:

- Improving the mental health of parents and of children.
- Improving social support networks among parents.
- Improving parents' knowledge, understanding and skills in dealing with their children's behaviour and supporting their development.
- Increasing the confidence of parents.
- Increasing parents' pleasure in their children.
- Reducing the number of childhood accidents.

- Improving parents' ability to make use of services and provision, and to ask for/organise provision where it does not exist.

Each of these possible aims will be discussed below. However, before looking at each possible aim, it is important to comment on the work and role of parents in current British society. It is generally accepted that the structure of family life in Britain has altered considerably over the last 25 years—reflected in more children living in households headed by a lone parent, in households where the parents are cohabiting rather than married, experiencing the separation, divorce and repartnering of one or both of their parents. The structure of society has also changed—patterns of work have altered; unemployment, low incomes and poverty are a feature of childhood for many children. A useful summary of these changes and their impact on parenting can be found in Pugh et al. (1994). The impact of the changes to family and society on parents is complex. A greater emphasis on individuality and diversity of styles of family life may be enabling for many people, but it is at the cost of a loss of shared values and practices of child rearing. The increased numbers of mothers and fathers who are working, if only part time, makes social support more fragmented and complex to organise within any local community or neighbourhood. Poverty lowers parents' abilities to access services, leisure and recreation facilities, and resources for health such as fresh foods (Judge & Benzeval, 1993; Bradshaw, 1993). Parenting has therefore become more isolated and unsupported (Cummings & Davies, 1994). At the same time legislation and policy have emphasised the importance, rights and responsibilities of parents, and in many areas of public service it is expected that parents should be involved as partners in the care and education of their children. Politicians of all parties have emphasised the responsibilities of parents for their children—there is little interest, it seems, in community or societal responsibility for children. This focus on individual responsibility of parents serves to isolate us still further. And yet, there is growing evidence, anecdotal and scientific, on the damage that family breakdown can cause to children (see, for example, Farrington & West, 1990; Kiernan, 1992); and on the ways that planned interventions can really make a difference (Rowe & Mahoney, 1993; Pugh et al., 1994). In this context it is important to consider the potential of each of the possible aims of parent education programmes, and their relevance to primary care practitioners.

It should be stressed that traditionally parent education has focused on work with mothers of young children. Parent education is relevant to both mothers and fathers, and to parents of older children and of teenagers. It is much easier to locate parents of young children, and there are far more opportunities for interventions with them as part of the routine work done by primary care practitioners. The section on 'Targeting programmes' (p. 108) will explore ways of reaching fathers as well as mothers, and of reaching and working with parents of older children.

Improving the Mental Health of Parents and Children

Parenting is a stressful experience for most parents, whatever their circumstances. The needs of child and parent may conflict; where there are siblings there may be further conflicts; parents who have not had their own needs met when they were children may have fewer resources on which to draw to help them meet the needs of their children. They may also lack material resources. The provision of opportunities to decrease stress and isolation has real potential to improve the mental health of parents, making it more likely that they will find it easier to cope with their children.

However, parent education programmes with this aim need to be designed very carefully, if they are to succeed. They may have the opposite effect, by exposing parents to what could be perceived as criticism by professionals. Health professionals are in a very difficult position, because of their child surveillance role, and the real power differentials between parent and professional (see Mayall & Foster, 1989, for a discussion of this issue). Moreover, reduced stress alone as an aim may not have any impact on what parents do with their children—this is likely to need a more careful and structured focus. If reduced stress and improved mental health are the main aims of a parent education programme, it might best be provided by community-based groups— voluntary organisations and self-help groups can provide peer support, which avoids the professional and parent inequality of power difficulty. The role of the primary care practitioner is perhaps best focused on being informed about local self-help and community organisations providing this kind of programme, and enabling parents to take advantage of the opportunities available.

Primary care practitioners, however, need to think very carefully about their relationships with parents, so that their opportunistic interventions are enabling and supportive, rather than critical and stressful. Parents interviewed about the role of health professionals in accident prevention frequently commented on the importance of good relationships with professionals, and on how vulnerable they felt to criticism (Combes, 1991). The need for mutual respect cannot be overstated. A parent who senses that the professional is hostile or judgemental about their parenting style will be quick to reject advice and intervention.

Improving Social Support Networks among Parents

This aim is a direct response to the isolation of parents. Research has demonstrated that parents value the support and shared experience of parent groups, and of meeting with other parents (see, for example, Combes, 1991). There are many opportunities within the routine work of primary health care practitioners to provide more structure to the occasions when parents are already together—child health clinics are a good example. An informal atmosphere, the opportunity to talk to each other while waiting to see a professional are often under-used as opportunities for more structured support. The professional needs to recognise the opportunities and provide a structure ensuring that parents are introduced to each other, arranging chairs informally, perhaps providing a theme of discussion at some clinics—weaning, sleep, behaviour, safety are all themes which are of interest and concern to parents. Showing a video, providing two or three questions for parents to talk about, asking them if their discussions have raised any issues which they wish to discuss with the professional present are all ways the time can be put to more effective use.

How can professionals know whether or not such interventions are successful? One indication is take up—how many parents attend the clinic regularly? Are they representative of parents who could attend? Are some groups under-represented, e.g. ethnic minorities or young parents? Another is to ask parents routinely whether or not they find attending is helpful—and why/why not. A periodic audit of the questions asked by parents can illuminate whether or not issues are being explored in response to parent interests or the interest of the practitioner. A periodic review with parents of whether and how they have put into practice advice and suggestions made at the clinic can illuminate strengths and weaknesses, and suggest issues which might need more attention.

In addition, when visiting parents or when they present at a clinic, professionals could put parents in touch with each other, enabling informal befriending and support to take place. Clearly, it is important to ask permission in advance, but this kind of individual concern, leading to increased social contact, is valued by parents.

However, setting up additional parent education programmes which go beyond the routine work already taking place which have as their main aim improving social networks is probably best left to community and self-help groups. Professionals rarely have the time for this kind of work, and arguably could put their professional knowledge and skills to other uses. There is no point duplicating work which others can do as effectively. Again, the professional has the responsibility of knowing what else is available locally, and enabling parents to make use of that provision.

Improving Parents' Skills

Improving parents knowledge, understanding and skills in dealing with their children's behaviour and supporting their development is an aim that is commonly found in parent education programmes organised by health professionals. It is a laudable aim, which is very difficult to implement. An informal structure at clinics such as that suggested above will improve social support networks but may have little impact on the knowledge, skills and understanding of parents.

It is important to distinguish between imparting information and education. Most of us need to reflect on what we are learning, and to actively engage in a learning process if we are to put new knowledge into practice. Information about an issue may raise awareness and may stimulate parents to seek involvement in educational work about the issue, but this is not the same as educating them. Many information campaigns about specific issues, e.g. child safety, do stimulate a desire for increased involvement by parents. All too often these campaigns are isolated events, with no planned follow up.

Education programmes which aim to improve knowledge, understanding and skills need to be carefully structured and planned. They need to be responsive to parents' real concerns, and to engage with parents, building on their current knowledge and experience. They need to be for groups of parents, to enable sharing of ideas and experience (see Braun & Schonveld, 1993, for a fuller discussion of this point). Running parent groups which deal with health issues can also decrease social isolation, reduce stress and increase parents' confidence. They can establish good relationships between parents and professionals, and demonstrate that the professional is responsive to the needs and concerns of parents. This is therefore a cost-effective and legitimate activity for primary care practitioners. In the section on structured programmes below (see p. 109), some practical suggestions of how this can be done are discussed. However, it is important to acknowledge that many primary care practitioners will be unfamiliar with techniques and approaches for designing education programmes (Combes & Schonveld, 1992). Some practitioners may therefore prefer to work in partnership with other workers or agencies, such as community educators or adult educators, so that the health professionals can contribute their expert knowledge while the educator can structure an educational approach. Given the time and resource constraints on all workers, however, joint working of this nature is best designed as a learning experience for both parties: the health professional learning about educational processes and the education worker learning about the expertise, contribution and role of the health professional, enabling both to work separately in the future, drawing each other in at the planning stage, or for specific input to a programme. There are a number of practical guides and resources aimed at health professionals who are unsure about designing educational programmes, which can be used by practitioners with more confidence in running groups (e.g. Braun & Schonveld, 1993; CAPT, 1991, 1993; Maternity Alliance, 1993).

What areas of knowledge are relevant for health professionals to work on with parents? Clearly accident prevention is one (see below); others include:

- The basic stages of child development and how parents can support their child.
- Dealing with specific behaviour difficulties in young children: sleep; discipline.
- Dealing with specific behaviour difficulties in older children and adolescents: boundaries; discipline; letting go and coping with adolescence.
- Child health issues: how parents can promote good health and how to deal with ill health.
- Dealing with specific child health issues that affect many children: e.g. asthma, allergies, feeding.
- Dealing with specific health concerns affecting older children and adolescents: the development of sexuality and sexual health; drugs and alcohol; depression.
- Parents/family health issues: diet, smoking, family routines, exercise.

How will you know if parent education groups are improving parents' knowledge, understanding or skills? This is a notoriously difficult question, and one which causes great frustration to practitioners and their managers in today's climate of an effective and efficient NHS. Attendance is an important indicator—if no one turns up, or numbers are very low, or attendance falls off it is not working. Groups may take a while to build up numbers, especially in areas where there is suspicion, hostility or unfamiliarity with the work of the professional. However, word of mouth is a powerful tool—if numbers do build up, and parents continue to attend regularly, this tells you at least that the group is meeting some of their needs. It is helpful to start any group by establishing why parents are attending and what they hope to gain; and then reviewing with them at the end how far their needs were met. 'Homework' can be set between sessions, where parents are asked to try a new approach with their child, or to reflect on what they know about an issue and how they learnt it; this can indicate to both parent and professional the extent to which they are able to put into practice ideas learnt in the group, and their further learning and support needs.

Evaluation will clearly need to be linked to the content of the programme, and should be planned into the work of the group so that for each piece of learning you plan, you consider how you will know if parents have in fact learnt what you planned. Be prepared for surprises—parents might learn about things you hadn't planned for! Making the evaluation explicit as part of the group's work not only helps you know what is being achieved, but also helps you identify further learning needs, and get ongoing feedback about your input. It shares the responsibility for learning with the group so that your responsibilities become more explicit—to provide a structure, contribute information and advice, respond to needs and issues as they arise, involve everyone in the group, follow up individuals if needed. Members of the group are responsible for what they bring to the group, and what they take from it. And if someone challenges you that this means you can never be sure that the programme will achieve your original intentions, you might want to remind them that most health interventions in primary care are just as uncertain, because of their dependence on patient compliance.

Increasing the Confidence of Parents

As with the aim of reducing stress and isolation, this aim rests on the perfectly valid premise that increased confidence will improve parents' ability as parents. However, if this is the only aim of a programme, it is somewhat limited. Increasing confidence needs to be built into any programme of parent education—without confidence parents cannot reduce their isolation or learn about specific issues. Evaluation of a successful programme will get feedback from parents about their increased confidence—but don't be content with that alone. Ask them how this has helped them—what it has enabled them to do, or to do differently.

Some parents are so lacking in confidence that they are unable to take advantage of self-help groups or parent education group. Health professionals are limited in the time they can offer such parents; voluntary organisations, such as Homestart, provide befriending schemes and home visits, and social opportunities can often offer more support. Liaison between such health professionals and such organisations is vital. It is not enough to merely refer a parent, the organisation needs to be linked into the other local opportunities available, so that when the parent's confidence is increased, they can link the parent back in to these opportunities.

Increasing Parents' Pleasure in their Children

The pressures and conflicts inherent in parenting can easily get in the way of parents' ability to enjoy their children—enjoy doing things together, enjoy what they have learnt and can do, enjoy seeing the world from their child's perspective, take pleasure in their company, and in the very many simple and small things that can give children so much pleasure. Parents' ability to be responsible, set clear boundaries, provide discipline, guidance and stimulation for their children can be very dependent on this enjoyment. Enjoyment is a powerful motivation for parent and child. Any and all parent education programmes should be based on buildings on, developing and enhancing the enjoyment that parents have in their children. This is something that is easily detected in evaluation—listen out for parents' comments on recent experiences with their children, and ask them about the things they like about their child. A few parents, for various complex reasons, may not like their child. This requires a professional response—one to one work with the parents about the underlying issues and possible referral to more specialist sources of help. Parents who do not like their child will find it extremely difficult to parent effectively, with possible serious consequences for the health and welfare of the child.

Reducing Childhood Accidents

The government's Health of the Nation Strategy sets accident prevention as a specific target, and many health professionals have responded with varying degrees of success. The Child Accident Prevention Trust have produced many resources to support such work (e.g. CAPT, 1991, 1993) which also contain ideas for evaluation. There is no doubt that parents are interested in accident prevention. However, it is not the only topic in which they are interested, and it would be good to see parent education programmes which take this as one aim but also cover other important areas of knowledge and skill, such as those discussed above.

Improving Parents' Ability to Ask for Assistance

Improving parents' ability to make use of services and provision, and to ask for/organise provision where it does not exist has been alluded to in most of the aims listed above. They have also alluded to the role of health professionals in signposting parents to other services. When parents lack confidence certain agencies can be used to enable them to gain confidence and then link them to other provision (see above). This means that primary care practitioners need to know about and liaise with other agencies and workers. Where provision does not exist, there is a role for health professionals, working with other local agencies, to support parents in organising provision for themselves. This is a valid role for health professionals, because the absence of other provision inevitably means that the health professional, being easily accessed, will spend a great deal of time with individual parents, working with them on issues which could be addressed by other agencies. In the long term this is not an effective or efficient use of the health professional's time. Agencies and workers who can help with organising local provision include voluntary organisations, such as Volunteer Bureaux, Homestart, The Pre-School Learning Alliance (PLA), welfare rights organisations, residents associations, community groups and organisations, churches and other religious organisations, and the larger charities concerned with the welfare of children, such as Save the Children Fund, Family Service Units, NSPCC, Barnardo's, NCH Action for Children and the Children's Society.

Summary

In sum, then, there are different opportunities for parent education programmes run by primary care practitioners.

- *Opportunistic*—built in to the routine work of the practitioner. Appropriate aims include: increasing parents' confidence, reducing stress and isolation; increasing parents' social networks, increasing parents' pleasure in their children, and signposting parents to other services and provision.
- *Structured*—planned educational groups for parents. Appropriate aims include: increasing parents' knowledge, understanding and

skills, in the context of increasing their confidence and pleasure in their children, reducing stress and isolation and signposting to other services and provision.

HOW SHOULD STRUCTURED PROGRAMMES BE ORGANISED?

I have argued that structured parent education groups can respond to the needs of parents, address legitimate health concerns and make use of the expertise of health professionals. I have also argued that such groups require careful planning and organisation if they are to be educational. There are a number of guides for health professionals which spell out the benefits of group work, and outline how to organise and structure groupwork on health topics (see, for example, Braun & Schonveld, 1993). Here, therefore, I will concentrate on two aspects which cause health professionals concern: community development approaches and negotiating the agendas of groups.

Community Development Approaches

Some primary health care practitioners are employed to work on community development projects; most are not. And even when they are, community development approaches in health settings are often driven by the medical model—set up in response to issues identified by health professionals which local people may not have asked for or identified themselves. Community development should be about working with and for communities about their own concerns. Good health is a major concern for all communities, but in areas of high social deprivation communities may not articulate or express these concerns in a way which health professionals can make sense of (see, for example, Braun, 1994). This requires patience, intelligence and trust on the part of the professional—and confidence in the relevance of the health agendas.

How do you work with local people? To start such approaches, you have to be out there, in places where parents are—don't expect them to come to you. There are places where parents gather—outside the school gates; in the park or recreation ground; in the launderette. There are also places where parents visit regularly—the local chemist, foodstore, housing office and post office. Think laterally about where parents might be found, and work with the workers in those places. Local pharmacists and school nurses are neglected resources for parent education in the opportunistic sense—if you keep them informed about groups you are organising, they can refer people on, or build up a list of parents who would like more details about a specific group or service. Don't attempt to do this in a formal way; questionnaires often put people off, and leaflets don't work on their own. Word of mouth is the best way of telling people about what is going on; think about how you usually find out about a service or a worry—you ask someone who might know.

At the start, ask open-ended questions, which allow people to express positives as well as negatives:

- What are the good things about living round here?
- Who do you turn to if you need advice about a concern with your child?

The answers to these questions will enable you to get a feel for the strengths and resources of a community, and to identify allies to work with.

- What do your children like doing?
- What do you like doing?

The answers to these questions will enable you to design programmes which build on the things parents enjoy. Don't forget that parents will not attend groups unless they are secure that their children are well cared for—for parents of school age children groups must be organised to fit in with the school day. For parents of younger children, crèche facilities will be needed. For working parents evenings may be better—or weekends, with childcare also on offer. The childcare you organise can be designed to fit with the things that parents have said their children like.

- What worries you about your child or children?
- Do you have any worries about yourself?

The answers to these questions will enable you to design programmes in response to parents' expressed concerns. What if these concerns appear to have little to do with appropriate health topics? This is actually very unlikely; I have yet to meet a parent who has not expressed concerns about health issues when asked this question. They may express it in a way you find hard to recognise:

'There's dog mess on the grass so the kids can't play there.'

This is a concern about child development—and the need for outdoor play. Responses can be about contact with environmental health to deal with the dog mess, about working with other agencies to organise outdoor play activities for children. And an invitation to a group on child development: 'I'm setting up a parent group to talk about how children grow and develop, and what we can do, round here, to give them opportunities and make the most of what we've got.'

'It's very cliquey in the playground, and I'm not sure about talking to other mums because I think their standards aren't the same as mine.'

This is about isolation, but also about discipline, boundaries and responsibilities, which are key areas for a group. Ask if they might like to come to a group where you will introduce everyone, and where there can be discussions on discipline using case examples: *What would you do if…* These allow debate which is not focused on one parent or child, and allow everyone to think about where he or she stands in relation to an issue. Then they can decide who they want to get to know better, and who they don't!

'My mum always gives me advice about the kids—she's a great help.'

You can probe a bit here: is she up to date with advice? Do you always agree? What happens if you don't follow her advice? Would you like to come to a group that is looking at various concerns (and give some examples) and different ideas that people have about how to deal with them?

'There's nothing round here for the kids. No one is interested. No one cares. I don't know why you're bothering.'

Well, you are interested, and you are trying to find others who are too. Ask if he or she would want to work with others when you've found them, and get back to the person. Ask what they would like to see round here, so that you can work on some of the ideas.

'This area is like a free car park for the office workers in town—it's really dangerous.'

A concern about child safety. Are others concerned about the same issue? Can you work with other workers and agencies to set up a meeting to discuss how the parking problems can be addressed—and follow up the ideas that are generated?

The trick is to spot the health concern, and to respond to the concerns of local parents. Once you have responded, new concerns will come to the fore, people will have confidence in you, and you will be able to negotiate to discuss issues which you think are important (see below).

When working with parents on the concerns they have raised it is vital that you acknowledge their interest and commitment, and that you work together to respond. Don't take over, and don't dump all the responsibility on them. When working on a specific project—e.g. safe play spaces—acknowledge the success that parents have already achieved; work together to decide how to move forward, identify who will do what, and what skills people may need in order to do their bit. Other agencies such as the local Volunteer Bureau can provide training and resources.

Negotiating the Agenda

So how do you introduce the health issues you see as important? And even when parents have come to a group about health issues, how do you ensure that the group responds to their interests and concerns as well as your own?

Many of the resources designed for professionals to use with parent groups contain suggestions and materials which will help you to do this (see, for example, Braun & Schonveld, 1993; DEC, 1991; CAPT, 1993). Here, it is worth discussing some key principles, and what they mean in practice.

Provide structure and boundaries—this is not a group about anything at all. You need to provide a framework which sets the limits of what the group can be about. At the first meeting, following introductions and some discussion of why people have come and what they hope to gain by coming, you need to structure a discussion about the rest of the group sessions.

If you have planned the topics for the group in advance, you could ask small groups (two or three people) to look at one or two topics and discuss what they think is most important to learn about that topic. Get each small group to report back, and invite everyone to comment. Go with the majority view; if one group has said that the most important thing about sleep is to learn about how to get a child to sleep in its own bed for the whole night, and most people agree, you will have to suggest to the one person who insists that the most important thing is about suitable bedding that this will not be the focus of the discussion, though it will be part of the discussion.

If you have decided that you want to negotiate the agenda for the remainder of the group sessions at the first session, after the introductions and discussions of why people have come, you could use a range of stimulus materials to help the group negotiate topics for the future. I particularly recommend using photographs, which work whatever people's level of literacy, and allow for a variety of interpretation, so opening up the possibilities. You can display photographs, ask people to select two or three that appeal, and pair up with another person who has picked at least one the same as them. Ask them to tell each other what you see in the photo—why you chose it, what interests you, what issues it raises for you. Take feedback and note down all the issues raised by the photos with the group. Discuss which ones they want to look at further in future sessions, and agree a running order. A good photoset for these purposes is *Us and the Kids* (DEC, 1991) which also contains many ideas for using the photographs with parents' groups. Other stimulus materials include adverts of children, headlines from newspapers, or a series of short statements for people to consider. These can be given to small groups to discuss, or you could do the Diamond 9 exercise to negotiate the group's priorities. This exercise is described in many parent education resources already referred to above. It involves giving pairs 9 statements, or photographs, and asking them to rank them in order of most importance in the shape of a diamond. Each pair feeds back on what they put top and bottom, and the group discusses the rankings, exploring the issues raised by the materials, and the importance they attach to each issue.

The exercises described above will do more than help you negotiate the agenda. They set a climate where everyone can participate, and all ideas are valued. They give you and everyone else a sense of where people are in their thinking about issues and topics, which is a good starting point for evaluation at the end of the group. They also acknowledge that group members already know a lot; and have ideas, interests and contributions to make. All of these are crucial in increasing parents' confidence. You need to acknowledge these things openly with the group. When people talk about an issue, and relate it to their experience with their child, you need to build from the success and achievements they have already had with their child.

Essentially this section has attempted to demonstrate that structured parent education programmes are about an educational process. It may be helpful to sum up by suggesting an educational framework which professionals could use when planning parent education programmes. This framework can be used for the whole programme and for individual sessions of the programme.

Introductions/setting the scene

When this is the first session of a programme, you need to think about making sure everyone has time to get to know each other, that you establish a climate where everyone feels able to contribute, and that you negotiate the agenda. Where this is the start of a session during the life of the group, it may simply be about giving an overview of what is planned for the session and why, but may also include an opportunity for group members to say what they are hoping to gain from the session.

Developing knowledge, skills and understanding

This is the 'bulk' of the work of the group—for the overall programme, this will be most of the sessions. Within each session, this part will take up most of the time. You need to identify very clearly what areas of knowledge, skills and understanding you plan to develop, and work out learning activities that will allow for this to happen. Learning activities don't have to be talks and videos—structured groupwork can be fun, and allows for more opportunities for parents to contribute their own experience. Where you use talks and videos, try to ensure that there is time for reflection and discussion about what people learnt from them. A useful discussion of the value of different learning activities for parent education can be found in Braun and Schonveld (1993).

Summing up and moving on

When this is the last session of a programme it is mainly about evaluation, and a discussion of what follows for individuals and for the group. At the end of a session it is about reflection: what did you get out of this session, how useful was it, how does it link with the future work of the group?

In reality this framework is more like an upward spiral: the introduction for a session may look back at the previous session, or look at what group members have done between sessions. The last session of a programme is not the end for group members, even if the group does not continue, but is the beginning of something else. The framework is also helpful for thinking about and planning for community development approaches. If you use this as a framework for planning it will help you retain a feel for the big picture, and avoid the common difficulty of feeling that the work is becoming disjointed and fragmented.

TARGETING PROGRAMMES

Clearly the work described here is time-consuming. Health professionals are a scarce resource, and have many competing demands on their time. Structured parent education programmes by health professionals need careful targeting to make best use of their time and skills. Programmes need to be targeted at groups who find it hard to access services (Benzeval *et al.*, 1995; Pugh *et al.*, 1994). Two groups where it is important to focus and target work are:

- Parents living in areas of high social and economic deprivation.
- Ethnic minority parents.

Other groups who are 'hard to reach' include:

- Teenage parents
- Parents with physical disabilities
- Fathers
- Parents of teenagers

With these groups the efforts of the health professional are best focused on linking and collaborating with other agencies.

Parents Living in Areas of High Social and Economic Deprivation

How do you know which are the areas of real deprivation? Obviously local knowledge is helpful, though beware of local prejudice and assumptions. Many health and local authorities have undertaken detailed analyses of the 1991 Census data, which provides a starting point (e.g. NHA, 1994).

A common feature of areas of economic and social deprivation is that they contain few resources and facilities to support parents. At the same time poverty increases the stress of parents and limits their resources to meet their children's health and care needs, (Bradshaw, 1993; Roberts & Press, 1995; Judge & Benzeval, 1993). Poverty and deprivation are associated with ill health (see, for example, Bartley *et al.*, 1994; Kumar, 1993). Parents who are struggling with the daily difficulties of low incomes and few services find it very difficult to access services, especially if getting to them involves struggles with transport and conflicts with their other responsibilities for other children. Health professionals often find themselves driving parents to appointments with specialist services, and find themselves referring to specialist services because no preventive low level local services are in place. A better use of their time is to work with other local workers and agencies to develop parent education and support locally.

The use of community development approaches outlined above is vital in areas of social deprivation. Not only will they help you locate who else is working in the area, they will also help you understand the local resources—people, groups and facilities—that do exist. Many health professionals based in primary care teams already undertake profiles of the local population, but often these are undertaken only to be filed away, because no one has planned what to do with the results. Frequently the people who ask for profiles to be undertaken have little understanding of the complexities of doing such work and of the need to build in time to respond to the local issues as an integral part of the work. Instead of trying to do a static and scientific local profile, primary care practitioners would do better to take a developmental approach to building their knowledge about the local area, and about local needs (see Braun *et al.*, 1997, for an account of the realities of such work).

A real difficulty for primary care practitioners in trying to develop work in areas of social and economic deprivation is that they are probably attached to a GP practice which draws patients from a wide catchment area, so that they may only relate to a few individual families on one estate. It is possible to negotiate with other GP practices, so that one professional undertakes work in one small neighbourhood, and others cover the work in other areas. Provided that a planned and developmental approach is taken, such as that outlined above, it should be possible for the professional to establish work with local groups and agencies, to support the development of appropriate local initiatives, to set up mechanisms for regular liaison and information sharing, and then to pull out from the role of initiator/community development lead. If community development approaches are used, the community will have become involved and the work will acquire its own momentum. It is worth GP practices devoting time and resources to investing in this community development work in areas of high deprivation in the short term, because it will mean that, in the medium and long term, parents will be better supported and therefore able to make more appropriate use of primary care resources.

Ethnic Minority Parents

Areas of high social deprivation usually contain an ethnic minority population. If you are unconvinced of the need to set up separate work with ethnic minorities, try checking the parents you are working with— do they reflect the proportion of ethnic minorities living in the area, or attached to your practice? There is evidence to show that ethnic minority women, particularly those from Bangladesh, miss out on antenatal care and education, and experience considerable difficulties when trying to access primary care services (e.g. Combes & Schonveld, 1992). Health professionals have spent many years arguing that because our services are universal, anyone can access them, and there is no need to make special provision. We need to recognise that this is not a level playing field. As with the need to target work in areas of deprivation, there is also a need to target work to ethnic minorities to ensure that services and programmes are relevant, and that they therefore have access to them.

What is special about the needs and circumstances of ethnic minority parents? It is dangerous to generalise, because situations and circumstances vary. Some common factors include:

- Dislocation from their families and support networks.
- Cultural and religious beliefs, customs and values which they wish to observe, and of which most provision takes no account.
- Lack of familiarity with the health care system, and other public service systems, leading to inappropriate use and poor access.
- Isolation and stress.
- Racism.

Many health professionals, while acknowledging the need for separate and specialist provision for parent education for ethnic minorities, are uncertain of how to go about it, and where to turn for help. For a sensitive account of the approaches which are required, see Dwivedi (1996) and Kemps (in this volume). Dwivedi argues that community development approaches which are designed around the needs and experiences of ethnic minority women are required. If you are not sure how to do this work, or cannot do it alone because you do not have the language or background knowledge, you need to identify people with whom you can work, such as: local community and religious groups— but beware of advice from male community leaders about what are regarded as women's issues; professionals working in anti-racist or multicultural education; local projects working with ethnic minority communities on other issues; a local translation and interpreting service. There may also be a specialist health professional whose role is to work with ethnic minorities. Not only can these groups and people provide you with help, they will be vital in identifying and recruiting parents to a parent education programme, and in suggesting venues where parents will feel comfortable and safe.

Teenage Parents

Teenage parents find most parent education programmes inaccessible, because they feel they are not designed for them, or for their particular circumstances. However, this poses a dilemma for the primary care practitioner, who may only work with one or two teenage parents at any time—not enough for a group. Many youth and community workers do run groups for teenage parents, but they often lack sufficient health input. It is worth trying to develop links with youth workers so that you can support them to introduce the health issues, perhaps by doing a regular slot at a group. In some local areas with very high numbers of young parents it is worth considering setting up special provision (see, e.g., Billingham, 1989).

Parents with Physical Disabilities

As with teenage parents, parents with physical disabilities may represent a very small part of the workload of primary care practitioners. Such parents may be linked to other support networks and groups—e.g. social services and self-help disability organisations. Try to link in with these organisations to see how to make best use of your skills and time, and to ensure that such parents also have access to parent education programmes that take account of their particular needs.

Parents of children with disabilities are usually well supported through the work done by specialist health provision such as child development centres who are working with their children.

Fathers

Lip service is often paid to the need to involve fathers in parent education groups. The reality is that very few fathers are involved. Changing patterns of employment and high levels of male unemployment in areas of social and economic deprivation mean that fathers could be involved. The problem lies in traditional ideas about who is responsible for childrearing and family health—a task usually assigned to mothers. Yet, if we are ever to enable fathers to really share the responsibilities of parenting, there is a professional duty to work with fathers as well as mothers. As with other 'hard to reach' groups, the answers lie in lateral thinking. Work with fathers where they are, even if this means the local pub, and work with other agencies and workers to ensure that you have a male professional involved in the work. Some voluntary organisations and family centres have had success in setting up fathers' groups (see Whalley, 1994); is it possible to contribute the health issues to those groups? Residents' associations, and voluntary children's organisations often include fathers—cubs, the boys' brigade, sports clubs. Try working with them to identify fathers who might like to become involved in a group about parenting skills. Remember to find out and respond to the issues they identify as important.

Parents of Teenagers

This group of parents are very hard to reach, yet can be desperate for support, information and education because of their concerns about their teenagers behaviour and anxieties about issues such as sexual health and drugs. Some secondary schools have managed to set up parents' groups with the involvement of the school nurse, but these are very difficult to sustain because the teenagers themselves seldom like the idea of their parents meeting their friends' parents to share problems and experiences! The workplace provides one possibility—many parents of teenagers are in full-time employment and could be recruited to groups via the workplace. A local health promotion officer will have responsibility for 'Health of the Nation' in the workplace, and may be undertaking such work, or willing to do it with some support from a health professional. Other voluntary agencies may also see the relevance of this work and be well placed to recruit parents—Relate, welfare rights organisations, and groups set up for single parents, such as Gingerbread. With some support and input from the health professional they may be able to organise programmes.

Summary

This section has argued the need to target and focus structured parent education groups, and has stressed the need to identify and work with other local groups, workers and agencies in order to make most effective use of the skills and time of the health professional. This kind of work is like designing and piecing together a jigsaw puzzle—working out what all the pieces are, and how they all fit together, so that you can clarify the most effective contribution you can make.

CONCLUSIONS

In conclusion, it is worth drawing out the implications of the work discussed above for the skills required by primary care practitioners, and by their managers.

Practitioners need confidence about what they can offer, to whom and why it might be beneficial to parents and children. They need to be able to negotiate the content of parent education programmes with parents. They need skills in running groups. They need to be able to liaise with other workers and agencies about what each can offer to parents, how best to work together, and how to develop new initiatives together where none exist. For this they also need to acquire and maintain a wealth of local knowledge: what services, self-help groups, community groups, or voluntary organisations exist, what they each offer and how parents can access them.

Managers, in their turn, need to recognise the skills required and support practitioners in developing them. They need to encourage and support flexible approaches and recognise the value of parent education groups. They need to support practitioners to liaise with other workers and agencies, by allowing flexibility and providing them with information and links with other agencies. And, finally, managers need to provide supervision and support—parent education work can be challenging and lonely for practitioners. Supervision needs to encourage practitioners to think creatively and laterally about their approaches; and to support them in evaluating its effectiveness.

This chapter has focused on practical approaches to parent education, but we should not ignore the policy context. The NHS reforms separate the responsibilities for service provision from commissioning of services. There is a new emphasis on a primary care led NHS. In this context practitioners and their managers need to inform commissioners about the implications of their work for future plans and developments, as commissioning is frequently too far removed from local issues to be able to respond in any meaningful way. Those working in the field, and the people who manage them, are well placed to provide information to commissioners. Never assume that they know what you know.

REFERENCES

Bartley, M., Power, C., Blane, D., Smith, G. D. & Shipley, M. (1994) 'Birth weight and later socio-economic disadvantage.' In *British Medical Journal*, **309** (6967, Dec. 3), 1475–1478.

Benzeval, M., Judge, K. & Whitehead, M. (1995) *Inequalities in Health—An Agenda for Action*. London: Kings Fund.

Billingham, K. (1989) '45 Cope Street' *Health Visitor*, **62** (5), 156–157.

Bradshaw, J. (1993) *Household Budgets and Living Standards*. York: Rowntree Foundation.

Braun, D. (1994) *Engaging with Local Residents: Report of an Action Research Project*. Northampton: Northamptonshire Health Authority.

Braun, D., Michel, T. & Scott, D. (1997, forthcoming) *Local Needs Assessment—Is It Worth the Effort?* Coventry: Community Education Development Centre.

Braun, D. & Schonveld, A. (1993) *Approaching Parenthood: A Resource for Parent Education*. London: Health Education Authority.

Child Accident Prevention Trust (CAPT) (1991) *Preventing Accidents to Children: A Training Resource for Health Visitors*. London: Health Education Authority.

Child Accident Prevention Trust (CAPT) (1993) *Keeping Kids Safe*. London: Child Accident Prevention Trust.

Combes, G. (1991) *You Can't Watch Them Twenty-four Hours a Day*. London: Child Accident Prevention Trust.

Combes, G. & Schonveld, A. (1992) *Life will Never be the Same Again*. London: Health Education Authority.

Cummings, E. M. & Davies, P. (1994) 'Maternal depressions and child development.' *Journal of Child Psychology and Psychiatry*, **35** (1), 73–112.

DEC (1991) *Us and the Kids: Ideas and Resources for Parents' Groups*. Birmingham: Development Education Centre.

Dwivedi, R. (1996) 'Community and youth work with Asian women and girls.' In K. N. Dwivedi & V. P. Varma (Eds), *Meeting the Needs of Ethnic Minority Children*. London: Jessica Kingsley, pp. 172–184.

Farrington, D. & West, D. (1990) 'The Cambridge study in delinquent development: a long term follow up of 411 London males.' In G. Kaiser & K. Kerner (Eds), *Criminality: Personality, Behaviour and Life History*. Berlin: Springer Verlag.

Judge, K. & Benzeval, M. (1993) 'Health inequalities: new concerns about the children of single mothers.' *British Medical Journal*, **306** (6879, Mar. 13), 677–680.

Kiernan, K. (1992) 'The impact of family disruption in childhood on transactions made in young adult life.' *Population Studies*, **46**.

Kumar, V. (1993) *Poverty and Inequality in the UK: The Effects on Children*. London: National Children's Bureau.

Maternity Alliance (1993) *New Lives and New Lives Together*. London: Maternity Alliance and Community Education Development Education Centre.

Mayall, B. & Foster, M. C. (1989) *Living with Children—Working for Children*. London: Heinemann.

Northamptonshire Health Authority (NHA) (1994) *Northampton Borough Locality Profile*. Northampton: Northamptonshire Health Authority.

Pugh, G., De'Ath, E. & Smith, C. (1994) *Confident Parents, Confident Children*. London: National Children's Bureau.

Roberts, I. & Press, B. (1995) 'Social policy as a cause of childhood accidents: the children of lone mothers.' *British Medical Journal*, **311** (7010, Oct. 7), 925–928.

Rowe, J. & Mahoney, P. (1993) *Parent Education: Guidance for Purchasers and Providers*. London: Health Education Authority.

Whalley, M. (1994) *Learning to be Strong*. London: Hodder & Stoughton.

7

GROUP WORK WITH PARENTS

Harold Behr

A group is an effective way to provide advice, support or therapy for parents who are experiencing problems with their children. However, groups can be hazardous as well as helpful. Like the individuals who make them up, they can be unpredictable, prone to the unexpected and caught up in emotional currents which can disturb the well-being of their members. It is therefore not enough to simply convene a group and rely on the natural chemistry of human interaction to carry the process forward. All the details surrounding the establishment of the group have to be carefully thought out in advance, and the group therapist has to constantly be on the lookout for signs of distress on the part of the group members and work towards making the group a safe enough place for people to talk openly about their problems.

This chapter provides a framework for setting up a group for parents and describes some of the techniques involved in achieving a therapeutic culture.

WHY A GROUP?

Parenting can be a lonely responsibility, especially when compounded by an anxious awareness that all is not well with a child or in the family. Probably the single most therapeutic element in a group is the discovery that one is not alone in one's plight. This discovery leads to others: that

Enhancing Parenting Skills: A Guide Book for Professionals Working with Parents.
Edited by K. N. Dwivedi. © 1997 John Wiley & Sons Ltd.

there is more than one way of coping with a problem; that one can have difficulty in a certain area of one's life and yet have the strength and skill to be of help to others; and that professionals are not the only source of useful information and psychological support.

A well-functioning group is a social laboratory, in which it is possible to experiment with newly learned interpersonal skills. For many parents the group becomes a place to which they can return each week and report in safety on the daily battles of their lives, the vicissitudes of family relationships and the thoughts and feelings which pre-occupy them. At the same time a group provides the space to think while watching and listening to others. Some parents say that they prefer being in a group to being in a relationship with just one professional because a group gives them respite from what they perceive as the relentless limelight of professional attention, with its connotations of expectation and disapproval.

Groups have a powerful way of casting light on the shadows of the past. Parents who have been unable to come to terms with sad, painful or traumatic events may have unwittingly transferred their own childhood attitudes onto their children. Groups are good at unscrambling these attitudes, first by helping parents to recall and retell their own early experiences, then by providing them with a corrective emotional experience and finally by presenting them with alternative approaches to parenting gleaned from the combined expertise of the other parents in the group. For example:

> A mother who had been forced to become independent in her early teens because of her own mother's feckless behaviour, had constructed her life around a rigid set of self-imposed rules based on the assumption that self-reliance and self-discipline were prized assets which had to be inculcated in her children. Determined to be a 'strong' mother she encouraged these values in her children, putting pressure on them to master social and educational skills before they were developmentally ready to do so. She became acutely depressed when her oldest child thwarted her efforts to bring her to independence by developing disabling psychosomatic symptoms, creating the very dependence on her which she so dreaded.
>
> The other parents in the group quickly picked up on her exaggerated emphasis on independence. They offered her examples from their own children's behaviour to show her how important it was to allow a child to be dependent in certain areas and at certain times. This surprised and intrigued her. She was able to take up some suggestions for relaxing some of her stringent rules. Another parent told her how much pleasure she got by joining her own children in play. Later the woman began to talk about her anger towards her own parents. She admitted that she had been reluctant to do this because it had felt like a betrayal of them, but that she had been enabled to do so by the openness of the other parents.

PLANNING A PARENT GROUP

Before making any practical arrangements for the group it is worth developing an overview of the group. Several key questions need answering: From which category of parent will the members be drawn? Will there be a specific focus or theme, and if so what will it be? How long will the group run for? What will the mechanism be for new members to join and old ones to leave? Who will lead the group, and how will the meetings be structured? Once these issues have been considered, practical matters have to be considered, such as arrangements for a venue which will be protected from disruption, and ways of letting colleagues, referrers and parents know about the group. It is also worth thinking about what therapeutic provision exists or will be needed for other family members (partners and children for example) while the group is running, and what liaison will be necessary with professionals and agencies involved with the parents.

FORMING THE GROUP

Parent groups can be formed either around children with similar problems or parents with similar problems or a shared life situation. Examples of the former are groups for parents whose children have a specific illness, developmental disability or behavioural difficulty. Examples of the latter are groups for lone parents, parents suffering from depression, and parents who have been through a similar experience such as abuse or bereavement. Frequently there is an overlap between these two categories of group. After a parent group has begun to meet, those factors which initially provided a powerful unifying theme become less significant as the members get to know one another and find other common ground.

LEADING A PARENT GROUP

Two styles of leadership can be distinguished: one which keeps the focus on the parent–child relationship, and one in which wider concerns are addressed, such as troubled family relationships, adult problems, and difficulties originating in the parent's own childhood. Most therapists settle for a compromise between the two, allowing the group to determine the focus and content.

Co-therapy

A group can be effectively led by one person. However, there are advantages to having two people leading the group, especially if complex problems are being dealt with. If the group is focused on a particular illness or disability it helps to have a professional with specialised knowledge of that condition (a doctor or health visitor for example) running the group alongside a professional with a psychological training who can attend to the interpersonal and group dynamic aspects of the group. A group of parents united by a shared cultural association such as membership of the same ethnic minority group, should have at least one therapist who can identify with them in more than a professional sense. In certain groups the gender of the group leaders is important. A group of mothers who have been abused by men, or whose children have been abused by men should be led by at least one woman.

A further advantage of co-therapy is that it offers a model to the parents of how two people can work together to solve problems. When differences or disagreements arise between the therapists the group can witness the attempt to resolve them. This provides a corrective emotional experience for those parents whose experience of disagreement has been breakdown into conflict and violence. Parents also welcome their problems being discussed by the co-therapists in their presence. Hearing themselves talked about thoughtfully and constructively, having their strengths and attributes acknowledged and their problems considered by professionals and fellow patients together are benefits unique to group therapy.

Sometimes training considerations come into play, such as the need to provide a learning experience for a student or a training opportunity for a staff member. If the group is to lend itself to this purpose the members have to be prepared beforehand. Groups do not take well to the unexpected arrival of a stranger, even in a professional role, or to the comings and goings of observers. When an observer is going to be present it is important to clarify in advance the extent to which that person can join in. An imposition of silence is generally artificial and unhelpful to both group and observer. A more relaxed atmosphere is achieved if the observer can be drawn into the interaction, and even the most inexperienced observer can contribute fresh and insightful observations.

SELECTING THE GROUP MEMBERS

In deciding whether a parent will benefit from a group the therapist has to take into account the needs of both the individual and the group. Groups can tolerate widely different personality types and problems but they also function on a basis of mutual identification. A parent whose expectations of help and psychological traits are conspicuously different from those of the other group members is likely to experience discomfort and become isolated. Social factors should be taken into account as well. A parent should encounter at least one other parent in the group who comes from a similar socio-economic, ethnic or cultural background. Some groups are better than others at tolerating difference and the therapist usually has to work actively to promote a common bond and a culture of acceptance even when group members are roughly similar in visible social characteristics and personality make-up.

> In one instance, a woman found herself the only lone parent in a group. Despite the fact that the other parents were in problematic relationships, she dropped out after a few weeks. During a follow-up interview she explained that she had found nothing in common with the other parents. Later she confessed that she had felt ashamed of her status and said that she had detected an attitude of condescension on the part of some of the other parents, which had reinforced her negative self-image.

In assessing someone for a group it is worth asking the question: 'What can this person contribute to the group as well as gain from it?' Groups are fairly good at 'carrying' group members who give little of themselves, but there is a tendency to close ranks after a while, and marginalise the 'ungiving' group member, leading to drop-out or even scapegoating.

Parents who are in the midst of a crisis may not be able to tolerate a group. In such cases a preliminary period of individual support may be required. The same is true for parents who are pre-occupied with a single traumatic event such as a recent bereavement, separation or serious illness. Unless the group consists of people who are going through the same process, these parents often find it difficult to tolerate the more leisurely pace of a group, where one has to find a way in, where there is an expectation of give and take, and where listening to others is as important as telling one's own story. Parents who suffer a crisis while in a group may, by the same token, need some individual sessions in parallel with the group to tide them over the crisis.

PREPARING THE GROUP MEMBERS

'Other people's problems get right inside me.'
'Will there be anyone else who's been through what I've been through?'
'How can people help me if they have problems of their own?'

These are some of the concerns frequently voiced by people contemplating a group. Parents in particular are likely to feel that they will be disapproved of and that their ability to parent will be called into question. Sometimes they fear that they themselves as people will be rejected. Feelings of shame, guilt, isolation and failure make it difficult for some parents to envisage sharing the intensely private world of their family life with a group of people who at the outset are complete strangers, not professionally trained to boot, and 'with problems of their own'. Such anxieties have to be anticipated and addressed in individual interviews before joining the group. Assessment is a two-way process. The therapist needs to get to know the parent but also owes the parent a detailed explanation of the group. Specific anxieties have to be addressed, for example:

> A parent expressed a worry that she might meet another parent who would know her, either from the school which her child attended, or from the religious community of which she was a member. The therapist knew that this would be unlikely but reassured the parent that in the event of this arising at a later stage she would not be expected to share the same group with that person, and that other therapeutic arrangements would be made for the new person.

More than one preparatory interview may be needed. It is worth asking if there are issues which the parent would prefer not to share in the group, and explaining that there will be no pressure to talk about matters which the parent does not feel ready to share. Misgivings about joining the group should be taken seriously. It is occasionally worth seeing the parent individually for a while to strengthen the working alliance and build trust.

THE PHYSICAL SETTING OF THE GROUP

The group room should contain the right number of chairs arranged in a circle and a low table in the centre to support a box of tissues, and refreshments if provided. Any detail of the physical setting can at one time or another assume significance for the group, as shown by the following example:

> A parent arriving late discovered that no chair had been left out for her, an absent-minded omission on the part of the two therapists which they hastily repaired. However the woman remained grimly silent. Later in the session an attempt by another parent to include her led to an angry outburst to the effect that the therapists did not regard her as important and did not respect her feelings. An apology by the therapists only partly mollified her, but other group members stepped in and gently confronted her with her oversensitive reactions. Subsequently she was able to reflect that the therapist's slight transgression had resonated with deeper feelings

of being rejected by her own parents, who had seldom acknowledged her presence at home. The problem she had come to the group with was a conflict between herself and her teenage daughter, who she felt did not appreciate her despite solicitous attention.

The group room should be well ventilated, well lit, adequately heated and spacious enough to give a feeling of personal comfort. Freedom from interruption and a sense of absolute privacy are required if people are to talk about themselves in a personal way. To minimise interference staff should be advised on the procedures for dealing with messages, late-comings, and any unexpected happenings which might impinge on the group.

Refreshments can create an atmosphere of informality and hospitality which makes conversation easier. However some therapists argue that a group can all too easily be diverted into a cosy, chatty mode and avoid exploring some of the more difficult issues which might only emerge in a more abstinent therapeutic culture. The following example, taken from a group in which refreshments were regularly served, illustrates how an incident arising in the catering area was turned to therapeutic advantage.

After handing round cups of tea to the other group members one of the parents accidentally knocked over her own cup while resuming her seat. Overcome with embarrassment, she burst into tears and was only persuaded with difficulty to remain in the room. Other parents tried to reassure her with accounts of their own domestic mishaps, some on a far greater scale than a spilt cup of tea. One woman described how she had thrown a plate of hot food on to the floor in a restaurant in the midst of an argument with her husband, with the children present. Another talked of how she had screamed abuse at her 8-year-old daughter for dropping a cake on the floor on the way to the table. The woman who had spilt the cup in the group was able to reflect on her own expectations of punishment and blame for trivial accidents stemming from her own childhood. The therapist commented on the woman's previously self-reported obsessional tidiness at home, and the way was open for an important therapeutic conversation on cleanliness and mess, which had relevance to all the parents in the group.

THE TIME-SCALE OF THE GROUP

The Duration and Frequency of the Sessions

Groups can have sessions lasting anything from half-an-hour to one-and-a-half hours, depending on the type of group and the setting. A group convened on a children's ward, for example, where parents do not have to make the journey to the hospital expressly to participate in the group, might only last half-an-hour to three-quarters of an hour. Shorter group sessions are easier to manage on a busy unit where there are constant calls on staff. Such groups tend to be more focused around a particular theme, and they often take on an educational and informative aspect. The therapist is actively supportive, responds readily to medical and psychological queries, and is careful not to open up emotionally charged areas which might demand more attention than the limited time allows. On the other hand, groups run along psychodynamic lines, where there is reliance on a gradually unfolding process and on the emergence of deeper feelings and issues through the spontaneous interaction of the members, generally have longer sessions, typically lasting an hour or an hour-and-a-half.

The frequency with which a group meets also depends on the psychological needs of the individuals in the group. A group for parents with high levels of anxiety or disturbance may need to meet more than once a week, although most parent groups provide a sufficiently containing environment with weekly meetings. Groups which meet at fortnightly or monthly intervals can constitute a useful support system for parents with chronically ill children or children with developmental problems. The longer interval between sessions allows the parents to implement tasks, suggestions, techniques and ideas generated by the group. Parents meeting in the context of a crisis or bereavement may choose to meet more than once a week for a limited period. Parents exploring complex and painful issues in a psychodynamic setting need to maintain therapeutic momentum and feel contained by sessions spaced at weekly or twice-weekly intervals.

Closed and Open Groups

A closed group is one which has a fixed number of sessions. The aim is for all the members to start and finish together. This model is appropriate for short-term groups, but can apply to groups which last as long as two or three years. The advantage of a closed group is that it can achieve a strong sense of togetherness over a short time, without the need to integrate new members along the way. The members come to know one another well and can work intensively on specific issues or themes. Closed groups develop a rhythm of their own. The members have a shared awareness that they have begun a process together and will end it together. The disadvantage of a closed group is that if people leave the group prematurely it remains depleted until its conclusion. Another problem is posed by the possibility that some group members may need continued support in a group beyond the natural lifespan of the group.

Groups which form part of an institution's therapeutic programme are generally run on an open model. Units through which clients circulate rapidly (acute wards in hospitals, for instance) need an open group in which the group members can come and go as the need dictates, perhaps attending for only one or two sessions. The model most frequently applied in a psychodynamic setting is the 'slow-open' model, in which the group itself has no pre-determined end point, new members can join along the way, and group members leave when they feel ready to do so. Slow-open groups place more emphasis on individual development and progress. These groups have a broader focus than closed groups, and often aim at a deeper exploration of issues, including the unconscious forces motivating behaviour and the psychological significance of interpersonal events. Therapists who run such groups promote a therapeutic culture of self-reflection, in which the irrational factors which complicate everyday relationships can be recognised and put into perspective.

A popular model for parent groups in clinics and educational settings is one which is intermediate between a closed and slow-open group. Such groups meet as closed groups for ten or twelve sessions, but with the option for parents to return for a further block of sessions. In practice, some parents use a group like this as a support system for several years, while others leave after perhaps one or two blocks, satisfied that the group has tided them over a difficult patch.

Breaks and Endings

Group members should be informed about holidays and breaks, and when the group is going to end. Breaks provide a useful therapeutic opportunity for parents to think about their own feelings of attachment and dependency, and how these might be affecting their relationships with their children. Holidays also enable parents to rehearse leave-taking from the group itself when the moment arrives. At the start of the group it is a good idea to give each group member a time-table containing the dates on which the group is due to meet, and when the breaks will be, and to encourage a culture in which members let the group know if an absence is anticipated.

Time-keeping during Group Sessions

It is important to begin and end each group session promptly. This shows that the time of the group meeting is precious and that the group is a valued occasion. Punctuality also contributes to the sense of predictability and containment provided by the group. Important conversations can develop in the first few moments of the group, and early questions such as 'Has the group started yet?' and 'Should I wait for the others?' soon disappear from the repertoire of questions if the therapist gets down to business from the moment that the clock-hand moves past the starting time.

Similarly the group should not overrun its time. Sometimes a group member becomes distressed near the end of the session. It is usually possible to help that person into a more contained frame of mind within the time boundary of the session, but, if not, the group should not be detained in order to achieve that purpose. If a crisis is evident it may be necessary to see the person outside the group, with a separately arranged appointment. It is often possible to anticipate a fraught ending earlier in the session and contain it at the time. Areas of discourse which are likely to become emotionally charged should not be opened up towards the end of a session, and non-verbal expressions of distress should be picked up as soon as they are perceived.

THE EARLY STAGES OF A GROUP

The main task of the therapist at the first group session is to reduce anxiety. A warm greeting to parents as they arrive and a few welcoming comments go a long way towards achieving this. It may be helpful to restate the purpose of the group and invite the parents to introduce themselves, perhaps asking them to say what they hope to gain from the group.

Prolonged silences are generally not therapeutic, and the therapist may have to step in with facilitating questions or comments, addressed to individuals rather than the group as a whole. If all goes well, the parents begin to trade information about themselves. This process is helped if the therapist joins in with interested questions and comments, a style of intervention which also demonstrates that the therapist is not the all-knowing, withholding professional so often imagined.

Establishing a Therapeutic Culture

The group soon moves from exchanges of social information towards discussions concerning the significance of events, a process led by the therapist.

PARENT A: Darren was thoroughly obnoxious when he came back from seeing his father yesterday. [*In response to interested questions from the*

group, she goes on to describe her 6-year-old son's fretful behaviour culminating in a tantrum after being sent to his room.]
THERAPIST: What do you think it might have been about?
PARENT A: I don't know. He's often like that when he gets back from his father's.
THERAPIST: Something is winding Darren up. I don't know what. [*Turns to the other parents.*] What do you think is going on with Darren?
PARENT B: I don't know. But I know that when my two used to come back from seeing their father they were just impossible. [*She goes on to tell how she sat them down one day and insisted that they tell her about their visits to their father. The story unfolds of her children having felt under pressure through questioning by their father and his new partner about their mother's personal life.*]
PARENT A: He never says a word to me about his father. [*The group gets into a discussion, facilitated by the therapist, about the pressures on children whose parents have separated. Parent A tells that she has not wanted to mention Darren's father to him because she has not wanted him to know how angry she feels towards the father.*]
THERAPIST: Somehow you need to find a way of talking to Darren about his father. That might give him permission to tell you what's on his mind.
PARENT C: I remember when my father left home I blamed my mother. I wouldn't speak to her for ages. I must have made her life a real misery.

In the group from which the above vignette is taken the focus moves freely between parent–child relationships and other relationships which affect the parents. There is no pre-arranged agenda. The therapist is guided by the conversation which develops, and responds with constructive comments. The group finds its own level, and if a theme emerges it is because the parents resonate to issues of common concern. The therapist follows the group wherever it goes, from present concerns to memories of past events, or into the imagined future.

The therapist is constantly alert to parents who are becoming tense or uncomfortable, states often only conveyed by subtle cues such as poor eye contact. Shy parents can sometimes be helped into the discussion by inviting their comments on other parents' problems. This enables the shy parent to get involved in the group without becoming personal too soon. The therapist may also sometimes want to steer the focus away from a parent who is demanding too much attention. This can occur when an anxious parent talks at length, but without showing signs of being reassured or taking in the reactions of the other group members. The therapist may have to interrupt the 'story' and invite the parent to listen to what the group has made of it. Parents who monopolise or bore a group should not simply be silenced but should be encouraged to contribute their solutions to other parents' problems.

The therapist will have prior knowledge of the parents' background, and can help less articulate parents to engage in the group by partly telling their story for them, in consultation with them. However, the therapist should be careful not to introduce sensitive new information into the group before a parent is emotionally prepared to deal with it. Family secrets and painful or traumatic family events should be respectfully held onto by the therapist until the parent gives a hint that it is safe enough to talk about them.

THERAPEUTIC AND ANTI-THERAPEUTIC SITUATIONS

The Emergence of Distressing Family Histories

Any therapeutic group is replete with stories of distressing life events which can be traced directly to the problems which bring people into therapy. A parents' group is no exception. Adversity strikes in many forms, and it is likely that the parents in the group will be collectively harbouring histories of family and social breakdown, physical, emotional or sexual abuse, physical or mental illness, and premature or traumatic death. For some, these histories will be well concealed, distorted by personal wishes and the passage of time, or even forgotten entirely. For others they will be ever present, intruding into their everyday lives and colouring their moods. Feelings of shame, guilt, fear, sadness and anger surround these histories, and are likely to surface when the story is told. Expressions of grief are common in a group, and often serve to bind the members closer together in a shared appreciation of loss.

When one parent begins to tell a story the others relate what they hear to their own inner world, privately matching it with their own stories. Another parent may be emboldened to share a similar story, and the therapeutic process gets under way. The therapist facilitates this process by empathic listening, questioning and commenting. In a well-functioning group this responsibility is largely shared with the group, which acts as a collective therapeutic agent for each of its members. Gradually, past events come to be seen in a different light, and new possibilities for conducting relationships emerge.

Recent Traumatic Events and Ongoing Crises

It is likely, especially in a long-term group, that some parents will bring news of a recent traumatic event or life crisis. In some cases this happens in the context of already existing problems, for example a parent reporting an episode of domestic violence or the break-up of a relationship. In other cases the traumatic event arises out of the blue, the onset of a life-threatening illness, for example, or the death of a family member. A commonplace traumatic event in everyday life, such as a theft or a minor traffic accident can have a devastating impact on a person already sensitised by earlier traumatic life events.

It is in the nature of a parents' group that the traumatic event reported is often one which has impinged upon the child, and is brought by proxy into the group. Groups often hear how a child has been bullied or victimised at school. They hear of accidents, illnesses, breakdown in a child's educational or care arrangements, or the discovery of a family secret.

Whenever such events are recounted in the group, the therapist has to bear in mind the impact of the event not only on the affected parent but on the rest of the group. The parent, who may become distressed in the group, has to be helped to tell the bad news and talk about the feelings which the event has generated. The therapist, assisted by the other parents, draws out the narrative with supportive comments and questions. Attempts to give meaning to the event in a more reflective or analytic way may have to wait for a later moment.

The account of a traumatic event often produces a shock wave in the group. The group may be faced with a parent who is emotionally numb, tearful, panicky or angry. Other parents who are vulnerable in the same area may have a profound emotional reaction too. The therapist may have to move the focus away from the content of the story to what is happening within the group itself. One way to do this is by discussing the impact which the news has had on the other parents, and the personal associations which it has stirred up in them. Traumatised parents discover that they are not alone, and a healing process is set in motion. A group is a good medium for the working through of traumatic events. Its members can collectively contain levels of distress which would place a heavy burden on one person.

Conflict in the Group

Parents who meet regularly to talk about personal issues become aware of their differences as well as their similarities. One parent may see in another traits which provoke dislike or disapproval, and this can translate into overt criticism, displays of irritability and even frank antagonism. Transference also plays its part. One parent may attribute to another qualities which call to mind a disliked figure from the past, perhaps a parent or sibling. There may indeed be a superficial resemblance which makes the problem all the more difficult to disentangle. The recipient of such feelings often experiences discomfort and begins to manoeuvre into a defensive or retaliatory mode which in turn can be complicated by transference feelings.

The therapist intervenes quickly to curtail tense, unpleasant or argumentative interactions between parents. These seldom lead to therapeutic change and can result in one or both of the protagonists (or even one of the other parents in the group) dropping out of the group. Once the group is back in a more reflective mode it is possible to work towards understanding the source of the conflict. Parents have to be helped to recognise and own their sensitivities and prejudices, and understand their origins.

Scapegoating

Scapegoating, the ancient human tendency to appoint a creature or person to carry the badness on behalf of the group, is a phenomenon which sometimes afflicts therapeutic groups. Some groups are more prone than others. A group made up of parents whose view of the world is bitter and persecuted, and who tend to find solutions to life's problems by blaming others, is likely to cast a vulnerable group member in the role of the scapegoat. Parents with this outlook frequently come from a background of deprivation or abuse. Their precarious self-esteem is easily threatened by someone who demonstrates the very characteristics which they hate and fear in themselves. On the other hand, a group whose members have had a more benign experience of the world is better able to tolerate vulnerability and difference in others, and will work assiduously to integrate marginal group members.

Scapegoating is less likely to occur if the group is carefully selected to ensure that no one parent is conspicuously different from the others. If the therapist senses that the group is isolating one parent, or behaving in a rejecting manner towards that person, swift intervention is again called for. Attacks in a therapeutic group can be quite subtle and well-disguised, taking the form of contemptuous or devaluating attitudes such as persistently treating someone as 'ill' or alien, 'not one of us'.

Even if the person being scapegoated invites attack the first priority is to protect that person before confronting him or her. This is achieved by manifestly 'taking sides' with the scapegoat and drawing attention to similarities between the scapegoat and the rest of the group. The therapist uses the power of the therapeutic role to confront the group with its disowning and blaming tendencies and help the individual members to acknowledge those aspects of themselves which they are projecting onto the scapegoat. Afterwards the scapegoat can be confronted with his or her part in the process. If scapegoating is carried through to its culmination, the scapegoat is expelled (which in practice means dropping out of the group) and the group closes ranks with a feeling of relief. But feelings of guilt, anger and inadequacy remain and the process is likely to recur unless confronted.

ENDING A GROUP

If the group has been a good experience, the prospect of ending is tinged with sadness. Parents can be helped to separate from one another and the group by thoughtful discussion well in advance of the ending. It is important for parents to talk about what they have gained from the experience as well as how it might have been improved upon. Sometimes the prospect of ending brings out earlier anxieties, and the therapist may be dismayed to see group members becoming more demanding at the last minute and slipping back into depressed and anxious states, but these are short-lived and generally give way to a mature acknowledgement of lasting change. Impulsive or premature moves to leave a group are usually picked up on by a mature group, and the therapist can count on the other parents to find sympathetic ways of pointing out to the would-be leaver the benefits of continuing. Groups are also generally good at giving their blessing to parents who have gained much and are genuinely ready to leave. Group members vary in their emotional reactions to endings. The therapist has to be mindful of those for whom a separation or departure has a deeper significance, perhaps reactivating painful experiences from the past.

LEARNING TO PLAY IN GROUPS

The above catalogue of problems and pitfalls associated with parent groups does not do justice to the rich tapestry of group interactions which develops around light-hearted, playful and humorous exchanges. Many of the parents who join such groups have had inadequate or negative experiences as children in the important areas of play and creative expression. Their experiences with their own children are consequently blighted by similar difficulties. Sometimes the parent's relationship with the child is too close or too demanding. In other cases the need for playful interaction may simply not have been recognised, and the requisite skills may have to be explicitly coached into existence.

When the relationship is complicated by anxiety or depression the underlying causes of these may have to be addressed and strategies introduced which are designed to lighten the parent–child interaction through play and shared enjoyment of pleasurable activities.

Far from being a place where only problems are brought, the therapeutic group creates a space in which the adult equivalent of play can take place. Laughter, humour and fanciful imagery enrich the group matrix and help to create a climate in which the members can work together on serious issues. The therapist models this by affirming the group members in their playfulness. Parents are also invited to report progress and expand on positive changes in themselves and their children. By bringing good experiences into the group, the parents convert the group itself into a good place, in which the task of tackling the difficulties which brought them into therapy is rendered safer and easier.

8

DEVELOPING HOME-BASED PARENTING SKILL PROGRAMMES, SUPPORTED BY GROUP SESSIONS OF PARENTING TECHNIQUES

Peter Marsden-Allen

INTRODUCTION

This chapter looks at a way of developing a model for practice of a 'Home-based Parenting Skill' programme and concurrent group sessions of parenting techniques. This programme is for parents referred to a child guidance or family centre setting.

Various techniques and use of video and other teaching aids assist in developing parenting skill. These ideas are explained and demonstrate how parents and professionals form a partnership in a process of parenting skill development. This partnership engages in an analysis of the parenting task, observation and validation of existing skills and development of additional skills which are relevant to parenting.

The programme is developmental in that members are both parents and professionals who are working on an adult learning and skill

Enhancing Parenting Skills: A Guide Book for Professionals Working with Parents.
Edited by K. N. Dwivedi. © 1997 John Wiley & Sons Ltd.

focused package of 'Home-based Parenting Skill' teaching. The programme is 'psycho-educational' in that both parents and workers are sharing new material in the application of theory to practice. The programme is also 'systemic' in that both parents and workers are members of individual family systems and the parenting technique group, which takes on an identity and experience of its own. This involves sharing personal feelings about these experiences in the group as a way of understanding the interactive patterns in parenting children.

Theoretical models that underpin the development of the 'Home-based Parenting Skills' programmes are drawn from a mix of psychological theories. The programme leader's experience of working with individuals and groups should provide a consultative and supervisory role for both the parents and the professionals. The team of professionals plays a crucial role in forming the 'worker system' that supports individual parents and their children on the programme. Home-based visits and the group sessions are a growth opportunity for both the workers and the parents. All participants are asked to monitor and evaluate both their individual and collective experiences of the programme, which are then evaluated continually to improve the programme for the future.

THE AIM AND REFERRAL PROCESS OF THE PROGRAMME

In a Family Centre or child guidance setting, it is necessary to contact the local social services office and other agencies that are likely to refer parents to the programme. At this stage the organiser of the programme would be providing two essential pieces of information. Firstly, a description of the programme which is clear about its aim and how it is to be organised and, secondly, a referral procedure.

The aim of the programme is to provide parents on an 'at home' basis together with a group experience; the opportunity to validate and develop their parenting skills.

The referral form would seek information about the parents and family members at home, together with details of relationships and ethnic origins as appropriate. The form should include the parents' details, their address and home telephone number, and a space should be provided for the address of the referring agency. The professional referring and the professional's telephone number should also be included. The form should then ask what issues the referrer feels that the referred parents might bring to the group. The form should also ask the referrer to comment on why he or she believes the programme might be useful to the parents. The form must seek out any specific requirements that the referred person has, in order to facilitate participation in the group. This could include a need for transport or other assistance with getting to the group or receiving home visits. The form should ask if the referred parents have a video and television at home, as this will form an essential part of communicating newly learnt techniques to the parents.

RECRUITING THE STAFF FOR THE PROGRAMME

As well as recruiting prospective parents, it is necessary to get together a group of professionals who are going to provide the input for the home-based visits, and run the parenting techniques groups. Some professionals will be required to operate the crèche facility, and the video for the home-based parenting skills input. It is important that the people providing the home-based visits need to be staff who are competent at communicating ideas to parents based on the psychological theories, in such a way that they come alive within the home setting. They must be familiar with the use of video cameras and flip charts to enable them to illustrate what they are putting across to parents. They must also be skilled in getting parents into role playing parenting skills in different ways. They must also be prepared to video record the parents' efforts, to play them back, so that parents can learn from watching their own experience growing, particularly in the home-based situations.

It is useful for the same team who do the home-based visits to be involved with the group teaching part of the project. This means that workers need to have the additional skills of being able to listen, involve people in the group exercises and group-based parenting technique training.

THE INTRODUCTORY PROCESS OF THE PROGRAMME

Weeks one and two are for setting up the programme and explaining the process to the parents. The first two weeks of the programme should be spent setting up the Home-based Parenting Skill visits as well as the Parenting Technique Group. This involves members of the team of professionals visiting all the accepted referrals to the programme during the first two weeks.

The parents are informed that home-based inputs occur for each parent at least once a week during the following six weeks of the eight-week programme. As in the case of the group sessions, which will be explained later, the sessions in the first two weeks are used to plan the work that goes on in the remaining sessions. This introductory process means that professionals visit the parents at home with the intention of making notes and recording as well as listening to as much detailed information as possible about the problems that parents are disclosing about the parenting of their children.

In addition, they explain about boundaries of confidentiality and the choice that parents have about sharing their experience in the home-based visits as well as the material associated with those visits, in the group sessions.

The parents are told how the video camera and the flip chart will be used to explain and to record existing and new forms of parenting skill behaviour. Parents can use this recorded material during the time between visits and group sessions to watch, evaluate and practice their new skills as they will be left with a video recording of their work to play back on their television sets.

The first two weeks will also contain two group sessions where the contract for participating in groups is made clear, including boundaries of confidentiality, respect for other people's points of view and respect for gender and race issues within the group. Parents are told that the final week of the eight-week programme will be used for evaluation purposes, both in terms of the group sessions and home-based visits.

THE THEORETICAL IDEAS BEHIND THE PROGRAMME

The author has found that Gordon and Sands' (1976) Principles for Parenting Skills are invaluable in developing such a programme. These are, that parents should:

(a) listen carefully to children; you must want to hear what the child wants to say;
(b) genuinely want to be helpful to the child with his or her particular problem;
(c) generally accept the child's feelings, whatever they may be or however different they may be from your own, or from the feelings you think your child should feel;
(d) have a deep feeling of trust in the child's capacity to handle his or her feelings; to work through her or his problems, and find solutions to them;
(e) appreciate that your feelings are transitory and not permanent;
(f) realise that 'a child is a person in his or her own right'.

Insofar as gender issues are concerned, it is interesting at this point to note the research such as that of Stratton and Webster (1985), which showed that the development of parenting skills by mothers was seldom influenced by father involvement but that father involvement is an important factor in maintaining the change that results from parenting skill training. In general terms, McCabe and McRobbie (1981) argue that parenting programmes working with women need to relate to the woman, assuming a degree of oppression and therefore lack of choices. They need to explain choices and challenge potential issues where there appears to be none. Additionally the choices of the parent need to be validated as well as the presence of any unhappiness in the life of the parent. It is also necessary to recognise that some women change with feminist views. Finally it is important to find language to describe and talk about women and their oppression which is understandable and addresses their circumstances, concentrating on limited tasks and achievable goals.

The context of the programme of six home-based sessions and group-based sessions begins with the first home-based session, when two workers visit the parents' home to assess, together with the parents, the way in which the child's behaviours are symptomatic of other problems which may exist in the family system. During the home visits there is a sense in which the analysis of the problem is both 'systemic' and 'behavioural'. A 'systemic' analysis suggests that the child's difficulties can be the result of a problematic interaction within the family system. Sometimes the child's behavioural problems are a direct result of those interactive relationships. Accordingly, if the intervention is to be helpful, it must be focused at the dysfunctional aspect of the family system. This is often known as 'punctuating' the system.

The systemic model is used as the basis of the analysis of what goes on in the family session. It is a relevant approach because it argues that the symptomatic behaviour is part of the transactional pattern peculiar to the system in which it occurs. It is therefore felt that the way to eliminate the symptom is to change the rules.

The notion of 'systemic' is essentially that, with the sea of interactions that occur in a family situation, the family balance or homeostasis is created by how those interactions serve a purpose in maintaining the functioning of the family system. So it can be argued that these interactions can be understood, possibly reframed and challenged. Thus the task is to identify what is happening in terms of interactions to find out how the problem is embedded and to understand the pattern of the family functioning, rather than individuals within it. This then requires the worker to work through a process of 'punctuation' to enable the family to understand that an individual's behaviour within the family can be seen as part of the family context in which it occurs.

THE CONTENT OF THE SIX INPUT SESSIONS OF THE PROGRAMME

The home-based sessions and the parenting technique group sessions take place in the programme concurrently through the remaining six weeks. They are outlined below in the order that they are described in this section.

The first home-based session deals with issues regarding uncovering the nature of the family system. Secondly, the first group session is described in terms of helping parents to relate in a more focused way, of listening to their children. The second and third home visits are then explained in terms of the material they are likely to cover. Following this, the second group session looks at input regarding listening effectively to children and gaining information from children which is child focused. The fourth home visit is then described, which focuses on a way of helping parents to get in touch with their own innermost feelings and how those feelings are likely to affect their parenting. Following this, the third group session is described, which looks at how techniques of 'Transactional Analysis' are explained to parents. After the third group session the fourth group session is looked at, in order to explain how parents are taught to analyse the process of irrational behaviours from their children and respond to them appropriately. The fifth home visit is then described, which looks at a particular example of applying 'behavioural' and 'cognitive' principles to a child's behaviour. The fifth group session follows, looking at how newly acquired skills are maintained and, finally, the sixth home visit session and group session are explained in terms of how the programme is evaluated.

The First Home Visit Session

During the first home-based session the workers invite the family to tell their story in order to understand the pattern that is occurring, and use a number of questioning techniques to help the family to see the pattern in its own family system. Therefore, in the first session the family are helped to think about

(a) the handling of their own child's behaviour;
(b) re-inforcing each other's understanding and skill development through the family process and discussion;
(c) how to improve their performance, particularly when related to their individual problems that are discussed during the home-based visits, which will occur along with the group session.

The parents are then informed that the second home visit would focus on listening skills. The third home-based visit would focus on communication skills with children, as indeed, would session four. Session five of the home visits would focus on behaviour modification skills for children and the final sixth session would provide further practice and evaluation of the work that has gone on in the previous sessions.

Second and Third Home Visits

The second and third home visits, which occur during the second and third week of the group sessions, use similar techniques to those used in the group sessions; that is, transactional analysis and other techniques which are described later, to explore with the family what it is that the systemic and transactional analysis has uncovered. The family members are then asked by the beginning of the third home visit to start to recreate a new script and associated new behaviours to tackle problems that have been uncovered. Again, this material is role played and recorded and played back to the family through the television sets. The completed video at the end of the third session, is left with the family to watch in the privacy of their own home, without the workers necessarily being present, in order for them to rediscover and practise their new found behaviours.

The First Group Session

In this session the input for parents in the group is that parents are asked that when listening to a child the parent should maintain eye contact and adopt a posture that is similar to or mirrors that of a child. They are told that they should be prepared to reflexively respond to the changes in the child's posture. Moreover, that they should be aware of the breathing of the child, which means to wait for the child's breath to exhale in a sentence or sentences, and then to respond adopting a lower tone, that is a quieter tone in response to excited chatter to reduce tension and/or temper in the child. They are then told that in maintaining eye contact they should be aware of the child's eye movements, e.g. to observe expression of feelings through generally downward movement of the eyes, and the expression of constructive visual and heard responses by generally upward movement of the eyes, in response to questions that are likely to ask for this kind of information. It should be noted that trends of optical processing have been found by Bandler and Grindler (1979) but based on subjective experimental observations.

Additionally, in the second group session, parents are informed that in order to join a younger child in play activities, it is important to allow the child to lead the way, whether it be doing a jigsaw or making a model out of scraps of waste material or drawing pictures. This means letting the child start the conversation and asking the child what object or objects are, rather than interpreting for the child. Parents are told that if a child is not talking about things which are important to him or her; one technique is to get the child to draw or write the names of the people and/or things it would like with it on a desert island for a week. Parents are shown how to draw the island and call it by the child's name.

The Fourth Home Visit

In this session parents are taught how to be aware of their own moods and feelings prior to listening and working with children. This is achieved through two exercises taken from Gestalt theory (Perls *et al.*, 1951). These exercises are begun by asking parents to sit comfortably in their chairs and asking them to tighten their toes and relax on the count of three. Subsequently, to tighten and relax their calf muscles, buttocks, abdomen, shoulders, forearms, hands, fingers and, lastly, their neck muscles all individually to the count of three, with their eyes closed. Once relaxed they are asked to keep their eyes closed and to imagine themselves on an island looking out to sea. Parents are then asked to visualise a boat coming towards them in which is the person or object they most want in the world at this time. They are asked to stay with the thought as to what that object or person is and why it is there. After a further two or three minutes they are asked to open their eyes and then to listen to an explanation of the idea that their inner motivation, or matters that are most important to them may have something to do with what is in their particular visualised or fantasised boat. They are told that this is what is known as a 'lead fantasy' technique and is being taught to the parents as a means of helping them in self-relaxation and to facilitate their inner awareness before dealing with their children in difficult situations. It is important at this stage to underline the importance of parents being helped to see the way in which their own feelings, and the way they project those feelings, has a direct impact on how they deal with their children and how their children will subsequently behave.

The Second Group Session

The second group session is designed to demonstrate techniques of communication with parents. They are shown two techniques from two models of communication with children and/or other people. These are 'Transactional Analysis' (Berne, 1961), and 'Rational Emotive Therapy' (Ellis, 1974).

Firstly, parents are asked that they are to work from the 'Transactional Analysis' approach. They are told that there are three ego states in the personality: the 'parent ego state' the 'adult ego state' and the 'child ego state'. It is explained that the 'parent ego state' is described as an 'introspect', of the parents and parental substitutes in the 'ego state' where we experience our own 'parent feelings' in a situation, or we feel and act towards others as our parents felt and acted towards us.

Finally, it is explained that the 'parent ego state', refers to the 'shoulds' and 'oughts' of our communication and can be both nurturing and/or critical.

The 'adult ego state' is explained to be the processor of data and information. Parents are then told it was the unemotional or non-judgmental objective part of the personality which uses available information to sort out problems.

A 'child ego state' is presented as the part of our personality that consists of feelings, impulses and spontaneous acts. Parents are then told that the 'natural child' is the impulsive, untrained, spontaneous, expressive infant in each of us.

Parents are then informed that a critical 'parent's transaction' often elicits a 'natural' or 'free child' response from another person, whether the transaction be between two parents or a parent and child or, indeed, between two children. Parents are therefore, made aware of their communications to children in terms of the 'ego state' they are using and the 'ego state' in the child they were 'feeding' with that transaction. Parents are then informed about the 'Redecision Theory' (Goulding & Goulding, 1979), where an early set of transactions towards a child may give a message such as 'don't be too close', which would encourage the child to grow up with the idea 'I won't allow myself to get too close'. This is to show parents how early messages to their children can powerfully affect the way in which the child will develop attitudes later on in adult life. Parents were then given other examples which were: 'Don't be a child, don't be sane, don't grow, don't be well, don't succeed, don't belong, don't be you, don't be, don't be important'. It was then explained that the injunction 'don't belong' could get the child growing up believing 'nobody will ever like me because I don't belong anywhere'.

The Third Group Session

In this group session, parents are told that 'rational emotive' techniques are communicated in terms of four basic ideas (Ellis, 1974). Firstly, that people condition themselves to feel disturbed rather than being conditioned by external sources. Secondly, people have the biological and cultural tendency to think irrationally and to needlessly 'disturb themselves'. Thirdly, humans are unique in that they invent 'disturbing beliefs' and keep themselves disturbed about their disturbances. Fourthly, that people have the capacity to change their cognitive, emotional and behavioural processes.

Parents are told the idea that the 'activating event' is generated by a belief that there is an emotional consequence to the event belief. They are also told that they could be victims of fallacious beliefs both in terms of themselves and on behalf of their children. Moreover, it is explained that parents tend to keep re-indoctrinating themselves over and over again in an unthinking way. Consequently 'beliefs' continue to occur as a basis for 'parent behaviours'. It is explained that the way to change, is to focus on the 'irrational belief'. Parents are told to think about children 'who wouldn't settle at night'. It is argued that some parents have an 'irrational belief' that all children must be in bed by 7.00 p.m.; there is no particular evidence to support 7.00 p.m. as being the right time to send a child to bed. It is further pointed out that a more 'rational belief' could be that children will go to bed when they are tired. As a result, a tired child is genuinely tired, so the child and the parent have a peaceful night. The right time might be 8.00 p.m. rather than 7.00 p.m. if the child's condition is the basis of a rational choice, not the mistaken belief that 7.00 p.m. is the only time suitable for bed.

Lastly in this session, parents are informed of the inadvisability of attaching sex roles to children with examples such as 'it's o.k. for boys to cook and take part in caring activities' and for girls to take an interest in traditional male activities. This is to get parents to think about sex role stereotyping as it can condition behaviour and attitudes.

The Fifth Home Visit

During the fifth home visit the session is started by workers having a discussion with parents about the ideas that were explained in sessions one and two using examples from the parents' own experiences. During the second half of the third session parents are told how to control and deal with difficult behaviour as well as listening and communication skills.

Firstly, the parents are taught to analyse their child's behaviour in terms of:

(a) what stimulated the feelings in the child
(b) how the child felt

(c) what the child's response was to its feelings in terms of the behaviour
(d) what the consequences were.

They are then given the example of the child and the fence. They are told that the stimulus was that a 7-year-old boy wanted to climb the garden fence to get out to the shops and factories outside, as he perceived these as exciting places. His feelings are ones of excitement and interest in climbing the fence and escaping to more interesting activities. His behaviour was to climb the fence when no one was looking. The consequence for him was the excitement and interest on the other side of the fence.

Subsequently, parents are informed of three ways of dealing with that behaviour. They are told that one way is to always let the child climb the fence but to be there on the other side to bring the child home. Thus the child learns that climbing the fence only means being brought home to an exciting reward once at home. Secondly, they are told that they could make the activities on the garden side of the fence more interesting, thus removing the child's need to go over the fence. Another possible strategy was that parents could encourage the child to climb the fence and always take the child to the same park when met on the other side, so the child becomes bored with the activity associated with climbing the fence. This example of analysing and constructing strategies in response to given behaviours, was applied in discussion with all the parents in home visits, in response to a child giving out a temper tantrum, or other challenging behaviour.

It often occurs during the fifth home visit that families start to discuss, in quite an aware way, their new found behaviours and the impact that is occurring with their family functioning.

The Fourth and Fifth Group Sessions

These sessions are used purely for maintenance purposes; that is, that the new found behaviours are revised and understood in the wider context of family functioning. It may be at this stage that those members of the family system attending the parenting technique groups, are able to share some of their newly learnt behaviour with the rest of the family system.

The Sixth and Final Home Visit

The sixth and final family session is to evaluate the effectiveness of the changes that have occurred within the family system as a result of the home-based inputs and, indeed, of the group sessions that have occurred concurrently. At this stage it is possible for the family to start to apply the different ways of thinking that they have learnt in their situation, particularly in terms of future problems that may occur. At this point the workers will use the flip chart, the video equipment and possibly play equipment to get the family to re-enact future scenarios that they may think about 'what if' questions that can be asked at this stage. The family should now move into role playing, to see how they might behave in the future, if certain situations occurred.

It is useful at this stage to invite the family to consider the use of video material about their behaviour, as a way of continuing to gather fresh material with which to look at their behaviour, particularly that of the children, in the future. Often such video material can become part of a family album or family life story, which is one way in which, for example, step families making sense of the stages they have passed through when they have come together. This whole process of externalising the family from its own behaviours, to help it become objective, as to what is happening within its system, is a useful means of helping the family to mature in its growth and to cope with problems which may occur in the future.

The Sixth and Final Group Session

This session is where the material from the home-based parenting skill inputs are tied together with those inputs from the group sessions, which have already been discussed. Essentially this session is an opportunity to 'tidy up' the remaining questions that parents may have as a result of their own inputs and some of the material they have been working with in the group sessions. There is a sense in which the last session is also used to evaluate the condition of the group—that is, how parents feel the group has helped them to express some of their own emotions with their peers and ways in which they have felt strengthened as a result of the support implicit in the group sessions.

CONCLUSION

As can be seen from this chapter, the idea of linking home-based inputs and group work with parents in the form of a Parenting Techniques Group is a useful combination to help families negotiate new ways of dealing with what they perceive to be problems within their own family systems. The key message which comes from this approach is that families are asked to gain a sense of objectivity and introspection about how the pattern of their interactions result in certain members of the family behaving in different ways and, above all, to understand that disturbed behaviour from the children is symptomatic of dysfunction in the family system as a whole.

REFERENCES

Bandler, R. & Grindler, J. (1979) *Frogs into Princes, Neuro-Linguistic Programming*. Moab, UT: Real People Press.

Berne, E. (1961) *Transactional Analysis*: New York: Grove Press.

Ellis, A. (1974) 'Rational Emotive Theory'. In Borton, A. (Ed.), *Operational Theories of Personality*. New York: Brunner Mazel, pp. 308–344.

Gordon, T. & Sands, J. (1976), 'Parent effectiveness training in action'. In *New Problems, Insights and Solutions in Parent Effectiveness Training*, New York: Wyden.

Goulding, M. & Goulding, R. (1979) *Changing Lives Through Redecision Therapy*. New York: Brunner Mazel.

McCabe, R. & McRobbie, R. (1981) *Anti Sexist Social Work*. B.A.S.W.

Perls, F., Hefferline, R. F., Goodman, P. (1951) *Gesalt Therapy*. New York: Jullian Press.

Stratton, P. S. & Webster, (1985) 'Prevention of childhood behavioural problems: long effects of treatment with mothers as therapist'. Paper presented at the AGM of Association for Advancement of Behavioural Therapy, New York.

9

HELPING PARENTS COPE WITH THEIR HYPERACTIVE CHILDREN

Jo Douglas

INTRODUCTION

Parents are often understandably confused about how best to manage their hyperactive child. Some see the child as difficult, disobedient and attention demanding while others recognise that attentional problems are at the root of the problem. Some arrive in clinics already well read and demanding medication or diets for their children while others are new to the concepts of attention deficit disorder and hyperactivity.

Historical confusion among clinicians about the diagnosis of hyperactivity has reflected the differences between North American and British clinicians in diagnostic criteria, terminology and prevalence rates. But more recently agreement over the terminology of ADHD (attention-deficit/hyperactivity disorder) to describe these children using clear diagnostic criteria has focused research.

SETTING THE SCENE
Understanding the Child's Behaviour

The first stage of helping parents cope is to empower them by providing knowledge about their child's behaviour. Parents may feel stressed,

Enhancing Parenting Skills: A Guide Book for Professionals Working with Parents.
Edited by K. N. Dwivedi. © 1997 John Wiley & Sons Ltd.

overwhelmed and helpless with the task of trying to rear a child with ADHD. The continual demands and activity, the need for constant vigilance, the lack of compliance, the impulsive and often dangerous behaviour shown by their child is far beyond their expectations of how they thought their child would behave.

Pre-school children show inattentive, overactive and non-compliant behaviour and require training by parents and teachers to be more sociable and compliant. ADHD is difficult to diagnose in the pre-school age range and it is the persistence over time and the continuance of the behaviour in new environmental settings that will confirm the diagnosis. A developmental perspective of the child's behaviour is necessary to see how the immaturities in social behaviour, concentration and self-control do not resolve as the child grows older (Douglas, 1991). Truly hyperkinetic children will often be more easily identifiable as their high level of undirected activity and restlessness will be so extreme as to make them very noticeable even in the pre-school years.

Parents often benefit from a clear analysis of their child's behaviour that discriminates different aspects of the problems they are experiencing. As the clinician draws out the parents' description of the child's behaviour and fits it into a diagnostic framework, the parents often experience a great sense of relief that someone is able to identify and understand how their child behaves and that their child is not just naughty (Taylor, 1986). There are five main areas of symptomatology which need to be examined during the diagnostic process.

Behaviour problems

Parents first concern is often their child's anti-social behaviour. This can include verbal and physical aggression to members of the family and friends; disobedience and non-compliance; temper tantrums; poor ability to share and take turns; and attention-demanding behaviour. Clearly these are all behaviours that are not specific to ADHD but occur in children who have conduct disorder, but they provide an important area of concern for parents of ADHD children and may dominate other problem areas that the parents have not fully recognised.

Attention and concentration problems

Detailed questioning is often required to identify symptoms that reflect the child's poor attention. Parents may consider that the child's non-compliance is disobedience when in fact it reflects the child's inability to listen and concentrate when spoken to; to remember a sequence of instructions and consequently to fail to carry out the instructions. The child may appear forgetful, make careless mistakes and be easily distracted and the parents may criticise the child rather than recognise this as an attentional problem. Difficulties in organising tasks and activities, losing possessions, or avoidance of tasks that require sustained attention, i.e. boring homework, may be interpreted as 'not trying' and 'being immature' rather than attentional difficulties. All of the symptoms of attentional difficulties are features that occur in young children and recognition of these symptoms as being inappropriate to the age of the child may occur only when the child goes to school, has to fit in with external expectations of their behaviour and is closely compared to other children of the same age (Barkley, 1990).

Hyperactive problems

Parents will readily report these symptoms as their child will be continually active, restless and fidgety. A child who can sit and watch a favourite television programme may still be continually on the move in his seat, changing position, flicking his fingers or drumming his feet.

Many pre-school children, particularly boys, are very active and restless and so this may be interpreted as developmentally appropriate, but in the child with ADHD the behaviour persists beyond the normally expected age or the child is unable to settle to any play task even one in which he is interested. Together with this the parents may see their child as dangerous due to their lack of anticipation and their impulsivity. The child often appears to have no fear. The irritating aspect of this is the continual interruptions in conversation or activities. The child is unable to wait and so often seems rude and selfish.

Social problems

The symptoms of ADHD often lead to such children being rejected socially by their peers. Children will not tolerate another child who interrupts or who will not take turns in games or fit into the rules that are developing in play. Children with ADHD will be lively and exciting but because they have difficulty seeing any activity to completion they will be irritating to other children. Parents often feel distressed because their child is rejected by others, is not invited to parties or to play. Parents may try to compensate by inviting other children around to play, but find that they spend a lot of the time peace keeping or keeping the visiting child amused while their own child flits around. Making friends requires a combination of skills including listening to other children, team work, cooperation and turn taking, all of which are difficult for children with ADHD.

Learning difficulties

The core problems of attention and concentration can often lead to failure in academic work. A child who is too poorly organised to follow tasks or too distractible to finish tasks at school will soon start to fall behind academically. If this is not identified early in his or her school career then failure to learn to read or write because of insufficient practice or support will compound the child's difficulties. Recognition that children with these problems require a different approach to other children in relation to teaching and learning skills is essential to support them through their school careers.

Supporting Parents of Children with ADHD

In addition to providing knowledge and an accurate diagnosis of the child's behaviour the clinician needs to progress onto putting the child's problems into the context of the family and providing some practical advice on how to cope.

Family tensions

Families of children with ADHD experience the same range of stresses emotionally, financially, environmentally and socially as any other family. The presence of a hyperactive child can exacerbate the stress experienced in relation to other strains of family life, but may also be unrelated to these other problems. These parents will have had the same difficult experiences in their own childhoods, have similar mental health problems and relationship difficulties to any other parents and they may need help for these problems in their own right, apart from the additional strain of parenting a hyperactive child.

Siblings also have their own needs and problems which may go unrecognised as the parents are preoccupied with the problems presented by the hyperactive child. Many siblings become resentful and angry at the hyperactive child who receives so much attention. They feel left out and may even start to misbehave in order to gain recognition. They are unable to leave their possessions around, have to guard their rooms against invasion and often feel helpless in trying to effect any change in their sibling's behaviour. Some children will instigate conflicts with their hyperactive siblings, out of sight of the parents, in order to get them into trouble. They may tell tales on them in the guise of trying to help their parents. Stresses between siblings do need to be recognised and acknowledged in order for families to be able to progress into a therapeutic phase. Balancing the needs of all of the family members is a difficult and complex process which needs to be flexible in order to respond to the fluctuating demands as children grow older and need different types and amounts of attention.

Removing blame

Many parents feel that they are to blame for their child's behaviour problems. A discussion about the aetiology of ADHD is often valuable in removing the guilt from parents. Psychosocial factors are not thought to play a primary role in the aetiology of ADHD but as interaction conflicts are more common in families of children with ADHD, the therapeutic orientation should be to focus on how to help the parents to cope with a very difficult situation rather than consider that they are the root of the problem.

The aetiology is unknown and it is unlikely that one factor will be found to explain all cases of ADHD. Some biological indicators are starting to emerge in the research literature, but it is too soon to have clear evidence (Cantwell, 1996). Family genetic factors also appear to be important as there is a heritability for attention deficit disorder. Adoption studies support the view that this is genetic rather than environmental. Other 'environmental' factors, i.e. diet, toxins, etc., have not received substantial support from research studies (Barkley, 1990).

Coping not curing

Once a diagnosis is made parents often feel that there must therefore be a cure for the condition. Unfortunately there is as yet no cure. All of the treatment methods to date only ameliorate the symptoms, they do not remove them so that they do not return. The effects of medication are transitory and dose related; the behavioural improvements that occur through parent training methods are only maintained as long as the parents work hard at applying the strategies. Parents need to realise that any intervention is aimed at helping them cope with a difficult situation, not remove it.

Understanding the ADHD symptoms as a chronic disability can often enable parents to recognise that they need to learn how to adapt to the situation and develop strategies to support their child to maximise their potential in the long term. 'Coping not curing' is an important perspective for parents to assimilate. ADHD is a long-term disability and parents will need to consider how they change their expectations and responses to their child for many years. Parents need to be much clearer about how to manage their child's behaviour, and to be more systematic, tolerant and consistent than they are with their other children.

Structure to the day

Assessment of the trigger points in the day that cause the most trouble at home is a valuable starting point for discussion. Parents often report difficulties in the morning when all of the family is getting ready to go to school or work. Coming home time from school, when again there are competing demands for parental attention, and unsupervised play periods, are times when the parents are busy and cannot keep an eye on their child; shopping, visiting friends and relatives are common trigger points for problems to arise. In order to prevent repetitive patterns of tension and conflict it can be helpful for parents to learn to anticipate the problem times and change their strategies of control or management in order to prevent problems escalating. Acknowledgement that their hyperactive child requires a different level of supervision and support from their other children is the first point for agreement. Parents can then work out strategies to contain the problem outbursts. The calmer the parents remain the less likely they are to exacerbate the child's behaviour problems.

Examples of a change of structure may be for father not to leave for work so early but to take prime responsibility for getting the hyperactive child up, dressed and breakfasted while the mother copes with her other children. Use of two parents is essential for survival in the family, and working out how they share the monitoring tasks and daily activities between them so that there is always one of them coping with the hyperactive child, can rapidly ease the tensions and explosions in the family. Acknowledgement between the parents that they each have a child care role and that each of them gets tired and exhausted can help remove blame, anger and additional sources of tension between them. Sharing the household tasks, e.g. one does the weekly shopping while the other cares for the child, avoids the stresses of managing a noisy, demanding and active child in the supermarket. Sometimes relatives, friends or paid child carers can help out by sharing the tasks of looking after the children. Help with getting children ready for bed is an important time when mothers benefit from an extra pair of hands.

Parents may need to plan meals and do the preparation before the children return home from school, so that as soon as the child arrives attention can be paid to his or her needs and monitor his or her behaviour. This avoids unsupervised times when the child may get into danger, be destructive or disrupt his or her siblings. Help with attention control on homework may also be needed and this will not be possible if the parent is distracted by household tasks.

Planning family outings also requires foresight and anticipation. Hyperactive children often respond better to a regular structure where they can anticipate what is going to happen, and so spontaneous outings can often disrupt them emotionally and behaviourally.

Safety in the home

Young hyperactive children can be of considerable concern when their impulsivity leads them into dangerous situations. Children will climb out of windows, unlock front doors and wander off or climb over balconies without any awareness or anticipation of the likely danger. Parents therefore need to be extremely vigilant but also think about how best to make their homes safe. Locks on cupboards, doors, windows and fridges may be necessary. Cleaning products, dangerous kitchen and electrical equipment will need to be out of reach and well hidden. Being aware of safety issues in the house with young children is important generally in all families but particularly so in families with hyperactive children. Altering the environment can often be an easier option than training the child not to touch or having to keep permanent vigilance.

Positive attitude

Parents who are exhausted and worn out by their hyperactive children are often extremely critical and negative towards them. The children's disruptive behaviour, lack of compliance, disorganisation will lead parents to repeatedly reprimand them. Help with parenting skills should enable them to focus on the positive behaviours shown by their children and to learn to praise them and identify small goals of change or behaviours that they can reward.

Concerns about the future

Many parents worry about what the future will hold for their hyperactive child. The prognosis is not particularly good for many hyperactive children and those who have co-morbid behavioural problems will have a worse prognosis. The child needs to progress through the developmental changes and academic developments expected of them at school so that they have some choice later in life to move into occupations that minimise the effect of their hyperactive symptoms (Weiss & Hechtman, 1993).

Parents can be helped to recognise the importance of supporting their child to maximise their social and academic skills but they cannot hold the weight of the future on their shoulders when they are coping on a daily basis. They need to face each day as it arrives and cope with the problems that emerge without being stressed by worries that they cannot immediately affect.

PSYCHOLOGICAL APPROACHES TO MANAGING HYPERACTIVE BEHAVIOUR: COPING WITH BEHAVIOUR PROBLEMS IN THE HOME

Compliance Training

Compliance training is an essential area of child management in which parents need to develop their confidence and skills. This is often the basis for much of the later behavioural training that is required. Parents may need to learn how to communicate effectively with their child, and this has several stages:

Establish attention control

Parents need to gain their child's attention by having their face at the same level as the child's, making sure that the child is facing them and making eye contact before the request is issued. The child must learn to stop what he or she is doing, look at the parents and listen to what is said. It is often helpful for the parent to ask the child to repeat the request to ensure that the child has listened to and understood what has been said.

Simple, direct request

Requests need to match the developmental level and memory skills of the child. For younger or very inattentive children one simple request at a time is important in order to train the child to listen and obey. Parents often make the mistake of issuing complex demands that have several instructions embedded in them. Alternatively they may issue a general demand that is not clear and specific. An instruction to 'clear up your room' is ambiguous as the child may just push clothes and toys to one side of the room or under the bed, while in fact the parent really intended the child to put away possessions in the correct drawers, cupboards and shelves. The parent needs to learn to be explicit about what is required.

Check on compliance

Parents often walk away once a request is made and expect the child to comply, but during this training phase it is necessary for the parents to maintain their attention on the child and wait for 10 seconds to ensure that the child has complied with the request. If the child complies then the parent should immediately reward the child with praise and a hug in order to provide positive feedback for the child's good behaviour. If the child has not complied then the parent needs to repeat the process and provide some additional physical or verbal prompts to encourage the child to comply. This is a process of teaching the child and can be used for teaching new skills.

Once the child has learnt the routine of what is expected of them at certain times of the day—e.g. get dressed by themselves, come to the table when they are called—then parents can use reward charts to provide the child with regular feedback about his or her compliant behaviour. The use of a simple star chart is a simple way of helping parents move out of a state of desperation when they feel that their child is not voluntarily doing anything that he or she should. A focus on small irritating problems can often produce a dramatic change in parents' feelings of competence.

Management of Aggression and Destructiveness

There are many good texts and manuals that describe parent training methods to manage antisocial behaviour (Bloomquist, 1996). All of the approaches follow a similar format of having a two-part process. Parents firstly need to be able to recognise positive qualities in their child and be able to praise the child genuinely and meaningfully. If parents have become emotionally distanced from their child and are being negatively coercive they may need to learn how to interact positively with their child before they can start to control the undesirable behaviours. Having a special play time with their child on a daily basis when they pay attention to their child's activity and join in positively in the play is a necessary starting point. Parents need to learn how to comment positively on their child during the play period by providing a narrative about what is happening without any evaluative or critical statements. This approach has been used successfully by therapists working with behaviourally disturbed children and their parents and has been called Child's Game (Forehand & McMahon, 1981; Barkley, 1987). The aim is for parents to become a reinforcing figure for the child rather than angry and negative in interaction.

The parents subsequently need to extend the range of their positive interaction outside the play setting and provide positive consequences for the child's good behaviour throughout the day. Reward charts, token, privileges, special leisure time activities or time with the parents can all be used as positive consequences depending on the age of the child and his or her preferences. Hyperactive children generally need to have a higher rate of positive reinforcement for their behaviour than other children. They tend not to habituate to reinforcers as do other children, and so parents need to be aware that the maintenance of reward programmes needs to be clear and consistent for long periods of time. The children need regular feedback about their behaviour and their attempts to control themselves.

The second stage of behaviour management is to teach parents how to withdraw their attention when the child is behaving inappropriately. Parents need to learn how to stay calm and ignore the child's behaviour. If such children are being destructive or potentially dangerous to themselves or anyone else, then ignoring is not possible. The parent has to carry out some action. Using a time out approach can be useful as long as the child is expected to stay in time out or to sit still only for short periods of time. The problem of trying to make a hyperactive child sit still may be inappropriate if the hyperactivity symptoms are too severe and the reason for time out is lost in the attempt to get the child to sit still.

With an older child a reward chart system may be established which provides concrete feedback to the child about his or her behaviour. This may be linked in with privileges, special leisure time activities with parents or special opportunities to purchase desired goods. Occurrence of destructive or aggressive behaviour may result in a response cost on such charts so that the child realises that there is an expense to behaving badly. Anger management training has also been used to teach children to control their emotional outbursts (Feindler, *et al.* 1984).

The parent training approach has been demonstrated to be very successful at managing the children's aggressive and antisocial behaviour but has not been shown to have any effect on attentional problems in children with ADHD (Pisterman, *et al.* 1992; Whalen *et al.* 1985).

Encouraging Concentration

Parents can help in providing incentives for the child to concentrate for progressively longer periods of time. They initially need to estimate the length of time their child is able to concentrate on any type of activity. It is possible to link positive consequences for defined increases of time spent attending and concentrating.

Some children are able to concentrate longer on a preferred activity but have very little perseverance with something that they find boring. There is also likely to be a difference between sedentary and active activities. Hyperactive children will generally find sedentary tasks related to school work difficult and parents can play a very important role in helping with concentration skills over homework tasks.

In order to help a child finish a task it can be divided up into discrete sections so that the child can complete one piece of the task within its defined concentration span and then have a break. Gradually by piecing together small sections of work the child can progress onto completing larger tasks and gain satisfaction from success. The child will require regular feedback and reinforcers for section and task completion.

If the task is sedentary then it may be appropriate for the child to intersperse this with a more active time as the break. In general it appears to be unwise to let the child race around frenetically as this tends to create over-excitement and it is then more difficult to settle down again (Taylor, 1986).

The child needs help and monitoring to achieve this type of progress and it takes a lot of patience and perseverance from the parents.

Children can be taught some direct measures for self-monitoring. For example, they may be able to keep a record of how often they get up from their seat during homework. They can be taught to evaluate their own behaviour and build in a reward process to successful attainments of targets. This process teaches a level of self-awareness and self-control but often it requires some backup reinforcement from the parents in order to maintain the child's attempts at self-control. If the parents do not care or do not show pleasure in the child's reports of their behaviour, then the child is likely to stop trying.

Reducing Impulsivity

In younger children this is related to teaching self-control. Many young hyperactive children have great difficulty in waiting for their turn in a game or to queue to use an activity at school or in the playground. Younger children will need to be physically prompted to wait by holding and guiding them until it is their turn. This can gradually be replaced by verbal prompts that indicate they are being good while they are waiting.

With older children impulsivity will be expressed in a variety of settings, both academically and socially. The children make careless mistakes in their work, don't check through what they have done, are disorganised and forgetful. The commonality is a high speed of response accompanied by many errors or inappropriate responses. It also can be seen as the result of a failure to think about the consequences of actions or the lack of ability to think about alternative actions and so can be viewed as a cognitive deficit (Baer & Nietzel, 1991). Self-instructional training is an approach that parents can teach and support (Kendall & Braswel, 1982, 1985). Children are taught to ask and then answer a series of questions that guide them systematically through the task. This has also been called self-statement modification and is applied to interpersonal tasks as well as academic ones (Dush *et al.*, 1989).

The Think Aloud Programme developed by Camp and Bash (1981, 1985) also developed this approach to attention control and reducing impulsivity. The children are taught initially to verbalise their thoughts. When the children are presented with a task they learn to focus attention by asking themselves aloud 'What have I got to do?' and then specifying the task aloud to themselves. They plan their strategy and actions by saying out loud 'How am I going to do this?'. During the task they say repeatedly 'Am I using my plan?' in order to check that they are doing what they set out to do. At the end of the task they say, 'How did I do?' in order to evaluate the task. Verbalising thoughts is one way of gaining control of actions, once the children have demonstrated sufficient control by talking aloud they can be prompted to whisper and gradually internalise their thoughts (Camp *et al.*, 1977; Meichenbaum & Goodman, 1971).

Children can use these techniques at school in the classroom but they often require prompting and encouragement to keep up their efforts, particularly if they are finding the work difficult. A range of additional techniques have been used to control impulsivity in children including modelling, strategy training and problem-solving training, and depending on the type of measurement used to evaluate the outcome of these treatment programmes, they have generally been shown to be effective although not to a dramatic level (Baer & Nietzel, 1991).

Improving Social Skills

Hyperactive children often have considerable social difficulty with their peers. Part of that difficulty can be their poor ability to negotiate peer group conflicts because of their impulsivity (Milich & Landau, 1982). This can occur within the pre-school age range and these children require help and training in how to react to other children. Some of the strongest predictors of social adjustment in children are their ability to offer alternative solutions to peer or authority type problems, and the ability to anticipate potential consequence to an interpersonal act. These skills are identifiable by 4 years of age. Children who have social difficulties, whether they are conduct disordered or hyperactive, can be helped by interpersonal cognitive problem solving (Shure & Spivak, 1978).

Children need to learn initially how to recognise and label feelings in themselves and others and that others can have different feelings from themselves. Once they can recognise emotions they need to learn how events relate and how one event can lead to another. The understanding of causal thinking is important in being able to anticipate possible outcomes of a course of actions. Children are then prompted to provide a range of solutions to either real-life social difficulties that they are experiencing or to hypothetical problems. The greater the number of different solutions to a problem that the child can produce, the greater is the child's potential for sociable behaviour. Aggressive children may only be able to produce ideas that are aggressive in answer to a problem where they want to get their own way, but sociable children will be able to suggest a range of methods including delayed gratification, e.g. waiting until the other children have finished what they are doing, asking someone else to help, pretending that they don't want the object, negotiating an exchange of another desired object, etc. Once the children can generate a range of ideas they need to be able to anticipate the consequences of each action and then choose the best solution.

This process encourages children to problem solve in social settings and realise their effect on other people. It provides a tool for them to use for more successful social interaction. Parents can also use it as a behaviour management method with their children directly.

CONCLUSION

This chapter has outlined the main psychological approaches to helping parents cope with their hyperactive children. In addition to these approaches many parents will have access to or be offered stimulant medication for their child or, more infrequently, a dietary approach to management. Medication is rapidly becoming the treatment of choice, particularly in the USA, but more recently in Britain. Research finding indicate that it has a marked effect on attentional difficulties and enables the child to benefit more from his or her educational experiences at school (Barkley, 1990). But medication alone is not likely to effect long-term improvement in academic achievement, antisocial behaviour or higher order cognitive processes (Shelton & Barkley, 1995).

Multi-modal approaches are important in providing a comprehensive package of care for families with children who have ADHD. Parent training has been found to reduce the increased stress experienced by parents of children with ADHD and will directly affect the co-morbid behavioural difficulties of antisocial behaviour that accompany ADHD (Anastopoulos *et al.*, 1993). It also supports behavioural improvements that are initially induced through medication. Approximately 20–30% of the school-aged population of children with ADHD do not respond to medication or show undesirable side effects, and so behavioural management approaches are then the only option. Multi-modal approaches combining the psychosocial and the medical interventions have the greatest chance of alleviating the multiple symptoms and areas of dysfunction that these children show. They have complementary effects and a wider range of symptoms can be treated than with either intervention alone. The use of both interventions together can allow lower medication dosages (Cantwell, 1996).

The complexity of symptomatology indicates that a package of care should include:

- medication to manage the biological components, i.e. attentional difficulties;
- special educational provision to manage the educational components, i.e. learning difficulties;
- family psychological support to manage the emotional and social components, i.e. family functioning and coping strategies;
- parental behaviour management training to manage the behavioural component, i.e. behaviour problems.

REFERENCES

Anastopoulos, A. D., Shelton, T. L., DuPaul, G. J. & Guevremont, D. C. (1993) 'Parent training for attention deficit hyperactivity disorder: Its impact on parent functioning'. *Journal of Abnormal Child Psychology*, **6**, 368-371.
Baer, R. A. & Nietzel, M. T. (1991) 'Cognitive and behavioural treatment of impulsivity in children: a meta-analytic review of the outcome literature'. *Journal of Child Clinical Psychology*, **30**, 400-412.
Barkley, R. A. (1987) *Defiant Children: A Clinician's Manual for Parent Training*. New York: Guilford Press.
Barkley, R. A. (1990) *Attention Deficit Hyperactivity Disorder: A Handbook for Diagnosis and Treatment*. New York and London: Guilford Press.
Bloomquist, M. L. (1996) *Skills Training for Children with Behaviour Disorders. A Parent and Therapist Guidebook*. New York: Guilford Press.
Camp, B.W. & Bash, M.A. (1981) *Think Aloud: Increasing Social and Cognitive Skills. A Problem Solving Approach for Children* (Primary Level) Champaign, Ill.: Research Press.
Camp. B. W. & Bash, M. A. (1985) *Think aloud. Classroom Program Grades 3-4.* Champaign, Ill.: Research Press.
Camp, B. W., Blom, G. E., Herbert, F. & van Doorninck, W. J. (1977) '"Think Aloud" : a program for developing self-control in young aggressive boys'. *Journal of Abnormal Child Psychology*, **5**, 157-169.
Cantwell, D. (1996) 'Attention deficit disorder: a review of the past 10 years'. *Journal of the American Academy of Child and Adolescent Psychiatry*, **35**, 978-987.
Douglas, J. E. (1991) *Is my Child Hyperactive?* Harmondsworth: Penguin.
Dush, D. M., Hirt, M. L. & Schroeder, H. E. (1989) 'Self-statement modification in

the treatment of child behaviour disorders: a meta-analysis'. *Psychological Bulletin*, **106**, 97-106.

Feindler, E. L., Marriott, S. A. & Iwata, M. (1984) 'Group anger control for junior high school delinquents'. *Cognitive Therapy and Research*, **8**, 299-311.

Forehand, R. & McMahon, R. (1981) *Helping the Non-compliant Child: A Clinician's Guide to Parent Training*. New York: Guilford Press.

Kendall, P. C. & Braswell, L. (1985) *Cognitive-Behavioural Therapy for Impulsive Children*. New York: Guilford Press.

Kendall, P. C. & Braswell, L. (1982) 'Cognitive-behavioural self control therapy for children: a components analysis'. *Journal of Consulting and Clinical Psychology*. **50**, 672-689.

Meichenbaum, D. H. & Goodman, J. (1971) 'Training impulsive children to talk to themselves: a means of developing self control'. *Journal of Abnormal Psychology*, **77**, 115-126.

Milich, R. & Landau, S. (1982) 'Socialization and peer relations in hyperactive children'. In K. Gadow & I. Bialer (Eds), *Advances in Learning and Behavioural Disabilities*, Vol. 1. Greenwich, CT: JAI Press.

Pisterman, S., Firestone, P., McGrath, P., Goodan, J. T., Webster, I., Mallory, R. & Goffin, B. (1992) 'The role of parent training in treatment of preschoolers with ADHD'. *American Journal of Orthopsychiatry*, 62, 397-408.

Shelton, T. L. & Barkley, R. A. (1995) 'The assessment and treatment of attention-deficit/hyperactivity disorder in children'. In M. C. Roberts (Ed.), *Handbook of Pediatric Psychology*, 2nd edition. New York: Guilford Press.

Shure, M. B. & Spivak, G. (1978) *Problem Solving Techniques in Child Rearing*, San Francisco: Jossey Bass.

Taylor, E. (1986) *The Hyperactive Child: A Parent's Guide*. London: Martin Dunitz.

Whalen, C. K., Henker, B. & Hinshaw, S. P. (1985) 'Cognitive-behavioural therapies for hyperactive children: premises, problems and prospects'. *Journal of Abnormal Child Psychology*, **13**, 391-410.

Weiss, G. & Hechtman, L. T. (1993) *Hyperactive Children Grown Up*, 2nd, edition. New York: Guilford Press.

10

STEPFAMILIES

Kathleen M. Cox

*A stepfamily is formed when a parent brings a
child from a previous relationship to a new
relationship*

INTRODUCTION

The need

Professional people encounter many members of stepfamilies in the
course of their working lives. Doctors, health visitors, school teachers in
the course of their routine work see patients, parents and pupils where
stepfamily issues are present to a greater or lesser extent. For social
workers, probation officers, educational psychologists, it is out of
proportion to the incidence in the population. They have seldom had
training working with stepfamilies and by trying to 'normalise' them
have done both positive harm (Visher & Visher, 1996) or offered no help
at all. Andrea, aged 19, found her husband's 16-year-old daughter hostile
and difficult to live with. Her GP, to whom she turned for help advised
her to 'be a normal mother', making her feel more inadequate than she
already did as a new wife and stepmother. Not knowing what to say the
GP used the inappropriate model of a 'normal family' for advice.

A different model is needed when the intergenerational boundaries
have been breached and the 'parent' and 'child' belong to the same
generation.

Some people, still say that 'this sort of thing does not happen in my
family', meaning that they marry, do not cohabit and once married stay

Enhancing Parenting Skills: A Guide Book for Professionals Working with Parents.
Edited by K. N. Dwivedi. © 1997 John Wiley & Sons Ltd.

married. As the Royal Family has discovered, no family is immune. Parents cannot control their adult children and still less their sons- and daughters-in-law. Vera suddenly realised that when her daughter-in-law left her son she could very easily lose her grandchildren if she did not desert the high moral ground and establish good relations with her son's replacement.

Many of the features of stepfamily life are embarrassingly obvious when pointed out. This does, however, have the advantage that when seen they are memorable and easily retained. The purpose of this chapter is to begin to show the gaps frequently left in professional training—to provide the spectacles to improve the vision. This is increasingly necessary as the numbers of vulnerable people grow. The General Household Survey, 1991 (1993) indicated that 8% of households with children included at least one stepchild and that 52% of all full-time stepfamilies has at least one child with the new stepcouple. In boarding schools it is not now uncommon for children to have two or more sets of stepparents in addition to their birth parents as second marriages fail more often than first—1 in 2 compared with 2 in 5 (Cockett & Tripp, 1994). Currently, 40,000 babies are born into stepfamilies and by the year 2000, three million children will be living in stepfamilies (Walker, 1995). These figures do not begin to refer to stepgrandparents and other members of the extended stepfamily, whose incidence is unknown but rising.

The Language

Writing about stepfamilies is problematic as the language is inadequate. To be precise can appear clumsy (he/she), or irrelevant to people who are not actually married but living as though married (divorced people are increasingly reluctant to marry again even though cohabiting on a long-term basis). Throughout this chapter, however, I shall use the word 'marriage' to mean a permanent relationship. I shall use the word 'traditional' for what is sometimes called a 'nuclear' family of the birth father and mother living together with their own joint children only. I shall use the word 'family' when adults take responsibility for children in a domestic situation; this can be part time and long term, as when children weekend with a natural parent. I shall use the plural form 'they' when the gender is irrelevant even when the situation more often applies to one gender than another, e.g. it is eight times more likely that the parent with whom the child does not reside is the father, but the issue is related to contact not gender. When, therefore, 'he' or 'she' is used the situation is gender specific.

The Situation

Stepfamilies are not new. The 1991 census of England and Wales reveals that about one in eight families had children being reared by someone other than their natural parent which is similar to the 1851 census (Stepfamily Fact File 3). In the late eighteenth century in Catholic France and Protestant England 30% of all marriages were second marriages for at least one partner (Clulow, 1988). Although the 'cornflakes' family, where beautiful happy healthy mother, father, son and daughter smile at each other over breakfast, is usually recognised as living somewhere other than 'our' house but it is all too frequently at the back of the mind when people talk about 'the family'. The mother at home, the father at work and their own two children is in fact only found now in 5% of households.

There has always been diversity in family forms. What is new is that they are now formed differently. In the past the parent died, whereas, while that still happens, most stepfamilies are brought about by the separation of the two parents who continue to live. One of them lives away from the children and either or both are inclined to form new partnerships, giving the children both stepfathers and stepmothers. The commonest stepfamily, 86%, is mother and children with stepfather in General Household Survey, 1991 (1993).

Stepfamilies are second choice; people do not fantasise in childhood about joining a stepfamily either as a parent or as a child. Quite the reverse is true. The stepmother in the children's fairy stories is an archetypal character to be feared. Children do not choose to have one for themselves and women do not choose to become one. (Stepfathers do not feature much in children's stories.)

THE NORMAL FAMILY (THE TRADITIONAL, NUCLEAR, STEREOTYPICAL FAMILY)

The stereotypical family is formed when a young man and young woman in their early twenties meet, get to know each other and marry. The wedding is a joyful occasion, a rite of passage, as the couple both move to the next stage in their lives. In the early stages of their marriage the bond between the couple strengthens, the household gradually develops its own norms, customs and lifestyle to suit them both.

When after some time together the first child is born the couple becomes a family. Both parents can see something of themselves in the baby. The baby's own personality and the pre-existing bond between the parents determine how the family develops. When a second child is born two or three years later, further changes have to be made and the family is complete.

It looks normal, the parents are a generation, i.e. twenty-five to thirty-five years older than their children, everyone has the same surname, the children have four grandparents and perhaps two or three aunts and uncles. Both parents believe that the other loves the children as much as they do themselves and have their children's best interests at heart. The children grow up in the family and repeat the process themselves some twenty-five years later (Figure 10.1).

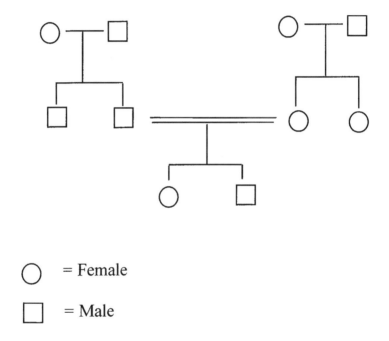

○   = Female

□   = Male

Figure 10.1:   Genogram of stereotypical family

At every stage there are possible variations. Few, if any, people will identify their family as exactly fitting this stereotype. Commonly there are more or fewer children born at different intervals, but staying married to the same person from early adulthood, living to old age and rearing their joint children together is the intention. Death and divorce intervene making first one-parent families and then reconstituted families creating infinite variations and the 'ab-normal' family more common.

HOW STEPFAMILIES DIFFER

The Members and Relationships

There are sixteen basic ways to form a stepfamily household when considering whether he, she or both bring children to the marriage and whether they do or do not have children together (Figure 10.2).

Part-time relationships, when children visit their absent parent, double this scenario and the history of death, divorce or single parenting is a further factor producing the 72 permutations of stepfamily (De'Ath, 1996) shown in Figure 10.3.

Most relationships are reciprocal, e.g. an aunt has a niece. In stepfamilies, however, anomalies occur when relationships are not reciprocated; a woman's child can have a stepmother whose own child has no relationship with her. Jennifer's ex-husband John married again. His second wife, Julia, is their daughter Jane's stepmother. Jane visits John often and knows Julia well. Julia and John's daughter, Gemma, however, never sees Jennifer, with whom she has no relationship socially or biologically.

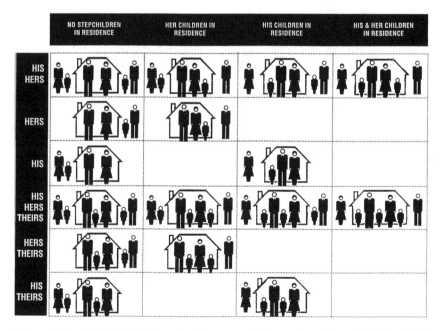

Figure 10.2: What kind of stepfamily are you? (Reproduced from De'Ath, 1996, p.76, by permission of The National Stepfamily Association.)

men

WOMEN	single — no children	single — resident children	single — non resident children	widower — no children	widower — resident children	widower — non resident children	divorced/separated — no children	divorced/separated — resident children	divorced/separated — non resident children
single — no children	■	1	2 part-time	■	3	4 part-time	■	5	6 part-time
single — resident children	7	8 stepsiblings	9 stepsiblings	10	11 stepsiblings	12 stepsiblings	13	14 stepsiblings	15 stepsiblings
single — non resident children	16 part-time	17 stepsiblings	18 part-time stepsiblings	19 part-time	20 stepsiblings	21 part-time stepsiblings	22 part-time	23 stepsiblings	24 part-time stepsiblings
widower — no children	■	25	26 part-time	■	27	28 part-time	■	29	30 part-time
widower — resident children	31	32 stepsiblings	33 stepsiblings	34	35 stepsiblings	36 stepsiblings	37	38 stepsiblings	39 stepsiblings
widower — non resident children	40 part-time	41 stepsiblings	42 part-time stepsiblings	43 part-time	44	45 part-time stepsiblings	46 part-time	47	48 part-time
divorced/separated — no children	■	49	50 part-time	■	51	52 part-time	■	53	54 part-time
divorced/separated — resident children	55	56 stepsiblings	57 stepsiblings	58	59 stepsiblings	60 stepsiblings	61	62 stepsiblings	63 stepsiblings
divorced/separated — non resident children	64 part-time	65 stepsiblings	66 part-time stepsiblings	67 part-time	68 stepsiblings	69 part-time stepsiblings	70 part-time	71 stepsiblings	72 part-time stepsiblings

Figure 10.3: A two-generational typology of stepfamily formation (72 permutations of stepfamilies). (Reproduced from Aleksander, 1995, p.17, by permission of The National Stepfamily Association.)

Values

The start of a stepfamily is more problematic than a normal family, more people, more complicated and more rush. There is not the time traditionally available before the children arrive in stepfamilies. Furthermore, they are not eagerly anticipated by both parties but come as part of a package with the desired adult. The children may not be wanted *per se*. They may also remind new partners physically of their predecessors and that there were sexual relationships with previous partners. Our stereotypic family were virgin adults. Both of these situations can be hard to admit.

Child-rearing practices differ. Stepchildren have been described as half formed to someone else's pattern. What can seem to be of major importance is often merely a different way of doing something.

Tina took on two children, in addition to her own two, when she married Doug. Every morning she was increasingly angry when Doug's children came down to breakfast in their pyjamas. They had been brought up to do this to ensure that their clothes stayed clean for school. Tina had brought up her children to dress first and then eat breakfast. The reality was that it didn't really matter which way it was done, but under the fraught conditions of getting four children ready for school it was becoming a big issue. Tina did recognise that it was just a different way even though not her way.

History (The 3 Gs)

Stepfamilies do not have the joyful innocent start of the stereotypical young couple. There is always a history, a death or a failure of a relationship and the powerful presence of Grief, Guilt and Ghosts. Sarah, aged 19, with her big white wedding, childhood dreams of marriage and limited life experience, tried not to think of her more mature new husband's children beyond dressing them up as cute bridesmaids. She was totally unprepared (as indeed was he) for his grief at not living with them, his guilt that he was not the good father he intended to be and the influence his former wife still exerted.

Grief

Stepfamilies are formed from loss. There may have been a death when the loss is recognisable, or more often the death of a relationship and the hopes that went with it. Even in these cynical days people do not enter marriage thinking it will end. When they promise 'till death do us part', that is the intention. When two people become responsible parents they do not foresee that one will live elsewhere and only know their child on the basis of visits.

When losses occur there are well recognised stages of grief through which the bereaved have to pass before they can make new lives without the loved person or ideal (Worden, 1983); the recognition of the loss, feeling the pain of the loss and finally establishing a life with a new focus.

The first stages are not pleasant. When John's wife died after a long distressing illness, he could not wait to give his children the family life they had been missing. He remarried within a year after which he began to be depressed and grieve for his first wife. His new wife assumed there was something wrong with her as she struggled to provide the family life she had agreed to do at the outset. John, trying to avoid feeling the pain of his loss, was actually making matters worse. Not ready to make changes he was expecting his new wife to be a replica of his old, and not giving her a chance to be a wife in her own way.

People need different amounts of time for each of the processes of mourning. In a family one member may be ready to move on when others are still in the earlier stages. It is not uncommon for young children to urge a parent to find a new partner. Gary, aged 5, told his mother 'we need a new daddy now', when his father left. The practicality of children can appear insensitive and be painful.

Conversely, children's need to grieve for both people and families can be ignored; too inconvenient or too difficult to handle. When Mary decided to marry Pete three years after her husband had died, her 13-year-old daughter Lisa refused to have anything to do with her new stepfather, made it very clear that he could not replace her father (which he had no intentions of trying to do) and generally made life difficult for the new family trying to establish itself. Her younger brother, Mark, liked Pete and what he brought to the family. As far as Lisa was concerned, this was unforgivable. Lisa had not been encouraged to go to her father's funeral, grandmother in particular stating it was 'not a nice place for children'. She was at an early stage in her grieving while her mother had moved on.

The early stages of becoming a one-parent family are often physically difficult with losses being all too apparent. There are often shortages of money, time and attention to children as parents are busy elsewhere. Parents unintentionally become dependent on their children for both practical and emotional support, and strong family units are formed. Children rightly take a pride in their contribution to this and often perform heroically. Debbie, aged 9, looked after her younger sister responsibly, bringing her home from school, making her tea and giving up her own time to play with her when her father left home and her mother, Patsy, suddenly had to take a full-time job. Patsy said she 'didn't know what she would have done without Debbie' and genuinely acknowledged her help. When, however, Patsy announced that their troubles were over and Dave was going to move in, Debbie became angry and declared that they didn't need him and were all right as they were. She felt rejected and that all that she had done was not valued. She became a 'difficult teenager', rude and difficult to Dave especially and Patsy wondered what had happened to her lovely daughter. What Patsy had needed as a transitional stage between her two marriages was a permanent family form for Debbie who tried so hard to make it work. Debbie saw her father and regarded him as such, although she recognised that he would never live with her mother again she did not envisage newcomers either.

When families are ended by divorce and the other parent is alive but elsewhere, unlike Debbie, children are often loath to accept the reality of the loss and harbour fantasies of their parents reunited and living happily ever after. The hopes and wishes of children of divorced parents persist for many years, frequently into adult life. They cannot accept the remarriage of either parent as to do so would be to accept the loss which they are both unwilling and unable to do. Fathers repartner more rapidly than mothers. Jane, aged 12, refused to have anything to do with her father when he married again a year after leaving an acrimonious marriage, the details of which she was only too well aware. Her solution was for her parents to stop quarrelling, not to start again elsewhere. Sadly, Jane's 12-year-old wishes were taken seriously by all concerned, and when she finally grew up and recognised the additional loss she had brought on herself, she contacted her father. She thinks with embarrassment of how she rejected her stepmother without ever meeting her, as she now recognises as an adult how many common interests they have and how much she likes her.

Guilt

Guilt is a feeling which is an essential part of the grieving process. It is also one which is often taken to a new family. Children frequently inappropriately blame themselves when their parents separate. The day James' father left home he had been naughty at school. Perhaps he sensed intuitively that all was not well and his naughtiness was really an expression of anxiety. At 6 years of age, he did know this and was even less able to say so. He just carried around with him for a long time a feeling that it was all his fault and if only he had been good his daddy would never have left. Because he did not say, no one knew what he thought and felt.

Guilt is about 'if only' and what should or should not have been done. When a person or a relationship is dying, feelings of helplessness predominate. When it is ended there are thoughts of what more could have been done either to avoid the loss or to make it easier to bear. It is always possible to have been a better wife, father, whatever. But the past cannot be made good in the present.

The slow ending of a relationship is often driven by guilt and triggered by the presence of a third party. Mike had an affair with Judy for many years. When he did eventually leave his wife he felt very guilty, especially about his children. His relationship with Judy was dogged by this guilt, his children were never refused any material things, his weekends were devoted to taking them out. His wife refused to allow them to have anything to do with Judy, a demand to which he acceded because he felt so guilty and did not wish to hurt her more. When finally the children did go to Judy's home he refused to check their bad behaviour for the same reason. He complained that his life was a nightmare 'piggy in the middle'.

Recognising that his guilt determined all his actions and actually caused many of his recent problems enabled him to assess his own wishes and priorities, recognise that Judy was the woman he wanted to spend the rest of his life with and assert himself. Paradoxically his new-found strength, when he stopped trying to be the 'good guy', meant that his worst fears were not realised; his children respected him more as he acted like a responsible parent disciplining them and he helped his former wife to move forward and establish a life of her own by not allowing her to remain in control of him. Although Judy insists that the marriage was over before she came on the scene her lingering doubts and fears that she might actually have taken the father from his children are what made her tolerate such poor treatment from Mike.

Guilt can also take the form of 'feeling sorry for'. Because the children have sustained loss, both parents try to compensate either by buying things or by making few demands on the children. At the age of 12 Alice had never washed a dish because her mother, Jean, felt sorry for her (as well as for herself) as her father had left home four years previously and she did not want to impose an extra burden on her. When Jean married Tom he was astounded at how little Alice could and would do about the house compared with his own 9-year-old daughter.

Stepparents also feel sorry for children whose childhood has been interrupted by loss and want to rescue them from their one-parent family state. Pauline, a career woman with no children of her own was determined to be 'a good mother' to her new husband's children. She spent the evenings cooking interesting and nourishing food for children who preferred beans and fish fingers to home-made moussaka and did not want to be rescued. They rejected her food and she felt rejected. The more rejected she felt the harder she tried, etc. Pauline needed to recognise that it was not only her desire to succeed but her image of childhood with its cosy home-made food which contributed to a rapidly worsening situation.

Ghosts

All stepfamilies have an absent parent. They may be absent through death or living apart but either way they are in the background exerting an influence. Fifty years ago the advice to absent parents following the rare event of divorce (Anna Freud) was 'have nothing more to do with your children', allow them to build a new life without you. Until relatively recently men often traded maintenance for contact. Colin left Hazel and their two daughters for Heather with whom he started a new family. He wanted to see his first children but, short of money for his new family, agreed not to do so in return for Hazel forgoing maintenance for both herself and the children.

The 1989 Children Act states that parental responsibility may not be shed, and specifying that contact is the right of the child and not of the parent, money and contact are separated in theory at least. The Child Support Act 1991 firmly acknowledges that each parent has a financial responsibility for any child they have.

It is the right of the child to know both their birth parents because this is beneficial to their mental health in adult life. Adults need to know their origins as a significant strand in their identity. Tom was reared in a loving home by his mother and stepfather but they could not understand his desire to be a violinist, pointing to the uncertainties and poor financial prospects. When he discovered his natural father was a talented amateur musician, he felt happier about his own wishes which had previously been so hard to explain.

Following divorce adults often want to have nothing more to do with their former partner and to make a clean break. Where the children's needs are considered this is not really an option even though contact visits can be very difficult. Stepparents often complain that the absent parent controls their lives by dictating when their children can and cannot visit, and that the influence of the former partner never goes away. It may be inconvenient with weekends frequently disrupted, and when the two parents live a long way apart it can also be very expensive of time and money.

When relations are strained between the parents, as they often are, contact visits can be dreaded for the after effects. In intact households parents disagree as to how children should be brought up. When the parents live separately this is heightened. Mothers complain vociferously that their children have been allowed to stay up beyond their normal bed-times and watch unsuitable videos on contact visits. Fathers express equally strong concerns that their children are not doing what they think important, often having to share with step and half brothers and sisters. Stepparents feel powerless and criticised.

Criticism is often veiled and indirect, a continuation of the quarrels in the marriage of former marriage partners. Nick had always disagreed with Josie's free-spending habits when they were married. When their son, Josh, visited Nick and referred to a recent extravagant purchase by Josie, with what Nick regarded as 'his' money for maintenance, Nick's ensuing criticism was habitual rather than related to the issue. Josie thought she was free of this, her new partner resentful and Josh confused.

There is also the less tangible influence of the absent parent in terms of the way we do things in this family; the practices and traditions which have grown up before the stepparent joined the family. When are Christmas presents opened? Linda was horrified in her first Christmas in her stepfamily when her stepchildren ripped open their presents in the very early hours of the morning before she and their father were awake. She and her own children always opened them together after breakfast on Christmas Day. An annual event can be anticipated and accommodated next year but many others are more regular. Do the children help themselves to what they find in the fridge or do they ask permission or wait for meals? Pat described 'It might have "just been a piece of cheese" to him (Dan, her adolescent stepson). To me it was a meal for four'. To Dan, Pat's display of anger was more evidence of her irrationality and impossibility and how his life had changed for the worse since her arrival.

If the parent is dead there can be a real feeling of having a ghost in the family. Sometimes the place is like a shrine, pictures of the deceased parent in prominent and respectful positions which is right for the children but not for the new spouse. For this reason it is better not to move into the house, bed and kitchen of the predecessor, however much economic sense it makes, as the presence and taste of the predecessor is everywhere. Helen, Jack's deceased wife, was left-handed. Every time Emma, this new wife, pulled the curtains or used a kitchen tool she was reminded of Helen (whom she had never met!). The past has to be included when a family gets new members but for a stepfamily to succeed it must change to suit all.

The dead can be abused and given undue power to the advantage of the living using both our cultural stricture of not speaking ill of the dead and the impossibility of ascertaining their true views. It is not uncommon to hear 'this is what your mother would have wanted', which cannot be verified but is a pressure not found in other families. When Meg died, one of her closest friends, Joan, married her husband Alan and became the stepmother to Ollie and Matt, whom she had known all their lives. Joan thought she knew what she was taking on, moved into Meg's old place and began by respecting her late friend's wishes. Joan soon found that she was becoming a cipher and her wishes irrelevant. Alan and the boys just had to say that was what Meg would have wanted and she was expected to do it.

The Couple

In all families it is the strength of the bond between the adults which provides security for the children. In the stereotypic family the couple know each other and develop their bond before the children arrive. In stepfamilies this is not the case. The courtship has often been conducted with the children very much in evidence; if both partners have children it can take the form of constant children's outings. Even without this, when a stepfamily is formed there are at least three people to consider (often more) who do not have the luxury of getting to know each other slowly. There is often a great deal of work to do, giving the new couple little leisure time to spend alone—a situation made worse if there are adolescent children who do not go to bed early enough to leave them with evenings to themselves. The failure to develop and maintain the couple bond is understandable but is also one of the reasons why more second marriages (1 in 2) fail than first marriages.

When parents remarry it is appropriate for their children to be present and involved. The ceremony reflects a change of status which applies to them as well as the adults and is a public recognition of that (Cox, 1995b). Many couples proudly proclaim that they are taking their children on honeymoon. This is a mistake as it is one of the few times the couple can be alone. It is an opportunity to be grasped for them to strengthen their relationship and begin the marriage.

TYPES OF STEPFAMILY

Five types of stepfamily have been defined, depending upon when it was formed in the life cycle of the child. Each type has its own characteristic strengths and difficulties.

The 'Normal Family'

The first is 'not really a stepfamily' (Burgoyne & Clark, 1984), formed when the child is a baby or even before it is born. This family looks like a normal family; the adults and the child learn to be a family together. There will, however, be some history and the inevitable question of whether and how to tell the child that the person who acts as the parent is not the birth parent. Origins form an important part in developing a sense of self and personal identity. These children need to know their parents, to understand their origins and subsequently themselves. Very often the mother convinces herself that it is better that they should not know their birth father as she makes a new life for herself. These children can become angry when they find their mother has kept them from their father.

Best opinion is currently to allow the child to grow up with this knowledge. This means that there is never a day when children are suddenly told that what they had hitherto believed is not true. This is to be avoided, not only for the shock but also because, when children begin to revise what they believe to be true, they may begin to wonder what else is there in their lives that they can no longer trust.

More practical reasons for telling children about their fathers are that it may not prove possible to withhold the information and others may reveal it in ways which are not as sensitive as the parent would wish. When Jake was 6, he overheard his grandparents say how much he resembled his 'real' father. He could not ask what this meant and didn't understand; he just got angry and remained so for many years. He developed a rich fantasy life about his 'real' father whom he regarded as successful, powerful and who must surely rescue him when life got difficult. There is always the danger that absent fathers are hero-worshipped.

There may also need to be genetic information related to risk factors in illness which people need to manage their health.

The Proud Stepfamily

The second type of family is formed when the children are older and always know that one of the adults in the household is not their birth parent. This family consciously pursues family life, expects difficulties, recognises the new start for all and makes up its rules as it goes along. All members are seen as important. The adults respect their children and listen to them but remain in control and make the decisions. The unexpected things which happen when stepfamilies form are acknowledged and not dismissed as irrelevant. For example, when two families come together the birth order will be altered; there can be only one eldest child and the other eldest or only child loses their previous status. Kate realised from the outset that her new stepson, previously an only child, found her three daughters noisy and rumbustious. As she managed to give him the quiet he was used to, he relaxed and came to be able to enjoy the rough and tumble of his three stepsisters.

Different families place different emphasis on sport, music, academic achievement. Mary had sent her daughters to music lessons and with considerable effort on her part they were passing successive exams. When she married George, he thought that practising in the holidays was a bit of a joke, formed an alliance with the girls and their musical success ceased. The family was, however, successful and the recognition of different values by Mary was part of what made it so.

The Embarrassed Stepfamily

The third type of stepfamily also has members who know their birth history and pursues family life but tries to look like a 'normal' family rather than accept its true stepfamily status. This is the family which most often has problems. It uses a pattern that does not fit. Gloria had lived with Lisa for twelve years as a single parent when she married Jim. Aged 14, Lisa liked Jim at first but when he wanted her to call him 'Dad' she refused. Jim, a policeman, was used to being obeyed; he refused to accept the advice given which did not support his wishes and the situation deteriorated rapidly. To Gloria's surprise, Lisa went looking for and found her birth father 'in whom she had never expressed any interest before'!

When Freda married Phil, she wanted her children to change their name to his so that they looked 'more like a family'. Ben, aged 9, refused adamantly to do so; to him this meant betraying, his dead father. Simon, aged 11, was more amenable to her suggestion, causing problems between the two boys which had never existed before. Mary's insistence of pursuing her family dream had unforeseen consequences and was Ben's 'reason' for rejecting Phil. (When the birth father is alive and living elsewhere a change of name can only be achieved legally, with his expressed permission, if the parents were married or there would be issues of contempt of court. For this reason many school registers and health records contain discrepancies with children named one last name but 'known as' another.)

Stepfamilies often have very limited resources of time as well as money, about which its members become increasingly resentful. Jed and

Jill had two children each when they got together in their two-bedroomed flat. Jill's children lived with them during the week and visited their father at weekends. Jed's children lived with their mother and visited them at weekends. Jill's life seemed to be an endless round of washing, changing beds and cooking. Her children resented their room being used in their absence; his children felt they weren't allowed to do anything or touch anything and were visitors in their father's house. The situation was not helped by Jed playing football every Saturday 'as he always had', 'his one relaxation'. The failure was almost inevitable, there was too much to do with too few resources, too many people, and too little time. There was also too little willingness to accept the consequences of the decisions made and the reality of the new situation and re-appraise what mattered.

The Mid-Life Family

The fourth stepfamily involves older children, teenagers, where the parents are described as 'waiting to become a couple'. The children live in the same house as their parent but there is little attempt on the part of either the children or the adults to function as a family. Parental behaviour on the part of the incoming adult is resented by the children and for the relationship to be successful the adult has to assume an avuncular rather than a parental role. Relations can be formed round mutual interests. Derek liked going to football matches with his wife Dot's son Dan. As long as he confined it to that (paying for the tickets, taking him, etc.) this was fine by Dan. Discipline, however, rightly remained Dot's responsibility and the household only worked when she assumed it, much as she would have liked Dan's help from time to time.

Teenage behaviour is often regarded as offensive or ungrateful even by birth parents. If the new adult has no experience of children this can be difficult, and if they have, invidious comparisons can be made with their own. Teenagers in particular feel no need to be 'rescued' from one-parent family status. This family can coexist satisfactorily by accepting its limitations and waiting for the time when the couple will be alone, as a couple, which was their intention from the outset.

The Empty Nest Family

The fifth type of stepfamily may not even recognise itself as a stepfamily initially. It is formed when people who have adult children living elsewhere marry. These children can be over 60 years old themselves when their longer living surviving parent chooses to remarry. On a day-to-day basis this is no problem although adult children often resent their widowed parents marrying again, seeing this as disloyal to the memory of the deceased, and can cause irrational resentments. There can be real difficulties over possessions and inheritance. A will needs to be made and the contents known to the children (Clout, 1993).

There are also less tangible problems as family members continue their previous ways regardless of changed circumstances. When Mollie married Brian, both in their late seventies, she went to live in the flat where he had formerly lived alone. His children had keys to this flat and continued to let themselves in at will, regardless of what Mollie was doing or where she was. This was aggravated by being acceptable to Brian who failed to recognise the need to change with his new situation or to accept his new wife's feelings.

PROBLEMS

Money is even shorter in stepfamilies than in other households with children (Fact File 2). They are more likely to live in crowded conditions (2.1 children per household compared with 1.8 and more likely to live in an inferior standard of housing). Poverty is also one of the main reasons for being taken into care. This necessitates both parents working even though they often have more children and more domestic duties resulting in tiredness, irritability and strained relations. Britain with its 'long working hours equals true commitment to the job' mentality, not surprisingly has one of the highest divorce rates in Europe.

Telephone calls to the stepfamily counselling help line reveal problems specific to women and to men (Batchelor *et al.*, 1994). Interestingly, although the majority of stepfamilies (one in eight) consist of a mother, children and stepfather the majority of callers to the help line (also one in eight) are stepmothers. The main problems for stepmothers are feelings of exploitation that they have only been married for the three 'C's, childcare, cooking and cleaning. A typical complaint of a stepmother 'I never thought it would be like this' relates to the childcare that her husband gave his children prior to marriage and which she assumed would continue (Cox, 1995a). As each slipped into stereotyped roles she found he was expecting her to provide childcare, giving very little support to do so. The husbands describe being 'piggy in the middle' when they feel the divided loyalties between their wives and children. The refusal to 'take sides' frequently means they fail to consider the issue.

The problems for stepfathers relate to the three 'D's; they feel they are only wanted for DIY, Discipline and 'Dosh' (Henry, 1995). When the mother is protective of her children, and the way she has brought them up, her new husband can feel excluded from any real decision making in the family. As a newcomer to an existing family unit he can have real difficulty in finding a role beyond bringing money and practical skills. Initially he does this willingly but in return he needs some personal recognition and status. His wife may ask for help disciplining the children, but he often complains that any attempts he makes to do so are rejected by her as 'too harsh', 'inappropriate', etc. The children themselves reject his authority if it has not been earned.

SUMMARY

Stepfamilies are formed from loss, and the individuals come together with previous family histories. The parent–child relationship predates the new couple relationship and there is a birth parent either in actuality or in memory with power and influence over family members. Children are often members of two households which have different characteristics and in which they have different roles.

The problems presented by stepfamilies appear to be caused mainly by a lack of understanding and acceptance of the individuals needs—whether parent, stepparent, child or stepchild.

Life in a stepfamily can be rewarding and satisfying but is even less easy than in a 'normal' family. There can, however, be big pluses to living in stepfamilies when the differences are acknowledged and their own styles found. Children can have two different homes where they are accepted as family members. They can have four parent figures to be there for them as needed and, at best materially, have two annual holidays and celebrate Christmas and birthdays twice. They can also learn that different styles of family can be equally valuable.

When unrealistic role models are abandoned and all the members of the family contribute to developing the norms, stepfamilies can be tough secure places from which children are prepared for the outside world. They do, however, need help at critical periods and the professionals to whom they turn for advice need to know about stepfamilies.

APPENDIX

- Many children are reared by people other than their birth parents. The correct names for their relationships and status are necessary for legal and social reasons.

- *Adoption*. When a child is adopted there is no distinction between their rights and privileges and those of a birth child. The parents have all the responsibilities. Stepparents are not legally responsible until they adopt formally.
- Half-brother or half-sister have one parent in common with each other.
- Stepbrothers or stepsisters have parents who have married, but they do not have a parent in common. They may or may not be brought up in the same household but do not have blood relationship. If their respective parents have a child together then they all have a half-sibling.
- Foster children are children in care to the local authority and the adults who look after them are paid to act as parents on a day-to-day basis but do not have full legal responsibility.

REFERENCES

Aleksander, T. (1995) *His, Hers, Theirs: A Financial Handbook for Stepfamilies*. London: Stepfamily Publications.

Batchelor, J., Dimmock, B. & Smith, D. (1994) *Understanding Stepfamilies: What Can be Learnt from Callers to the STEPFAMILY Telephone Counselling Service*. London: Stepfamily Publications.

Burgoyne, M. & Clark, (1984) *Breaking Even: Divorce, Your Children and You*. Harmondsworth: Penguin.

Clout, I. (1993) *Where there's a Will, there's a Way: Making a Will in a Stepfamily*. London: Stepfamily Publications.

Clulow, C. (1988) Proceedings of Conference: *Working with Stepfamilies*. London.

Clulow, C. & Mattinson, J. (1989) *Marriage inside Out; Understanding Problems of Intimacy*. Harmondsworth: Penguin.

Cockettt, M. & Tripp, J. (1994) *The Exeter Family Study: Family Breakdown and it's Impact on Children*. Exeter: University of Exeter Press.

Cox, K. M. (1995a) 'The "Cinderella Complex" in men with children (how stepmothers are made wicked)'. *Forum*, No. 81. Leicester: British Psychological Society.

Cox, K. M. (1995b) *Another Step: Weddings in Stepfamilies*. London: Stepfamily Publications.

De'Ath, E. (1988) *What is a Stepfamily?* Proceedings of Conference: *Working with Stepfamilies*. London.

De'Ath, E. (1996) *Families in Transition: Keeping in Touch when Families Part*, London: Stepfamily Publications, p.76.

Henry, M. (1995) *Training Day for Stepfamily Telephone Counsellors*, (Personal Communication).

Visher, E. B. & Visher, J. S. (1996) *Therapy with Stepfamilies*, New York: Brummer & Mazel.

Walker, J. (1995) *The Cost of Communication Breakdown*. London: The BT Forum.

Worden, J. W. (1983) *Grief Counselling and Grief Therapy*. London: Routledge.

The National Stepfamily Association has many booklets on specific aspects of stepfamily life in addition to a series of Fact Files. National Stepfamily Association, 3rd Floor, Chapel House, 18 Hatton Place, London EC1N 8RU.

11

PARENTING OF GIFTED CHILDREN

David George

This chapter is primarily for parents who are seen as partners in the educational process with the professionals to make children whole. However, the chapter will be helpful to all concerned in the education of children and, of course, many teachers are parents themselves. It is based on the assumption that children are the most precious natural resource in the world and that parents are the most important teachers a child ever has, particularly in the early crucial years. Parents need to be familiar with the language of education and to know what is going on in schools. If very young children could articulate their feelings, they might well say 'learning about myself and the world around me is my work. Your part is loving and supporting me'. Good parenting, then, is an essential part of educating children, but there are some obstacles, risks, challenges, errors and joys that accompany the parent of a child with gifts and talents. This is where it is essential for teachers and parents to be sensitive to each others' problems and help one another.

This chapter will emphasise some practical approaches to the education of gifted and talented children and aims to be different from what has already been written.

We will begin this discussion by looking at what every child needs. The healthy status of an individual is considered to be governed by the biological integrity and the dynamics of the social cultural factors within the individual's environment. A child's health, due to his or her dependence, is greatly influenced by the health of the family unit and the

Enhancing Parenting Skills: A Guide Book for Professionals Working with Parents.
Edited by K. N. Dwivedi. © 1997 John Wiley & Sons Ltd.

qualitative nature of the relationship between members of the family and the wider world. The fact that education has recognised the influence of such factors upon a child's learning is reflected in official educational documents which consistently emphasise the relationships between the child's home, community and school. Space does not allow further discussion on the health of a child, but to remind readers, the World Health Organisation defines health as 'the state of complete physical, mental and social well-being and not merely the absence of disease and infirmity'. With this definition in mind, health is a vital aspect in the total development of all our children, and parents have an important role to play in ensuring that children have adequate sleep, nutrition, exercise and peace of mind.

The interaction of negative emotion and needs of an individual is outlined admirably in Maslow's Hierarchy of Human Needs (1954)—see Figure 11.1.

Maslow's model asserts that it is necessary that an individual's needs are satisfied before higher levels can be met, and suggests that emotions reflect the level of satisfaction which an individual experiences. These levels are dynamic, and are dependent upon the individual's capacity to meet the safety, psychological and self-actualisation needs. This self-actualisation means the full development of a child's capabilities and talents. It is essential to have a child's physiological needs met first, and unfortunately in the world, there are too many children wallowing at the base of the pyramid. Secondly, there is a need to feel that the world is organised and predictable and a child feels safe, secure and stable within that basic need. Thirdly, a child needs to have some self-esteem, as well as the esteem of other people. This means to achieve the best of which they are able, to be competent and independent and to have a need for recognition and respect from others. All children need to feel secure, loved and to have the opportunity to love others. When these basic needs are met, motivation will direct behaviour towards fulfilling the higher level needs, which means the needs to live up to one's fullest and unique potential, to know and understand, and the needs for beauty and order and, finally, self-actualisation.

From these basic human needs, both parents and teachers will note that gifted and talented children will need to learn skills to develop their effective base before the acquisition of competent skills can occur, and they need to integrate their skills to meet the fundamental needs of their children.

THE EARLY CRUCIAL YEARS

One of the ways to help our ablest, very young children, is to admit them to school earlier than is normal and, indeed, most children now have the

```
SELF-ACTUALISATION        * self concept
       ↑                  * benefiting others
       |                  * independence
       |                  * persistence
       |                  * concentration
       |                  * developing your talents

SELF-ESTEEM               * vision
       ↑                  * significance
       |                  * positive attitude
       |                  * confidence
       |                  * knowing your talents
       |                  * esteem of others

AFFILIATION               * caring
       ↑                  * expressing yourself
       |                  * understanding
       |                  * listening
       |                  * love and friendship

SAFETY                    * comfort
       ↑                  * consistency
       |                  * predictability
       |                  * security

PHYSIOLOGICAL             * exercise
                          * sleep
                          * liquids
                          * food
                          * fresh air
```

Figure 11.1:   Maslow's hierarchy of human needs (from George, 1992).

opportunity to go to school in England soon after the age of 4, and this has been well supported by research (Reynolds, 1976; Proctor, 1986). While these studies have varied in their criteria for selecting students and in their methods for ascertaining success, the general conclusions have consistently been in favour of early admission to school. It is, however, important that these children are well screened before being admitted and some teachers are very cautious, in that early entry into school may cause personal as well as academic and social problems. This is where parents and teachers should work closely together and look at some of the variables before making the decision. The following are some other points that should be carefully considered.

Reading readiness

This is a skill which is most crucial to early school success and, of course, many gifted children are able to read prior to school entrance.

Gender

We have to remember that males do mature later and that it is often young girls who are more physically mature and, therefore, are ready to go to school earlier than boys.

Eye/hand coordination

Children admitted earlier should have reasonable motor skills, otherwise this could put unnecessary stress on a young child who is unable to draw, cut materials and write.

Health

The early years are a time for common ailments to be caught by children and the child who has a history of good health is more likely to attend school regularly and be able to concentrate.

Social, emotional and physical maturity

This is largely the decision of the parent, in consultation with the teacher, because it is essential that the child is really ready to appreciate and gain from going to school early. This means the support of the family that values education.

Many parents are sensitive observers of their own children and know when their children have special talents. This is where parents can inform teachers that their youngsters have unique abilities, and a joint evaluation can then take place.

Teachers may be able to help parents by discussing the following:

1. Is your child curious about the world and keen on exploring and discovering its meaning?
2. Is your child interested in the whys and wheres, as well as the hows and the whys, as well as always asking questions?

3. Is your child really well above the age level and is possibly even self-taught?
4. Does the child have a good vocabulary?
5. Did your child start to walk and talk earlier than average ?
6. Does your child show special abilities in such areas as problem solving, art, music and even mathematics?
7. Does your child appear to be unusually attentive and able to concentrate?
8. Does your child show advanced motor skills and is your child good at physical activities?

This would be a useful checklist to help schools assess a child's base line on entry to the reception class. An honest discussion of these characteristics would be most helpful in identifying gifted and talented children and in coming to a decision as to early admission to school.

To find out whether your child has gifts and talents is one thing, but we have to remember that this is a continuing process, because your child's needs, interests and behaviour change with time. Also, a child's growth and development is uneven, and therefore, continuous assessment and recording of behaviour in discussion with the school is very important. Likewise, children make sense of their world by using their senses and should be given every opportunity to expose them to a variety of experiences. For example, your child needs the experience of playing the piano to show outstanding talent in that field. The more opportunities your child has to take part in a wide range of activities, the more likely it will be that his or her gifts and talents will be detected. This is not to say that you should be rigid, but be flexible in the use of time to accommodate interests and encourage perseverance.

We know that the environment begins to exert an influence on the child before birth and that a favourable pre-birth environment will enhance intellectual growth and development. Young children are unique genetically and their IQ has a strong inherited base, but that intelligence is manifold and more than the narrow quality measured by IQ tests. We also now know that they need optimum environments to maximise their potential, and that domains other than the cognitive must be considered in our search for the early precursors of giftedness, and should not be studied apart from the environmental factors. Education in the early years in general has long practised individual learning by the children, creating a unique environment for each child and, ideally, this should carry through to the secondary phase of education, although it is harder here because of the needs of the individual and the demands of society for a flow of trained manpower. There is some incompatibility between an individual's needs and those of society, as witnessed by the controversial debate in education at the present time, but basically, as indicated earlier, individual learning is sound both educationally and biologically.

The concept of gifted infants is unwarranted and the reality is probably that, during this period, there is only potential for giftedness that requires an optimum environment for full development.

Burton White (White, *et al.*, 1979) described the work of his Harvard project, in which he studied the development of several hundred children over some twelve years. In these studies, it was found that the average Western environment can be expected to contain all that it needed for the development of most human abilities during the first few months of life, and that there is evidence that the rate of achievement of abilities in these first months can be substantially increased. In addition, children can learn to use their hands as reaching tools by three and a half months, rather than by five. Brierley (1978) states that at the age of 5, the brain has reached 95% of its adult weight and, by this time, he suggests that half of the intellectual growth of a child is complete.

The Harvard project discovered that by the end of the second year of life, an infant has gained two-thirds to three-quarters of all the language she will ever use in ordinary conversation for the rest of her life, including all the major grammatical elements in her native language and a receptive vocabulary of about a thousand words. In addition an infant at this age will have developed thinking skills, most of the attitudes towards learning and a full range of social skills.

Parents, who are the most important teachers that a child ever has, should be aware of this rapid development of intelligence during the early years, as well as the crucial development stages, and that a child craves experience.

The brain has a timetable of development altered by experience. For instance, a child is able at about the age of 3 to start searching systematically for experiences and, therefore, children at play is a serious business. It is about work learning, not about relaxation. With this in mind, play is sophisticated and toys need to look and sound as real as possible; for example, a graded abacus and a toy telephone. This is also why pre-school education has lasting benefits and a diversity of provision will reap many rewards in terms of the quality of life of a child into adulthood.

The effects of early nutrition on the brain's mature capabilities are crucial. Poor nutrition in pregnancy may not be as important as nutrition in the first two or three years of life, because the mother's foetus may be protected from poor nutrition, but by the end of the first two years of life, the growth spurt of the brain is over. Relatively lethargic children may be so for reasons of poor diet and late nights; they can be less stimulated and not develop well. We need to take note of the evidence of crucial periods of any child's learning. Flexibility of mind and exceptional immaturity at birth compared with other animals gives humans a unique capacity for development. Interaction with a stimulating environment, including language, is critical to the mind's development. The brain contains a model of the world built up through the senses. The model creating the brain cells depends on the quality of experience a child has.

Each of us has different models and information fed into the brain through the senses is scanned against the model and decisions taken as a result of the scanning process. A child needs to explore, talk and play with others to refine the model and the quality of environment influences the model. If deprived, then a poor state of mind is created which learns to expect little out of life. Evidence suggests that memory is stored rather diffusely within the brain tissue and cognitive development is a reflection of interest and maturation, as well as biological and inherited ability.

In this age of computers and space travel, our understanding of our own mind is only just beginning, and much more research is needed. Scientific evidence now indicates that only the left half of our brain is capable of expressing its thoughts in words fully, and the right side of the brain has its own separate train of thoughts, which are not in words. Though these non-verbal thoughts are a crucial part of our personality and abilities, they continue to be ignored and misunderstood because they are so difficult to translate into words. Since the right side of the brain is capable of controlling our actions, remembering things, solving problems and having our emotional selves developed, it fully qualifies as a mind by itself. In spite of this fact, we have continued to look at our mind as a single entity that thinks only in words. When you look at a human brain, it is difficult to see how anyone could ever have thought of it as the physical basis of a single mind, for the human brain is obviously a double organ consisting of two identical looking hemispheres joined together by bundles of nerve fibres called the Corpus callosum. Certainly the billions of neurons in the two hemispheres are not so identical that they can simultaneously conceive identical thoughts on each side, yet the human mind resides strictly in one of the hemispheres. What could the equal amount of brain power in the other hemisphere be doing? Most of the organs of the body are in pairs and evolutionary forces simply do not allow the kind of waste that would be represented by having one hemisphere sit idle. In fact, measurements of the rate of metabolism of the two hemispheres indicates that both are doing the same amount of work.

Contemporary understanding of human brain functions establishes that each side of the brain is unique and that brains in general are specialised. While experts argue about the degree of specialisation (Herrmann, 1987), there is a general agreement on the fact of specialisation. For example, there is agreement on the concept of dominance—eye dominance, hand dominance, foot dominance, ear dominance and brain dominance. While the body is symmetrical in terms of organ duality—that is, we have two eyes, two ears, two hands, two feet and two hemispheres—in the use of these dual organs, there exists a general asymmetry. In other words, we use one to a greater degree than the other. When combined, the concepts of specialisation and asymmetry, or dominance, produce within each human being a distribution of specialised preferences that affect general behaviour. Specifically included is a unique individual's learning style. This has important implications for both parents and teachers of children, in that intelligence is no longer one-dimensional, but rather includes the notion of multiple intelligences.

Each individual is a unique learner with learning preferences and avoidances different from other learners.

All this points to the need to provide optimum conditions for all children from birth and we should not be satisfied until all children are born into homes where parents have the knowledge and skills to meet all the needs of the growing child and are sufficiently affluent to do so. Experiences that a child has in the early primary years seem to matter for the rest of life, because of the physical changes in the cortex, which are perhaps unchangeable, but deprivation cannot be solved by schools alone. The influence of the streets, television, homes and youth organisations, to give a few examples are crucial. Parent/school liaison is of the greatest importance and a difficult art. The school should not undermine the dignity and authority of the parents with the children. Perhaps of the early years 0–5 are the most crucial; then the brain is undergoing maximum growth and is probably at its most plastic. This is when the quality of the environment can be crucial. To give one further example, the brain is built to mop up language incredibly quickly. Babies are born with the left (language) hemisphere larger than the right. Therefore, language, like food, is a basic need and it is essential that children are talked to and not treated to 'shut up' answers.

An excellent book was published in 1993, entitled *Talented Teenagers*, by Czikszenmihalyi *et al*. These American professors undertook research among an equal number of boys and girls in the age range 13–14, looked at those who achieved highly in art, athletics, mathematics, music and science, and came to the following conclusions:

- Teenagers must develop skills that can be recognised.
- Appropriate or supportive personality traits recognised in the successful teenagers were energy, endurance, openness and responsiveness.

- Productive habits:
  - limited socialising
  - concentration on school as their main focus in life
  - time to be alone
  - no after-school jobs
  - as much interaction with parents as possible
  - limited TV viewing.
- Conservative sexual attitudes.
- As much family support as possible, in families that are cohesive and flexible and where parents model discipline, intellectuality and productivity.
- Teachers who were good role models, who had a romance with their discipline, had a professional identity, and were involved in their field.
- Teenagers required rewards and recognition.
- Talent and talent development are complex processes which necessitate both differentiation and integration of the curriculum.

This sounds very idealistic, but one has to be optimistic if we are to fully help these children in our care.

LOOK AT THE WHOLE CHILD

This chapter has suggested a new model which should have as its basis the provision of a rich, stimulating experience which extends all children to the highest potential of which they are capable in a climate which fosters creativity and allows some freedom of choice. As gifted behaviour is observed to emerge under these conditions, the sensitive teachers and school, as well as the parental support, will provide opportunities for further development.

The tendency in education, and this will probably increase, is to develop the cognitive areas of a child to the detriment of the cultural, physical and the spiritual dimensions. For example, there is a growing interest in the idea that we can all take more responsibility for our own health and a recognition of good health is more than freedom from disease or infirmity. The idea of a holistic living programme is now the fastest growing and most important development in the domain of health and healing. It is a programme of self-care in which a person is seen as a whole—body, mind and spirit and the parts interrelated. Despite the tendency in schools for physical education to decline, it is essential to develop a healthy mind and healthy body.

Parents have an essential role to develop the whole child and to encourage health and religious education. This neglected affective area of education, which in addition to developing spirituality includes self-concepts, self-esteem and moral thinking, social adjustments, altruism and motivation, is essential for the development of well-rounded, fulfilled and outgoing students. In an earlier book the author discussed the fact that most gifted and talented children are well able to understand moral issues and have the ability to discuss them, as well as being basically honest, ethical and truthful.

The home has a vital role to play here because teachers are under considerable pressure with large classes, testing and the National Curriculum to implement. The school should look at all the positive attributes of a child and tell each child of his or her capabilities and worthwhileness. Developing a good self-concept is a goal of every school and is a motivating force to give children higher aspirations and achievements. There are many perceptions of self, including:

- Body Self—which includes understanding changes and the use and misuse of the body.
- Sexual Self—understanding sexual development and the role of sexuality in relationships.
- Vocational Self—making contributions to society, lifestyles and developing awareness.
- Social Self—understanding others' perspectives, their relationships, coping with conflicts, working with others and making sense of others.
- Moral Self—the making of judgements, resolving moral dilemmas, taking actions on issues.
- Self as a learner—understanding strengths and weaknesses and reflecting on approaches to learning.
- Self, the organisation—becoming an active member of the school, giving and gaining benefits.

Given time, commitment and opportunities, schools can teach a humanistic, caring curriculum which includes exposing children to problems of the elderly and handicapped, involvement in community service, raising money for worthwhile projects, recycling materials in school which raises awareness of environmental issues, debates about pollution, overpopulation, AIDS, abortion and other current issues of real concern. Table 11.1 could form the basis of a holistic home curriculum for gifted children to discuss with their parents. This is a fundamental area of concern if we are to have a caring society and one to which parents can contribute so much at home.

Table 11.1

Body	Mind	Spirit	Relationship	Environment
Exercise	Thoughts	Beliefs	Family	Soil
Food	Feelings	Values	Friends	Plants
Illness	Ideas	Experience	Community	Animals
Health	Knowledge	Faith	Society	Air

HELPING CHILDREN AT HOME

1. They are still children. They need love, but controls; attention but discipline; parental involvement, yet training in self-dependence and responsibility.
2. Often the gifted child feels isolated from the rest of the world because of exceptional abilities he or she possesses. Facing these feelings of difference alone can create emotional problems, disruptive behaviours or withdrawal from the frustrating situation.
3. Consonance of parental value systems is important for their optimum development. This means that there should not be wide disagreements over values between parents.
4. Parental involvement in early task demands, such as training them to perform tasks themselves, to count, tell time, use correct vocabulary and pronunciation, locate themselves and get around their neighbourhood, do errands and be responsible are all important.
5. Emphasis on early verbal expression, reading, discussing ideas in the presence of children, poetry and music are all valuable. Parents should read to children. There should be an emphasis by parents on doing well in school.
6. Encourage children to play with words. Even in such common settings as a car ride or shopping trip, word games, like rhyming, opposites and puns can be used to their full advantage.
7. Provide a variety of books, magazines, puzzles and games which promote use of the imagination, logical thinking, drawing inferences and making predictions.
8. Help gifted and talented individuals become critical viewers and readers by discussing influences; the mass media such as television and literature may have personal and social values.
9. Lack of disruption of family life through divorce or separation, and the maintenance of a happy, heathly home is an important aspect in raising able children, as well as other children.

10. Since able children often have vague awareness of adult problems such as sex, death, sickness, finances, war, etc., which their lack of experience makes them unable to solve, they may need reassurance in these areas.

11. Encourage children to play an active, real role in family decisions. Listen to their suggestions, applying them wherever possible. For example, when planning a trip or vacation, have gifted children participate in decisions about places, routes, food and activities. Respect their suggestions and assign important tasks appropriate to their abilities—such as map reader on a trip or book-keeper of the family budget.

12. Explore ways of finding and solving problems by asking questions, posing hypotheses, discussing alternative solutions and evaluating those alternatives. Personal and family situations may be used, as well as the larger social issues of the town, the country or the world.

13. Help the child relate to friends who may not be so gifted. While gifted children should recognise their abilities, they should also learn to put them into perspective with the abilities and interests of others. Instead of setting themselves above others, they should learn to look for strengths in friends as well as for ways to share their abilities in a productive manner.

14. The role of good books, magazines and other aids to home learning, such as encyclopaedias, charts, collections, are important.

15. Parents should take the initiative in taking able children to museums, art galleries, educational institutions and other historical places where collections of various sorts may enhance background learning.

16. Parents should be especially careful not to 'shut up' the gifted child who asks questions. In particular, he or she should not be scolded for asking, nor should it be inferred that this is an improper or forbidden subject. The parent may, however, insist that questions not be asked at inappropriate times, and he may require the child to sharpen or rephrase his or her question so as to clarify it. Sometimes questions should not be answered completely, but the reply should itself be a question which sends the child into some larger direction. When the parent cannot answer the questions, he should direct the child to a resource which can.

17. There's a difference between pushing and intellectual stimulation. Parents should avoid 'pushing' a child into reading, 'exhibiting' him before others or courting undue publicity about him. On the other hand, parents should seek in every way to stimulate and widen the child's mind, through suitable experiences in books, recreation, travel and the arts.

18. Prize and praise efforts and accomplishments. Support children when they succeed as well as when they don't succeed. Create an atmosphere where risk taking is OK.

19. Encourage the gifted and talented to challenge themselves. Because of their superior abilities, the gifted often work at only partial capacity in various areas and still succeed. This approach to learning, however, may ultimately create difficulties because the individuals may acquire extremely poor learning habits which they may not be able to overcome when they are sufficiently challenged.

STIMULATING ACTIVITIES TO DO WITH YOUR CHILDREN AT HOME

1. Play Scrabble *ad lib* using only words around a theme. For example, farm, Christmas, weather. Children must give rationale for words used.

2. Pick a household item and invent ten new uses for it apart from the obvious. Design the perfect broom, vacuum cleaner or sink.

3. Listen to a foreign radio station. Pick up a foreign newspaper and explore it with the child; listen to music. Borrow records from the library. Plan a dish from that country and then create your own, using products similar to the native recipes. This is a good introduction to global education.

4. Plan a trip and mention problems that arise. Let the children solve the problem with Yellow Pages, newspapers and maps.

5. Write letters to manufacturers praising or complaining about their products. Make suggestions for improvement. Include a catchy commercial jingle. Discuss commercials for obvious and hidden messages. Enter a manufacturer's contest.

6. Invite an elderly member of the family to discuss old times and life 50 years ago. Design a family crest or flag depicting family history and symbols of the family's value system. Prepare a motto to accompany the crest. Work out a family tree. Keep a diary of family or personal events and make each entry different, such as a poem, slogan, illustration, song lyrics.

7. Investigate various forms of communication in your home, body language, facial expressions, conversation, animal communication, media. Design your own code of communication.

8. Chart the routine of animals and plan a change in habits. Record the changes in behaviour in the development of a habit. Design the perfect fictitious household pet, borrowing characteristics of other animals.

9. Have the child redesign his bedroom to accommodate his hobbies and interests. Allow suggestions for architectural and structural changes on paper. Have the child find a new way to make a bed, decorate a window or set a table. Have a child give the rationale for his changes.

10. Listen to a different kind of music such as jazz, calypso, swing, as well as classical. Discuss mood and interpretation of music and encourage free dance expression to the music. Rent or borrow an instrument and investigate musical patterns.

11. Discuss a favourite TV programme and plan two plots and sub-plots for the characters. Relate characteristics of characters to friends and relatives. Discuss plausibility of the present plots and relate them to their own personal experiences.

12. Star gaze and investigate astronomy. Learn about calendars to which other different cultures adhere (Hebrew, Chinese). Create a new month with a new holiday. Children are fascinated by the sky at night.

13. Watch a new sport. Play your own invented sport and make logical rules, uniforms and equipment.

14. Scour the newspapers for local problems and plan logical solutions. Write letters to the Editor.

15. Learn a new craft.

16. Ask the child to condense a film, book or TV programme to four sentences or four words.

17. Create and illustrate a cartoon strip featuring original animated characters or a hero.

18. Devise a weather station for recording conditions and predictions. Plan novel ways of conserving energy and water based on your findings.

19. Devise a new maths value system and plan equations in your system. Explore unfamiliar operations on a calculator.

20. Learn about perennial and annual plants and plan a timetable for flowering.

21. Plan a simple chemical experiment from household items. Explore the chemical components of household items and food stuffs. Discuss chemical changes in food and additives.

22. Solve crossword puzzles or anagrams and construct your own. Plan riddles and pantomimes.

23. Explore infrequently visited spots in your home for 'antiques'. Critique the value of items. Discuss economic concepts such as appreciation/depreciation. Have the children plan a car boot sale and evaluate the items for sale.

24. Read current world news items. Analyse the articles for solutions

and discuss how the possible solutions will filter down to affect their lives.

For more ideas see George (1994).

Our society has made two promises to its children. The first is to prepare a world which accepts them and provides them with opportunities to live, grow and create in safety. The other is to help them develop their whole beings to the fullest in every respect. Education is the vehicle through which we try to keep these promises, in partnership with parents. What a challenge to parents and teachers, but what a joy!

REFERENCES

Brierley, J. K. (1978) *Growing and Learning*. London: Ward Lock.

Czikszenmihalyi, M., Rathund, K. & Wholen, S. (1993) *Talented Teenagers—The Roots of Success and Failure*. Cambridge: Cambridge University Press.

George, D. R. (1992) *The Challenge of the Able Child*, 2nd edition. London: David Fulton.

George, D. R. (1994) *Enrichment Activities for More Able Children*. Milton Keyens: Chalkface.

Herrmann, N. (1987) *The Application of Brain Dominance*, 7th World Conference, Salt Lake City.

Maslow, A. H. (1954) *Motivation & Personality*. New York: Harper Row.

Proctor, T. B. (1986) 'Early selection of children'. *Journal of Education Research*.

Reynolds, M. C. (1976) *Research on Early Admission: The Intellectually Gifted*. New York: Grune & Stratton.

White, B. (1979) *The Origins of Human Competence*. Arlington, Mass: Lexington Books.

FURTHER READING

Bragget, E. J. (1992) *Pathways for Accelerated Learners*. Sydney: Hewtar Brownlow.

Butler-Por, N. (1987) *Gifted Underachievers*. Chichester: John Wiley.

Clark, B. (1988) *Growing Up Gifted*. Columbus: Merrill.

Colengelo, W. L. & Davis, G. A. (1991) *Handbook of Gifted Education*. New York: Allyn & Bacon.

Davis, G. A. & Rim, S. B. (1989) *Education of the Gifted and Talented*. Englewood Cliffs, NJ: Prentice Hall.

Denton, C. & Postlethwaite K. (1985) *Able Children—Identify Them*. Windsor: NFER-Nelson.

Dunn, R. Dunn, K. & Treffinger, D. (1992) *Bringing Out the Giftedness in the Young Child*. Chichester: John Wiley.

Edwards, B. (1992) *Drawing on the Right Side of the Brain*. London: Harper Collins.

Eyre, D. & Marjoram, T. D. (1990) *Enriching and Extending the National Curriculum*: London: Kogan Page.

Gardner, H. (1994) *The Unschooled Mind*. New York: Basic Books.

Gallagher, J. J. (1985) *Teaching the Gifted Child.* New York: Allyn & Bacon

George, D. R. (1995) *Gifted Education.* London: David Fulton.

Gross, M. U. M. (1993) *Exceptionally Able Children.* London: Routledge.

Heller, K. A., Monks, F. J. & Passow, H. A. (Eds) (1993) *Research of Giftedness and Talent.* Oxford: Pergamon Press.

Leyden, S. (1990) *Helping the Child of Exceptional Ability.* London: Routledge.

Sisk, D. (1987) *Creative Teaching of Gifted.* New York: McGraw-Hill.

Young, P. & Tyre, C. (1992) *Gifted or Able: Realising Children's Potential.* Open University Press.

12

PARENTING LEARNING DISABLED CHILDREN: REALITIES AND PRACTICALITIES

Ruchira Leisten

Let us recognise that the work of parents, as parents, is of immense value to our society. Parenting is probably the most demanding of all human roles, especially where the child or children of those parents have learning disabilities. This chapter is not primarily for parents of learning disabled children; it is for professionals working with those parents to provide professional care for the child with leaning disabilities. It is through sensitivity to the needs of the whole family that professionals can really make a positive difference to the life of the child with a learning disability.

This chapter is about parents, because through insight into the parenting role professionals can engage in a more effective partnership to ameliorate difficulties. Through appreciation of the work of parents, professionals can see the merits of assisting parents, empowering parents and encouraging parents rather than simply dictating to them.

In reality the quality of care available to a child with a learning disability depends on the quality of life in its family unit. This in turn depends on the effectiveness of parents in coming to terms with the condition of the child with learning disabilities. This chapter will have succeeded if it convinces professionals that the best way to help the

Enhancing Parenting Skills: A Guide Book for Professionals Working with Parents.
Edited by K. N. Dwivedi. © 1997 John Wiley & Sons Ltd.

learning disabled child is through collaboration with parents. Above all parents should not be viewed *'from a pathology based model, but rather from a health promotion framework that [supposes] that family members are basically competent individuals'* (Roberts & Magrab, 1991, p. 144). In other words, we should prefer to think of the family as a group of people who are achieving what they can in adverse circumstances rather than as incompetent individuals requiring supervision.

ACCEPTING A CHILD'S LEARNING DISABILITIES

The impact on a family of the birth of a child with learning disabilities can be devastating. If the disability is known about at birth it complicates the postnatal psychological health of the mother. The feelings of elation and triumph that are normally present are replaced by dread of what the future holds and a deep sense of disappointment and victimisation. Wider family and friends often do not find it easy to support the helpless parents, who become isolated.

If the existence of the learning disability appears after birth then the parenting experience turns sour in another cruel way. In this case the parents have to accept that the happily anticipated development will not perhaps occur. Once again the happiness at the birth of the child is replaced by grief for the loss of the 'perfect' child.

As the child grows the ramifications of the child's learning disability draw heavily on the parents' resources. The caring demands and medical facilities that may be necessary place constraints on the possible career developments that may otherwise be available to parents because they restrict time and the chance to move away from facilities that are necessary for the care of the child.

Depending on the specific needs of the child concerned the family may be the recipients of help from numerous professionals. These may include health visitors, community nurses, general practitioners, physiotherapists, speech therapists, teachers, social workers, link workers and counsellors. Often parents looking after a child with learning difficulties experience a cocktail of problems which, together, make the caring role of professional workers particularly important because they can collectively cause the parents to withdraw from friend and family networks. For example, the parents of the child may experience problems of acceptance, adaptation, social isolation or coping with stress due to the demands of the child and also they may face an inner battle to come to terms with the situation. In these circumstances it can potentially be from these professional people that the parents can derive vital support. Although the provision of this support may traditionally be considered beyond the brief of each individual professional worker, it is increasingly becoming accepted that professional workers should widen their focus to address these needs.

In a regime of scarce and stretched professional resources it is necessary to make a careful examination of the evidence before it is clear that it is worth extending those resources. The true caring role, involving the care of the whole family, is far more demanding of the professional's time and resources than the traditional role of just providing professional care to the child. However, to form a balanced view the agreement should not be viewed from the caring institution's viewpoint only. It can be argued that a family that is adequately supported will help itself more than a family that is not. A family that is coping well with the demands of caring for a child with a leaning disability may make less demands on professional workers than another that is not. From an overview position it may be most advantageous, therefore, to provide closer support rather than simply the traditional narrowly defined professional discipline of the individual professional workers. To prove this point it is necessary to analyse the needs of the parents, define appropriate roles for professional workers and finally to test the effectiveness of the service they provide. Let's start with a more detailed examination of the psychological and practical needs of parents caring for a child with a learning difficulty.

Swick (1984, p. 37) has pointed out that:

> Parents of handicapped children, for example, experience an intense sense of isolation from the usual life routine. It appears that they use so much energy in coping with the child's problems and their new life context, that feelings of resentment and insecurity temporarily isolate them from their former friends and acquaintances.

The first thing that professional workers can do to help is to counter this unhealthy development. As Swick goes on to say (p. 37)

> It is essential that all who work with parents in such situations establish some basis for helping them re-establish self-confidence and social linkages with the outside world, so they can foster constructive family living and be functional community participants.

To fulfil this need professional workers need to really get to know the family. Roberts and Magrab (1991) have convincingly argued that 'The child is best understood in the context of his or her family ecology' (p. 2). If the impact of caring for the child with a learning disability is causing disruption of normal friend and family networking, then professional workers should do what they can to repair the situation. A more normally oriented family environment promotes a more positive environment for the child with a learning disability. The creation of a healthy psychological environment is probably the most important objective.

It is important to recognise and understand what Dunst and Paget (1991, p. 25) have called the 'dilemma of helping'. An inappropriate strategy might create dependencies causing the parents to rely on some service provided by professional workers, lose independence, self-esteem and this can probably actually compound their sense of isolation. On the other hand, a well-conceived strategy can promote independence, dignity and normalise relationships with the community of family and friends. The key to the operative distinction between these two approaches is concerned with empowerment and partnership. To provide help that is truly beneficial to parents, professional workers should seek to build up competencies and the strengths of those parents. They should concentrate on enabling the parents to accomplish things themselves and should avoid exercising professional authority. In fact the ultimate corollary of this argument is that they should recognise and respect the parents' authority over the care of the child with a learning disability. This authority is naturally placed with those individuals (in this case, parents) who are full-time carers for the child. Professional workers should empower and partner those parents in the pursuit of looking after the child and should accept whenever possible that the overriding management responsibility rests with the parents.

Roberts and Magrab (1991, p. 144) have defined the collective role of professional workers in this context as:

> The professionals . . . make determinations about the most effective methods of achieving prioritised goals compatible with the personal style and cultural patterns of the family. (Families are considered as being) basically competent individuals. The role of the inter-disciplinary team of professionals is to help the family meet the development, mental health and social goals that they have set for themselves.

DEALING WITH A CHILD'S LEARNING DISABILITIES

There are problems with participating in the dynamics of a family caring for a child with a learning disability if the character of the family in circumstances without that child is not known. Merton, et al., (1983, p. 21) have commented that because the 'professional consulted when the client needs help may never [have] seen the client in a state of general well-being [the help giving professional] can therefore have only an indirect sense of the client's capabilities and strengths'. This limited perspective reinforces the already ingrained tendency for the professional to exercise paternalistic authority. Bearing this in mind, it should be important discipline for professional workers who need to take into account the difficulties the families are in when forming impressions of the strengths these families possess. In order to help a family help itself, the professional worker should get to know the family very well. This is an important part of the empowering and partnership ideal which has been gaining in importance in recent years.

Fine and Gardner (1994) and Roberts and Magrab (1991) have provided two excellent contributions which argue for and state the principles of a family-centred approach for administering professional care. Fine and Gardner chart the history of professional care for children with learning disabilities from the traditional medical model which supported the authority role for professionals. The ethos was child centred with parents expected simply to implement the prescribed case of treatment unquestioningly. This manner of professional behaviour in Fine and Gardner's American context was questioned as parents began to assert rights based on articles and amendments of the constitution of the United States of America. American parents sought legal remedies for what they increasingly regarded as unacceptable lack of involvement in the decision-making process. In the United Kingdom, 'Care in the Community' (Department of Health, 1990) and the Children Act have provided a strong stimulus for change to a community/family-centred approach. Both these influences have promoted a rethink of the whole professional approach to a vision of one which, as far as possible, subjugates professional roles to parental management.

Hobbs (1975, pp. 228-229) pointed out that 'It is the parent who firmly bears the responsibility for the child, and that the parent cannot be replaced by episodic professional service'.

Parents have to be supported to function as the embodiment of consistent support for the child with a learning disability. In terms of ability to support the child directly, a professional worker is not generally in a position to provide commitment that is even close to that which can be provided by parents. In all normal circumstances, supporting the parents and thereby improving the caring capability of the parents is very clearly the most effective way of assisting with the care of the child. Professional workers need to hold this principle as a most important pillar of guidance because the condition of the child may seem so complicated that the needs of the supporting family can easily be forgotten.

In order to be able to assist in building a good family environment for the child with a learning disability, it is helpful for the professional worker to have established a realistic appreciation of the properties of a contemporary family. Definitions are rather difficult to provide in this context because family structures have diversified significantly away from the traditionally religious models. Fine and Gardner (1994, p. 288) have the following offering:

> Families are generally thought of as a group of people who are genetically or emotionally connected to each other. The nuclear family has traditionally been seen as the parents and children in the home setting, with the extended family including a multi-generational collection of relatives and others of very close emotional ties living in another home. As understanding of the contemporary family requires awareness of the varieties of structures that exist, including single-parent, multi-generational, blended or reconstituted families, as well as parents and children residing in other homes.

THE SWICK CYCLE

In the course of liaising with families, performing the often difficult task of caring for children with special needs, professional workers should recognise that they are dealing with a family unit operating under stress. Behavioural abnormalities that may be apparent in these circumstances may not occur in more tranquil and 'normal' times. Swick (1984, pp. 42-44) has identified certain patterns of reaction in families encountering highly stressful experiences. Although the reaction of each individual family is unique, it is worth proposing Swick's model of the cycle of reactions as a developmental journey in which the professional worker will often see opportunities to assist (Figure 12.1).

In order to assess the coping performance of the family it is helpful for the professional worker to be able to draw conclusions about the position of the family unit on the Swick 'cycle of reactions' train. A little more detail adapted from Swick is helpful.

Most people about to encounter a stressful life event say that they experienced a sense of foreboding as they anticipated the coming disorder. It may be that prior to diagnosis of the child's learning disability the parents were beginning to suspect it. Alternatively, they may have knowledge of genetic or congenital circumstances that promote the chance for the disability to occur. This is the anticipation stage of the reaction cycle.

When the actual confirmation or discovery of the learning disability is obtained, the parents may suffer the shock or disbelief stage. Swick has suggested a number of psychological symptoms: 'disregard for reality, psychological malaise, social isolation, extensive moodiness, cognitive malfunctioning and physical illness (often of a psychosomatic nature)' (p. 43). People only come out of this stage of the cycle when they

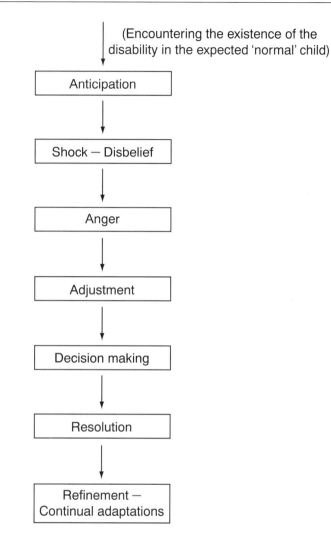

(Encountering the existence of the disability in the expected 'normal' child)

Anticipation

Shock — Disbelief

Anger

Adjustment

Decision making

Resolution

Refinement —
Continual adaptations

Figure 12.1: A model for the cycle of reactions for a special needs family. (The headings in this flow chart have been extracted from Swick, 1984, pp. 42–44.)

perceive once again that there is an acceptable reality. This may take some time, depending on personalities and circumstances, but it is certainly a stage in which professional help is very valuable.

As families start to accept the reality of their difficult caring task they often become angry as they pose the question 'why us?' and feel victimised. Unfortunately this anger can be expressed through parental arguments or child misbehaviour and it is possible for families in these circumstances to appear highly dysfunctional. However, anger is actually a necessary stage towards effective resolution of the problem because (as Swick points out, p. 43) 'if a person is upset enough to reach a state of anger, it is obvious that there is a desire to find ways to handle the situation'. Professional workers should be alerted to finding ways to get the family to channel their anger positively and to be prepared to let the parents 'vent their feelings'.

After the anger reaction has run its course the family generally starts the adjustment phase of the cycle: in which the anger feelings are directed towards a more constructive adjustment process. Feelings are still likely to be raw in this phase but communication between partners may develop a more positive character. Basically the family are ready to plan strategies to adapt, having realised that the negative feelings of anger and victimisation bring nothing but misery. The professional worker's role at this stage might be to very subtly engage in planning dialogue, but it is very important that the family passes the adjustment stage by itself.

There is a risk that taking over ownership of solutions in this stage, from the viewpoint of the family, may slow the passage through the adjustment stage. Families are striving to recover their lost dignity and need to maintain their pride, independence and self-reliance.

The adjustment process should eventually lead families to a desire to plan long-term methods of dealing with the situation. They need methods of creating a workable life pattern that adequately accommodates the new demands on them. At this stage families may actually seek advice and be willing to discuss solutions with professionals. However, once again it is wise to foster a helpful back-up role as far as possible and to help implement and develop ideas offered by the family. Positive influence towards a more workable lifestyle is very possible here but families will gather strength and vitality from the pride they take in implementing their own solutions. Professionals should strive to enable the family to retain as much autonomy from outside services as possible, even when families are reluctant to accept this independence. It is generally true that fulfilment of a measure of self-reliance is necessary for recovery to a 'workable life pattern' in the long term. Hopefully the family ultimately arrives at the resolution phase of the 'Swick Cycle'. Resolutions implies nothing permanent in this context; only that the family has found a pattern of life which is sustainable. Each member of the family, while accommodating the care needs of the child with a learning disability, has found a stable life pattern that is acceptable. It is important to recognise that this stage will be reached most satisfactorily if isolation of the family is avoided and integration with the community around the family is achieved.

The last stage of the reaction train is what Swick called the stage of refinement and continual adaptations. This stage is included to acknowledge the fact that, as a family grows, life changes—sometimes gradually and sometimes abruptly. The family needs to develop and create strategies to cope with these changing circumstances as they occur. Professional workers assigned to the special needs of that family should be involved in the planning of solutions as necessary.

The greater level of experience of caring for the child with learning disabilities should hopefully have imparted a confidence in both the family and the professional worker. It is possible that a very friendly and creative relationship may exist between the professional worker and the partners by this stage.

The challenge faced by the professional worker is to get to know the family well through any stage of the Swick reaction cycle. The primary purpose is to be able to identify and enhance the family strengths that will provide the most important component of care for the child with a learning disability. Fine and Gardner (1994, p. 291) have defined this task as follows:

> The identification of family strengths requires an openness by professionals of learning how the family has generated and used its resources to cope. The movement away from a deficit or pathology model allows the professional to engage the family in discussion and enquiry regarding its organisation, patterns of support, and ways of meeting crises.

Many problems exist for a family caring for a child with a learning disability. The main tools the professional worker can use to improve the situation are objectivity and informed judgement. It is likely that there may be aspects of the family life which are not satisfactory for all members of that family and there is a possibility that some carers may not be coping well. Again it is worthwhile addressing these defects while avoiding labelling the family as being dysfunctional; just in need of compensatory support to balance its increased burden of responsibility and care. Fine and Gardner (1994) have some useful insight on how this professional involvement can be applied in a way which is effective and collaborative. Remember, we are trying to avoid taking over management of the care from the family because we recognise that such arrangements can only be transitory and, in the longer scheme of things, merely disruptive.

To summarise so far: we have stated that the central mission statement for professional workers should be that they work in collaboration and partnership with families caring for children with learning difficulties. To do this, professional workers have to get to know the family well and to understand the stage in the cycle of reactions—from adaptation to accommodation of the care burden—the family are in. The professional worker should not feel critical or judgemental about the performance of the family, but rather compassionate and, wherever possible, complimentary. When necessary and mutually acceptable to the family and to professional care-providing agencies, the professional worker should act to facilitate help that may be required to complement the care provided by the family. It is in the management and fulfilment of this need that we should further examine the needs of families caring for a child with a learning disability.

CARING FOR A CHILD WITH LEARNING DISABILITIES

The value of professional advice can be illustrated by a case from the author's research (Bose, 1990). In the course of a passive survey of families of children with learning difficulties in Kent one family stood out as one which was suffering unnecessary hardship. A couple occupying a house with three upstairs bedrooms had a 21-year-old child who was unable to move, so the mother had to actually carry this child up and down the stairs. The husband worked as a taxi-driver and worked during the night, so that the child had to be downstairs while the father was sleeping during the day.

Unfortunately, the child had sleeping problems too, so that the mother, in addition to having the physical hardship of moving a 21-year-old child up and down stairs, also suffered from lack of sleep at night. There were countless things that a collaborative partnership with professional workers could have achieved which would have improved the quality of life for this family. They could have helped to organise better accommodation, reduced the difficulty of managing the child in so many ways and perhaps even improved the child's sleeping habits. The ability of this family to cope with this huge burden of care was truly amazing and yet the contribution the family was making was apparently completely unrecognised.

Over time, the daily care demands of a child with learning difficulties can affect a family's way of life in ways that can relatively easily be modified positively. Each member of a family may have a different experience of and reaction to the stress of caring for the child with learning difficulties. It may be the case that some members of the family assume too many responsibilities while others shun responsibilities. Fine and Gardner (1994, p. 293) have put it like this:

> Some persons become 'over-functioners', whereas others in the family may appear to be 'under-functioners', side-stepping or withdrawing from responsibilities. From a systems perspective, the involved professional can

explore how the various family members found themselves in certain roles, how shifts may occur that will be more productive for the family and how members can work more supportively with each other. In helping to open up communications amongst family members, the professional can assist the family in clarifying feelings and respecting each member's position in the situation.

Often it is not principally the action of caring for the child with learning disabilities, but rather the consequences of having to provide that care which causes stress in the affected families. For example, the child may require care that is only available in a certain region. Also some of the health or education needs may be expensive to provide. The family may have fewer wage-earners due to the care demands of the child. The primary wage earner may have to forgo career opportunities to stay in a region where facilities necessary for the care of the child are available. Also, the living expenses of a family caring for a child with learning disabilities may be significantly higher than is normal. The sacrifices that are having to be made to accommodate the special needs of the child with learning disabilities may cause resentment among siblings. Equally, siblings may possess a commitment to help provide for the welfare of the child with special needs. In a family the human reactions of each member of that family affect the other family members and can place family life under strain. The range of individual responses to these circumstances vary from excessive interdependence to complete disengagement. Families can become so interdependent that they completely deny any of their members any measure of healthy independence or, alternatively, they can become so uncommitted that they leave other members feeling alone and unsupported. Professional workers can seek to influence families to adopt a more 'normal' and fulfilling family relationship with appropriate sharing of care responsibilities.

Fine and Gardner (1994, p. 290) have proposed examples of how certain family dynamics could benefit from being modified to enable family members to relate in more productive ways, as follows:

> Boundaries, roles of family members and the coalition of certain family members need to be understood and may become a focus of intervention. Older siblings may have become 'adultised' in terms of being given excessive responsibilities. There may be a blurring of boundaries between parental and child prerogatives, with some children in the family assuming inappropriate decision making power. The professional, for example, may work with the parents to strengthen the parental subsystem and help the children remain children. This in turn may require helping the parents to relate more supportively with each other and to diminish unhealthy coalitions with the children.

Turbulent family relationships can seem to many of us to have a destructive momentum that denies well-intentioned intervention of any measure of success. It is worth pondering the question of whether the gentle interventions that have been advocated above are actually practically helpful and worth while. Is it reasonable to expect professional workers who have hitherto been able to keep to narrow professional routines and procedures to adopt the wide counselling role that has been recommended? These are powerful questions for in reality they elicit bold and provocative answers. However difficult these tasks may seem to professionals, the methods advocated here are in reality both ethical and pragmatic. Confrontation with families has not been advocated—in fact a family's ultimate right to self-determination must be fully respected. Families taking on the role of caring for a child with learning difficulties have had to adapt to rapid change and are often very accessible to the participation of professional workers in that process. It is probable that the professional stature of the professional worker lends his or her suggestions a greater significance than those ideas that come from family members. The power to facilitate use of appropriate institutional care resources may be another helpful influence. Nevertheless, it is undeniable that there is a need for professional workers to acquire considerable counselling skill to be able to fulfil these roles adequately. Commenting on the role of psychologists in this venture, Roberts and Magrab (1991, p. 147) have predicted:

> . . . the role of the Psychologist in the 1990's will require both an attitude shift and a behavioural change. To effect change within the family, Psychologists must see themselves as consultants to the child and the family with a goal of developing supports that will promote the behavioural changes that are desired by the family. Psychologists must not import their values on the desired changes. The changes must be ones that will be supported in the environment after the formal interventions have ceased. Psychologists must learn to draw on informal supports to behavioural network of resources. In addition, Psychologists can plan a major role in the reorganisation of the formal systems of care that will help them to be more responsive to the needs of families.

Of course, psychologists are only one of the many classes of professional workers who will come into contact with the families. It is very worth while for all of the professional workers supporting such families to support the same philosophic role. The principle task is to gain the trust and friendship of the families and to empathise with them. To the extent that it is possible in the particular professional worker's role, the worker should make himself or herself as useful as possible and also as psychologically supportive as possible. The word that is often used in this context is 'collaboration'.

There have been numerous attempts to define what is meant by 'collaboration' in terms of the actions by professional workers that it implies. Friend and Cook (1992, pp. 6–8) have cleverly stated six characteristics which distinguish collaboration from other forms of professional interactions.

1. Collaboration is voluntary.
2. Collaboration is required for parity among participants.
3. Collaboration is based on neutral goals.
4. Collaboration depends on shared responsibility for participation and decision making.
5. Individuals who collaborate share their resources.
6. Individuals who collaborate share accountability for outcomes.

In order to be able to collaborate it is necessary for the professional worker to gain the close working relationship with the family that is implicitly required. The professional worker must be able to demonstrate a credible responsibility for the welfare of the child as well as a strong friendship for the family.

The professional worker comes into the life of a family caring for a child with a learning disability just because of the existence of that child in the family. This purpose can be a tremendous advantage in promoting a good basis for friendly collaboration with parents who may otherwise have reduced capacity to form friendly relationships with members of their general community. Families are likely to value the professional credentials of the worker as one who provides professional assistance to people adapting to facing the demands of caring for a child with learning disabilities. The professional worker should try to direct this professional expertise in a way that convinces the family of the value of this contribution. If this can be done in a collaborative way it is likely that friendship and trust can be built up very quickly, and the professional worker can gain the privilege of being perceived as a collaborator in the care of the child by the family. Ideally it should then be possible to act as a conduit to the restoration of friendship with friend and family networks as the family can be encouraged to confidently look outside for some of the solutions that it needs.

To gain the ability to work closely with parents in this way the professional worker must show an ability to do things for the family and also to relate to the family. It is worth while fostering the language of collaboration very strongly. This avoids all traces of professional authority, arrogance or disrespect and substitutes sensitive, polite and friendly language. The personal pronoun 'we' should be used instead of 'I' in as many instances as possible. Fine and Gardner (1994, p. 230) give the example of substituting the phrase 'I wonder how we can get him to smile more' instead of 'He is so irritable'. It is important to give the family clear feedback that their input is being listened to and respectfully considered. Avoidance of technical professional language in favour of more down-to-earth practical forms is also helpful. Remember that families under pressure have neither the time nor the inclination for what they may see as excessive frivolity or time-wasting self-indulgence on the part of the professional worker.

The form of practical help which can be provided by the professional worker can best be described as 'enablement' of the family, to achieve its goals and liberties, as far as is possible. In order to conduct this role effectively the professional worker should be able to count on the support of his or her sponsoring organisation. Basically, the task is to demonstrate how to get services to which the family are entitled. A well-informed and empowering professional worker can give the family the pleasure of planning its own support from available welfare, health and educational institutions. The family can benefit both from the relief of burdens that this support can provide as well as from the organisation of their lives that the professional worker can help to expedite. Again the objective is not to control, dominate or even determine the lives of the family members. All decisions have to be taken by the family members themselves, the professional worker's role is simply to influence, organise or expedite them. The practical training and experience of the professional worker can be used collaboratively to empower the family to achieve a more satisfactory lifestyle.

The management role of the professional worker is the most important aspect of the empowerment and collaboration ideal. The professional worker who supports a family in this way can make that family feel truly supported but able to retain an independent and individual family character. Success in this effort gives the family pride in its achievements. The family can be enabled to meet its normal goals as well as to provide a good quality of care for a child with learning disabilities. If successful this process leads to a level of care and nurturing for the child with learning difficulties which might not be available from any other form of state provision.

CONCLUSIONS

This chapter has argued for an 'enabling and collaboration' role for professional workers by stating its operation, philosophy and advantages. In the course of this argument, questions have been raised to facilitate a fair appraisal of the effectiveness of this approach. Basically these questions concern the effectiveness and cost-efficiency of provision that is based on this method. The argument has been that the appraisal derives its cost-efficiency from the way it is designed to empower the people who most intensively care for the child with learning disabilities: the child's family. In terms of units of caring support for units of cost, the method's efficiency must compare well with more invasive methodologies because it seeks to emphasise the psychological health of the caring family. This is basically the same argument that prevention usually costs less than care, thus enabling families to provide 'good enough care' for their children.

It has also been questioned whether the 'enabling and collaboration' role for professional workers is able to effectively support families experiencing the potentially intense pressure due to the care demands of the child with learning disabilities.

Professional workers familiar with a more authoritative role may be feeling impotent and professionally ineffective when sustained to a merely collaborative level of influence. This question can be answered convincingly if the psychological scenario present in a family caring for a child with learning disabilities can be shown to be addressed naturally by the enabling and collaboration approach. The basic point here is that only methods which restore family pride and individuality can provide support to the family which genuinely meet its needs. Invasive supports of that kind traditionally provided by caring institutions take autonomy from the family and leave it with a continuous sense of unease that might be regarded as an unfulfilled quest for life without burdens and constraints. Families want their happiness, pride and character but they also need support. The 'enabling and collaboration' approach meets their needs as they perceive them and leads them to meet their goals, build their family experience and, most importantly, provides the most harmony for the care of the child with learning difficulties. This approach can restore family pride, give them the feeling of control of their environment and circumstances and perhaps lead to fulfilment and happiness. It most effectively mitigates the emotions of embarrassment, anger, disillusionment, sadness, disorientation and isolation which can accompany families caring for children with learning difficulties. It utilises and marshals the power of the community to care for itself and, most of all, it brings a pride into the task of nurturing the child with learning difficulties.

REFERENCES

Bose, R. (1990) *Innovations in community care: an evaluation of the Canterbury and Thanet link family scheme.* PhD thesis. Canterbury: University of Kent.

Department of Health (1990) *Caring for People and the Children Act: Similarities and Differences*. Department of Health Discussion Paper, London: HMSO.

Dunst, C. J. & Paget, K. D. (1991) 'Parent–professional partnerships and family empowerment.' In M. J. Fine (Ed.), *Collaboration with Parents of Exceptional Children*. Brandon: Clinical Psychology Publishing Company, pp. 25–44.

Fine, M. J. & Gardner, A. (1994) 'Collaborative, consultation with families of children with special needs: why bother?' *Journal of Educational and Psychological Consultation*, **15** (4), 283–308.

Friend, M. & Cook, L. (1992) *Interactions: Collaboration Skills for School Professions*. New York: Longman.

Hobbs, N. (1975) *The Future of Children*. San Francisco: Jossey-Bass.

Merton, V., Merton, R. K. & Barber, E. (1983) 'Client ambivalence in professional relationships: the problem of seeking help from strangers.' In B. DePauls, A. Nadler & J. Fisher (Eds), *New Directions of Helping*, Vol. 2. *Help-Seeking*. New York: Academic Press, pp. 18–44.

Roberts, R. N. & Magrab, P. R. (1991) 'Psychologists' role in a family-centred approach to practice, training and research with Young Children.' *American Psychologist*, 144–148.

Swick, K. J. (1984) 'Understanding special needs families.' *Journal of Instructional Psychology*, II, No. 1, 37–47.

INDEX

Related titles of interest...

Teaching Children with Autism to Mindread
A Practical Guide
Patricia Howlin, Simon Baron-Cohen, Julie Hadwin and **John Swettenham**

For professionals in educational psychology and caregivers for the autistic child, this is the first practical book on applying theory of mind to children with autism. Leading the reader through the underlying experimental and clinical principles, a graded programme is provided for teaching children each of these skills.

0-471-97623-7   approx 336pp   Publication Due Jan 1998

Controlling Your Class
A Teacher's Guide to Managing Classroom Behaviour
Bill McPhillimy

Aimed at teachers and student teachers of both primary and secondary pupils, this book provides a short, readable set of ideas and guidelines that a busy student or teacher can relate to his or her own experience, and put into practice. The author is directive and down-to-earth in his advice throughout the book.

0-471-96568-5   200pp   October 1996   Paperback

Troubled Families - Problem Children
Working with Parents: A Collaborative Process
Carolyn Webster-Stratton and **Martin Herbert**
Foreword by **Thomas H. Ollendick**

Helps the mental-health clinician understand the most effective 'therapeutic processes' for supporting families who have children with conduct disorders. Help for these families is particularly urgent as the children are not only at increased risk of abuse by their parents but are more likely to be involved in school dropout, alcoholism, drug abuse, juvenile delinquency, etc., and also to suffer from poor physical health.

0-471-94251-0   368 pp   May 1994   Hardback
0-471-94448-3   368 pp   May 1994   Paperback

Understanding and Managing Children's Classroom Behavior
Sam Goldstein

This book distills the best current findings about behavior management and offers practical suggestions for applying new techniques in the classroom.
0-471-57946-7   526pp   1994   Hardback

Visit the Wiley Home Page http://www.wiley.co.uk